Latin American Fiction and the Narratives of the Perverse

Latin American Fiction and the Narratives of the Perverse

Paper Dolls and Spider Women

Patrick O'Connor

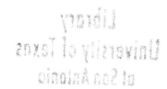

First published in 2004 by
PALGRAVE MACMILLAN™
175 Fifth Avenue, New York, N.Y. 10010 and
Houndmills, Basingstoke, Hampshire, England RG21 6XS
Companies and representatives throughout the world.

PALGRAVE MACMILLAN is the global academic imprint of the Palgrave Macmillan division of St. Martin's Press, LLC and of Palgrave Macmillan Ltd. Macmillan® is a registered trademark in the United States, United Kingdom and other countries. Palgrave is a registered trademark in the European Union and other countries.

ISBN 1–4039–6678–8 hardback

Library of Congress Cataloging-in-Publication Data

O'Connor, Patrick, 1958–
    Latin American fiction and the narratives of the perverse : Paper dolls and spider women / Patrick O'Connor.
        p. cm.
    Includes bibliographical references and index.
    ISBN 1–4039–6678–8 (HC)
        1. Spanish American fiction—20th century—History and criticism.
    2. Sexual deviation in literature. I. Title.

PQ7082.N7036 2004
863'.6093538'098—dc22   2004050144

A catalogue record for this book is available from the British Library.

Design by Newgen Imaging Systems (P) Ltd., Chennai, India.

First edition: December 2004

10 9 8 7 6 5 4 3 2 1

Printed in the United States of America.

Contents ᑫ

Preface and Acknowledgments ᏶

> [Molina]—But did you really like it?
> [Valentín]—Well, it made our time go by faster, right?
> — But you didn't really like it then.
> — Yes I did, and it's a shame to see it ending.
> — But don't be silly, I can tell you another one.
> — Honestly?
> — Sure, I remember lots of lovely, lovely films.
>
> (Kiss of the Spider Woman, 37/43)[1]

Here are some lovely, lovely stories.

One Argentine prisoner seduces another by telling him the plots of movies . . . Although homosexuality among his own friends is punished in the traditional ways of fiction, a young Cuban poet/narrator approvingly narrates his father's adolescent homosexual escapades. . . . A rich Uruguayan commissions a life-size doll for himself and his wife; he then falls in love with it, cheats on it with still another doll, and eventually goes mad. . . . Two Argentines in Paris obsess over a Hungarian countess who murdered peasant women in order to bathe in their blood. . . . A Cuban transvestite goes to Morocco for a sex-change operation couched in a parody of Lacanian analysis. . . . On the California/Mexico border, a man's fetish for navels induces him to find and marry the daughter of his father's mistress. . . .

I like to study moments of Latin American fiction such as these; and in *Paper Dolls and Spider Women* I hope to use some of these stories strategically, to question or to extend the narratives which we have inherited from the fin-de-siècle and especially Freud about the nature of the perverse. As I hope to show, the perverse does not resist narration, as do some of the other terms one might privilege in an investigation of the negotiations between sexuality and textuality; indeed, unlike the hysterics who can only speak by means of their symptoms, perverts are often compulsive narrators. But their narrations are not necessarily reliable as they trope the master discourses of normality. Molina, the homosexual in Manuel Puig's *Kiss of the Spider Woman* alluded to above, is quite the representative figure for this project. He and his cellmate Valentín's mutual creation, The Spider Woman, is just one of the many phantom figures of powerful if vulnerable women that haunt the narratives of the perverse. As my book hopes to do, Puig in *Kiss* moves from one level or kind of storytelling to another, in order to compose a defense of certain kinds of perversions and to satisfy a certain kind of perverse desire to tell stories.

Psychoanalysis is the discourse that promises to tell us the true story of how some people become perverts, and for that reason the "narratives of the perverse" which need to be examined most closely are Freud's narratives. As Peter Brooks has done in his work on narratology and *Beyond the Pleasure Principle*, I find at work in Freud's writing on the perversions various powerful narrative strategies. Here the concept of polymorphous perversity, and especially the notions of stages, fixation, and regression, create an intelligible model of characterization which relates but also subordinates the pervert to the norm of "mature" sexuality. Because psychoanalytic theory's thoughts on the construction of female sexuality have been definitively challenged, and because male deviance has been more tolerated in practice in sexist societies but more invigilated theoretically than has female deviance, my book takes as its center of gravity the "male perversions," or what Kaja Silverman has called "male subjectivity at the margins."

For convenience's sake, the chapters are divided according to recognizable male perversions: one on male homosexuality, one on voyeurism and fetishism, one on sadism and masochism, and one on male transvestism.[2] My principal objects of study come from mid-century and beyond: first, some precursors of the Boom of the 1960s and 1970s; then the Boom authors themselves; and finally, a U.S. Latino author after the Boom.

The first chapter of the book begins with a reading of the Spider Woman in Manuel Puig's novel. It also establishes my methodology, by offering a critical reading of one of Freud's narratives of the perverse, in this case that of male homosexuality in Freud's *Three Essays on the Theory of Sexuality*. (Puig himself, in the novel's long footnotes, also summarizes the debate over the origins of homosexuality, privileging Freud's account.) Like other critics (Paul Julian Smith, Ross Chambers), I find the writings of Foucault to be a good point of departure to think critically through Puig's deployment of a gay liberationist discourse; however, I am more sympathetic than they are to Molina's strategy of "identifying with the heroine," and I try to work this figure of the glamorous/phallic mother back into Freudian accounts of the vicissitudes of sexuality.

Latin American culture has generated at least one autochthonous "perversion," namely, machismo. Although machismo is arguably everywhere in Latin American relations, its power as an explanatory concept derives to a great extent from being embedded in a prestigious narrative, the "The Children of La Malinche" chapter of Octavio Paz's much-anthologized *The Labyrinth of Solitude*. In the context of a Third World cultural nationalism, Octavio Paz's grounding of machismo in the relationship between the conquistador Cortés and his betrayed translator and mistress La Malinche is a potent and dangerous variant on Oedipus and historical mythmaking: while seeming to lament it, Paz paradoxically renders machismo "normal" for Latin American masculinity while also implying that it can be one way to defend against the modernization and Yankeeification of Mexican culture. Framed this way, "Oedipal colonialism" will be hard to undo, and I suggest a few polemical strategies to undercut the power of Paz's formulations.

In quite a much more general way, the sexual perversion of incest has also functioned as a paradoxically "normal" sexuality. Machismo separates Latin Americans from other masculinities; the incest taboo unites them to all other masculinities. Yet the discourses of cultural and structural anthropology, through figures as diverse as Levi-Strauss and Oscar Lewis, have had in the twentieth century a privileged position in formulating Latin America's incomplete modernity to itself. Thus, by declaring, through the Oedipus complex, that incestuous desires are characteristic of the human condition, Freudian discourses erect a sort of normality around incestuous desire which Latin American authors such as Paz and García Márquez are eager to exploit in their attempt to describe (or impose) a normal, healthy modernity for Latin American fiction. There are subtle indications in *Kiss of the Spider Woman* that even Puig is willing to abide by this normalizing discourse.

Chapter 2 takes on the most important homosexual novel of Latin American literature, José Lezama Lima's *Paradiso*. Lezama's novel is a grand, double embarrassment to the literary tradition: traditional critics who wish to canonize it for its complexity and theory of poetic genius wish that it didn't have so many gross sex scenes in it; the (anti-Castro) leftist and feminist authors who might wish to canonize Lezama as a "minority voice" wish that *Paradiso* were written in a more accessible style, and that it were not so visibly sexist (indeed, gynophobic) and classist. I am actually rather sympathetic to these positions, certainly the latter; it is more relevant to criticize those readings by Lezama's contemporaries that argued that a Barthesian *jouissance* offered the reader a textual pleasure that had no relation to the sexuality of the author or his characters. For this task it is necessary to look to the side of the rather asexual protagonist, José Cemí, and instead read the novel through two important secondary characters, José's revered yet ambivalently presented father José Eugenio Cemí, and his abjected yet ambivalently honored homosexual friend Eugenio Foción. Such a reading goes against the grain of the text. But Lezama makes his own attempts to situate himself to the side of a patriarchy he does not wish to abandon in his portrayal of his uncle, providing us with an example of what queer theorist Eve Sedgwick whimsically refers to as the "avunculate," a familial, homosocial (perhaps even homoerotic) yet non-Oedipal image of a relationship to literary creativity.

Chapter 3 examines the writings of Felisberto Hernández, the solitary vanguardist writer of short fictions that return constantly to the thematics of voyeurism and fetishism. My main subject will be his novella *Las Hortensias* (The Daisy Dolls, 1949), where I hope to show that Felisberto understood far better than Freud did the complexities of erotic attractions that have unmoored themselves from the heterosexual normal narrative; however, in his 1927 essay on fetishism, Freud seems to have understood better than Felisberto did how to construct a story that includes some (but not all) of the sort of insights we see in Felisberto's ramshackle fictions. Felisberto's protagonists grant power to the female body (often inanimate, often large or fat and therefore usually coded as maternal) over themselves, and this primary situation unleashes on the one hand a torrent of small episodes and mini-narratives, and on the other hand a plot mechanics that punishes the protagonists for abandoning their male privilege so completely. Felisberto remains outside Oedipus, as does the fetishist narrative, insofar as the punishment (or castration threat) does not come from a father figure. His anti-modern conservatism, while supportive of fetishistic desire, criticizes the commodity fetishism of consumer capitalism, and *Las Hortensias* maneuvers between these different uses of the concept of fetishism as it brings down its protagonist.

Chapters 2 and 3 studied pre-Boom authors. In chapter 4 we move into the writers of the Boom and into the milieu of the 1960s. Julio Cortázar's *A Manual for Manuel* shares with the footnotes of *Kiss of the Spider Woman* a roughly Marcusean perspective on sexual politics: liberation in one sphere requires liberation in others. Sexual violence that disrupted one's bourgeois habits was, so to speak, the party line of the Paris of the 1950s and 1960s, and Cortázar's enthusiastic adoption of this strategy in some of his writings suggests a willingness to follow that fashion. Nevertheless, this field of sexual theorizing was unstable: against the Freudian notion that sadistic and masochistic impulses were vicissitudes of the same instinct, other theories emphasized the radical disjunction between sadism and masochism.

While the writings of the Marquis de Sade were deplored or praised as anti-humanist, a writer such as Gilles Deleuze would examine the writings of Masoch as an independent source of both an ethics and a poetics. Yet we should also note the stance of an Argentine poet who, though much younger than Cortázar, was as aware as he was of new trends in French thinking about the relationship between violence and sexuality: Alejandra Pizarnik. Basing her ideas more directly on George Bataille's view of Sade than on Lacan's 1963 "Kant With Sade" or Deleuze's Bataille-inflected readings of Sade, Pizarnik upbraids Cortázar for abandoning the potential of a Sadeian aesthetics. Not just in her famous prose piece "The Bloody Countess" (1966) but throughout her prose oeuvre, Pizarnik positions herself in the role of "the Satanic daughter," visible in some of Sade's writings. The Satanic daughter goads the Sadistic father to new levels of violence, often against a mother figure. The two Argentines provide conflicting versions of The Bloody Countess, Pizarnik in her 1966 essay and Cortázar in his 1968 novel *62: A Model Kit*. Nevertheless, it is only in poems he published in 1983, many years after Pizarnik's 1972 suicide, poems situated in a fin-de-siècle lesbian boudoir, that Cortázar can defend himself from Pizarnik's rigorously Sadeian demands upon him.

My last chapter remains in the 1960s as it takes up a motif in a variety of texts written almost exactly contemporaneously, the figure of the transvestite in José Donoso's *Hell Has No Limits* (1966), Carlos Fuentes's *Holy Place* (1967), and especially the works of Severo Sarduy in a variety of genres, from the novels *From Cuba With a Song* (1966) and *Cobra* (1972) to his literary criticism *Written on a Body* (1969) and *La simulación* [also collected in the English translation of *Written on a Body*] (1982). While each of these fictions deploys the phantasmatic phallic woman of the transvestite differently, they all bespeak an anxiety about the relationship between fiction and reality, in which the feminized term threatens to usurp the masculinized term or in which a castrated masculine position can only speak by inhabiting the feminine (yet an insubordinate feminine) position. In this chapter I descend to the rather insubordinately feminine genres of gossip and literary innuendo to explain some of the formal inconsistencies in Fuentes's novel; then, in a short extra chapter, I resituate Sarduy's transvestite Cobra in a broader landscape of his day, "the Queer Sixties," to complicate the text's desire to turn Cobra into a pure sign, and to keep us all a little anxious about the relationship between fiction and reality.

Where do we go from the Boom, into an environment in which Freud is no longer canonized, and "perversions" no longer so clearly stigmatized or demarcated? An epilogue to my book examines *Poison River* (1988–94), by the Chicano graphic novelist Gilbert Hernández, and reflects on the challenges that literary history will have to face as it assimilates both the more overt alternative sexual narratives of the last twenty years and the critique of "master narratives" heralded by multiculturalism and the new cultural studies. As I have been suggesting throughout, in both theory and practice the perverse has defined itself against an intelligible narrative of the normal. As that narrative becomes gradually unintelligible, the concept of a subculture or an alternative culture becomes more complex, especially as it is related to the one master narrative that won't go away, global capitalism. Under such a regime, the taste for reading and writing complex Latin American fictions may itself be understood as a perverse taste, a stubborn, persistent desire for the unproductive pleasure that both reinforces a marginal self and casts doubts upon other, confidently normal subjectivities.

This book owes much to many people, at many institutions. My own family, of course. From my first job at Saint Ann's School, I would like to thank Ruth Chapman, Cristina Reyes, and especially Victor Marchioro; and from my New York friends and family, Daniel Jacobson, Ellen Kushner, Delia Sherman, Steve Novak, Noah Millman and Carolyn Schiff, and especially Mickey Dobbs. This book owes much of its thoughts about literary affiliation and much of its enthusiasm for Cuban authors to Roberto González Echevarría at Yale University; other Yalies and/or Cubanólogos I'd like to thank are Jacques Lezra, Anne Gebelein, Benigno Sifuentes, Simon Stern, César Salgado, Arnaldo Cruz-Malavé, Óscar Montero, and Guillermina de Ferrari. The book itself was imagined while I taught at Deep Springs College; in particular I'd like to thank Joshua Malbin, Mark Boulos, Steven Singer, John Dewis, Damon Rich, and Geoff Andersen at various points along that journey. It was written at The University of Chicago, thanks in part to the Franke Institute of the Humanities, but mostly thanks to support from Elizabeth Amann, Lauren Berlant and George Chauncey of the Center for Gender Studies, my students there (especially Janis Breckenridge, Olga Vilella-Janeiro, Dan Russek, Stephanie Frampton, Jen Insley, and Katherine Ostrom), and the graduate students and faculty of the Sexualities and Normativities Working Group (Sharif Youssef, Rebecca Zorach, Mark Miller, Candace Vogler, and Sandra Macpherson most particularly), and above all Mario Santana. My Chicago home team of Sean Sullivan, Abe Lentner and Abby McGrath, Charles Horecker, Jim Walsh, and especially Colin Davis and Charlotte Henkle helped keep me on (so far) this edge of sanity. Behind the scenes but everywhere for the last eight years Dianna Niebylski has been a comrade, sounding board, and true friend. At Oberlin College all my colleagues but especially Ana Cara and Sebastiaan Faber have been welcoming. And from beginning to end and on every page of this book, the work and example of Eve Kosofsky Sedgwick from a distance and Sylvia Molloy from very close up have helped make these ideas happen and helped me get them down on paper. I thank them all.

1. Enter the Spider Woman: An Introduction to the Narratives of the Perverse ⟋

> [Molina]: And now I have to put up with you telling me the same old thing every-
> body tells me.
> [Valentín:]—Is that so ... What is it exactly I'm supposed to tell you?
> —You're all alike, always coming to me with the same business, always!
> —What?
> —How they spoiled me as a kid, and that's why I'm the way I am, how I was tied
> to my mother's apron strings and now I'm this way, and how a person can always
> straighten out though, and what I really need is a woman, because a woman's the
> best there is.
> —(That's what they tell you?)   Kiss of the Spider Woman, 19; 25)

Manuel Puig's *Kiss of the Spider Woman* (1976) confronts one compulsive narrator with another. Not that it looks that way at first
glance: the story of two men imprisoned during the military
crackdown just before the *guerra sucia* mostly brings together opposites, not
similars: not just an effeminate homosexual and a macho young revolutionary, but also a speaker and a listener. Of course there is no doubt that
Molina is a compulsive storyteller. He is in many ways the hero (the heroine) of the story—certainly the one with whom Puig identifies the most.[1]
Over the course of the novel Molina tells Valentín the plots of no fewer
than five movies, and during the period when, angry with Valentín over his
insensitive responses, Molina refuses to speak to him, Molina tells himself
the plot of a sixth movie; and later, while he is retelling one of the movies,
he free-associates thoughts which take the form of still another narrative.
He pretends to be reluctant to talk about his possible romance of a waiter

named Gabriel, but he turns out to be very eager to tell this story, too, and the reader can discern that the romance is mostly an invention of Molina's. Of course, there is one story in which he is involved which he must not tell his cellmate (we'll get to that in a minute), but we have no reason to believe that keeping that story secret is the font of his loquacity: Molina would be a compulsive storyteller wherever he is and under whatever circumstance.

But if I say that there are two compulsive storytellers in the novel, I do *not* mean the other occupant of his cell, the young political prisoner Valentín, who hears these stories beginning from the position of a willful silence (despite threats of torture he has not yet divulged the secrets of his revolutionary cell). Over the course of the novel he answers Molina's stories first only with (Marxist and Freudian) analysis (chapters 1–3), but soon with autobiographical remarks about his love life (chapters 4–6), then with involuntary fragments of violent imagery (chapter 9–10). It is only in the novel's finale under the influence of morphine that Valentín becomes a storyteller proper, narrating the story of the Spider Woman to himself, with enough conscious will to keep his secret information secret even under morphine. Valentín has opened himself to a broader notion of love, friendship, and pleasure, but his newfound love of story remains within bounds.

No, in the passage I have quoted above, Molina correctly, vaguely describes the other compulsive narrator in *Kiss*: "everybody." "Everybody" in different contexts can mean different things: it can mean the dream machines of the cinematic industries of Hollywood, Mexico City, and Nazi Germany, each internally inconsistent and historically all quite different but all purveying an ideology of romantic love; it can mean the state apparatuses whose documents are reproduced in chapters 8, 11, 14, and 15, more successfully and consciously univocal, certainly more repressive. But here in this passage "everybody" has a more homely pedigree: "tied to his mother's apron strings" (*pegado a las polleras de mi mamá*), Molina reproduces clichéd language in order to seem to disagree with it. Indeed, one of the ways that Puig's oeuvre is supposed to usher in post-Boom or postmodernist literature is in its understanding of language and social relations as swimming in cliché.[2] Molina's refusal of "everybody"'s compulsive storytelling is only partial, however. He accepts the story, but reinterprets it to suit him (much as he edits out the Nazi ideology of the most notorious of the films he tells to Valentín). Indeed, he insists on putting this cliché into Valentín's mouth, as if teaching Valentín to speak like "everybody" in their attempt to oppress him.

Although a compressed and abbreviated one, this one-sentence story—
"they spoiled me as a kid, and that's why I'm the way I am, how I was tied
to my mother's apron strings and now I'm this way"—is a full-fledged
narrative of the perverse. It focuses on aetiology, on the cause of a perversion; it places the blame on the pervert's parents, especially the mother. In
all these aspects it is clear that these clichés were generated by, or at least
sanctioned by, the writings of Freud. Molina has an answer to this narrative
that is equally practiced: "And my answer is this . . . great! I agree! And
since a woman's the best there is . . . I want to be one" (19; 25). This language of choosing between *having* a woman or *being* one is the flip side of
the language of a different psychoanalytic theory, Jacques Lacan's division
of the genders according to being or having the phallus. This is a structure,
not a narrative; we will return to it in another chapter. More relevant for us
to begin with is the strategies that Molina employs to bring Valentín
into his conversational circuit. He offers him the position of "everybody"
because he has a witty ready answer to the criticism that everybody
makes of him. All of his favorite narratives are all at least a little different,
although he interpellates himself into the same position every time:
"Who do you identify with? Irena or the other one?" asks Valentín, and
Molina answers, "With Irena, who do you think? She's the heroine,
dummy. Always with the heroine" (25; 31). Against a central sameness
amidst glittering worlds of differences, Molina claims that everybody only
has a single narrative to tell about people like him and how he got this way.
Can this compulsory storytelling, from everybody, be successfully parried
by Molina's compulsive storytelling? This question is the emotional center
of the relationship between narrative and seduction in *Kiss of the Spider
Woman*.

Molina is probably uninterested in whether the similarity between
Freud's narratives of homosexuality and the popular narrative he claims he
faces from everybody is a case of ideas trickling down from a European
intellectual and new discourse of sexology, or whether it is a case of Freud
"inventing" a theory that reflects most of the popular prejudices of his day,
prejudices carried through to the Italo-Spanish mix of lower-middle-class,
mid-century Buenos Aires. But Molina does have a stake in bringing
Valentín to the same initial position of other people with whom he deals,
even if that initial position is extremely disadvantageous to him. It seems
perverse in the other sense to put such negative words into Valentín's
mouth at the beginning of their relationship like this. Good rhetoricians
and good storytellers alike must know their audiences; in practice, they
offer a place into which their audience is encouraged to place themselves,

and it is shrewd on the part of a rhetorician or storyteller not to ask them to accept something that is too much to their own advantage, or too unflattering to their listeners. And the stakes for this particular narrative contract are particularly high, much higher than Valentín realizes. In exchange for a reduction of his sentence Molina had been sent into Valentín's cell as a spy, to befriend the Marxist, learn his secrets, and betray him. In that sense, Molina's storytelling is both compulsive, and compulsory.

Yet, just as Molina deflects the demands of compulsory heterosexuality, he deflects the demands of the Warden; his compulsory storytelling is never placed at the service of the police state but towards his own ends, and he successfully seduces Valentín, who retains the active role in their sex (Molina wants sex with a "real man"). Suspecting that they are being double-crossed, the police free Molina, who, now in love with Valentín, hopes to prolong their relationship by asking Valentín for the relevant information to pass on to the rebels; a police report describes trailing Molina to a meeting with the rebels, where he is murdered in a shootout between the rebels and the police. The novel ends with a dream by Valentín under the influence of morphine administered after he has been tortured, in which Molina appears to him in the guise of The Spider Woman, and in which Valentín acknowledges both the importance of stories and storytelling to the beauty in life, and the importance of Molina to him, even after death.

Such a bare recounting of the novel's many storytelling threads already suggests that *Kiss of the Spider Woman* deserves a prominent place in the investigation of the relationship between narrative and the perverse. This investigation follows in a long narratological tradition comparing narration to seduction, a subtradition within theorizing and practicing rhetoric that goes back to the *Phaedrus* and to the works of Ovid.[3] Yet stories can be used not only to win over or pervert the listener but also to reinforce one's own sense of self; and a fragile, marginal, beleaguered sense of self might need constant reinforcement. Hence the mood in *Kiss* oscillates between a sense of freedom in language and the sense of compulsion from without and from within in storytelling.

A nineteenth-century tradition also links perversity to the misunderstood self-destructive behavior we call compulsions in a more general sense: the voice that tells us to do exactly the opposite of what is in our interest stands in opposition to utilitarian notions of the self, pleasure, and society. This tradition of confronting the maddening pleasure to be found in rejecting the useful has a particularly nineteenth-century inflection, one that extends from Poe's "The Imp of the Perverse" through Dostoevsky's Underground Man until Freud's analysis of the repetition compulsion, which leads him to formulate a theory that goes "beyond the pleasure principle"; finally, self-destructiveness becomes almost an ethical imperative in 1930s writers like (post-Nietzschean) Georges Bataille or Argentina's (post-Dostoevskian) Roberto Arlt.

Both Molina's life and his death can be discussed in terms of utilitarian strategizing and self-destructive compulsions. Whereas Valentín earnestly defends utilitarian Marxist values yet is committed to an ascetic pleasure-hating practice, Molina defends the right to pleasure in the everyday yet is committed to a fantasy life of tragic altruism that is almost certainly his motive for meeting with Valentín's rebels. Valentín, discussing it with his dream-lover Marta in the morphine vision of the last chapter, would like to think otherwise: "*the only one who knows for sure is him, if he was sad or happy to die that way, sacrificing himself for a just cause [...], 'For a just cause? hmmm ... I think he let himself be killed because that way he could die like some heroine in a movie, and none of that business about a just cause,' that's something only he can know, and it's possible that even he never knew*" (279;284–5). Valentín prefers that Molina's psychology be enigmatic but also altruistic, recalling the way they discussed the ending of the last film Molina told him: "Such an enigmatic ending, isn't it, Valentín?" to which Valentín replied, "No, it's right, it's the best part of the film ... It means that even if she's left with nothing, she's content to have had at least one real relationship in her life, even if it's over and done with" (259;263). Molina (could have) put those words right in Valentín's mouth, even if he argues with Valentín about the ethics of pleasure which these thoughts entail.

One possible position for the relationship between narrativity and the perverse, then: storytelling can be a repetition compulsion which reinforces a perverted, self-destructive self-image, censurable even when altruistic. Rather than seducing the other, it produces a self that traps itself, or so the Spider Woman seems at first: "*poor creature ... she can't move, there in the deepest part of the jungle she's trapped in a spider's web*" (280; 285). A second possible position is the strategist's: storytelling can be a successfully repeated skill that merely simulates abjection, resituating speaker and listener for everybody's good (and the speaker's pleasure): "*or no, the spiderweb is growing out of her own body [...] she's smiling but a tear rolls out from beneath the mask [...] and I ask her why she's crying and in a close-up that covers the whole screen at the end of the film she answers me that that's just what can never be known, because the ending is enigmatic, and I answer her that it's good this way, that it's the very best part of the film*" (280; 285). Is the Spider Woman actually trapped in her own web? Valentín's dream leaves this enigmatic, and those who understand storytelling about sexuality as an activity ambiguously between repeating the stories that everybody tells and deploying the stories that you choose to tell will prefer to leave it that way. No matter what its pretense of irony or neutrality or even condemnation, imaginative literature will always be on the side of the perverts because they have the best stories.

THE PERVERT AND THE NORMAL

[Molina]—Curiosity, that's all you feel.
[Valentín]—That's not true. I think I have to know more about you, that's what, in order to understand you better. If we're going to be in this cell together like this, we ought to understand one another better, and I know very little about people with your type of inclination.

(Kiss 59; 65–6)

This book, then is a contribution to queer theory, not merely content with studying the experiences of lesbians and gay men, but questioning the categories and narratives that define these experiences. Queer theory, like the concept of the perverse, is suspicious of giving too much weight to the distinction between homosexuality and heterosexuality; thus, many of the authors studied in this book are nominally heterosexual. When queer theory takes advantage of the vocabulary and the techniques of psychoanalytic criticism, it does so somewhat against the grain of Freud's own writings, not so much writing against Oedipus as circumventing its most blatant imperatives. Like feminist psychoanalytic theory that can trace its genealogy from Klein to Dinnerstein to Jessica Benjamin, some queer theory accepts that the Oedipal complex describes the imposition of a patriarchal (and a heterosexist) order but nevertheless dwells in the complexities of the pre-Oedipal, examining the infant self's formation through its relation to the mother, the breast, and the mirror image: even Freud says that such pre-Oedipal satisfactions and anxieties are never fully renounced, and I will exploit the lush resources of such pre-Oedipal theorists. Queer theory is notoriously diffident about attributing fixed identities to individuals, and our diffidence about sexual identities often extends to similar reservations about political, national, and racial identities; my project is full of more than the usual share of Latin America's biculturals, borderlanders, exiles, and cosmopolites, writers who can't always decide whether living on the margins of various identities is a blessing or a curse, a mark of living between a past and a present regime or a harbinger of some future world with no fixed identities. Alas, like much queer theory, this book will find it easier to show the operations of stubborn perverse desires in the texts of already well-known prestigious male authors, rather than in a female canon still struggling for visibility.[4] Indeed, the structure of this book is somewhat similar to that of Kaja Silverman's *Male Subjectivity at the Margins*, insofar as different chapters hope to show the logics of different male perversions (homosexuality, voyeurism/fetishism, masochism, and transvestism) at work in different narratives.

So all in all Molina and his cohort of compulsive storytellers and their often compulsory narratives prefigure my own project as a chronicler of the narratives of the perverse. Yet in one important way my storytellers of the perverse strike me as inherently different from the major thrust of queer theory. Whether infused with the rabble-rousing rhetoric of the first years of gay liberation or enamored of the more intricate feints with empowerment in Foucault, queer theory takes on its projects in the hope of effecting change. Perverse narrators, on the other hand, are often politically conservative, or at any rate quietistic; living in makeshift subcultures or zones of tolerance, perverts do not necessarily espouse the subversive or revolutionary rhetoric that informs much of queer theory. This unwillingness to rock the boat of their life's pleasure cruise goes all the way back to Freud: while obsessive-compulsives and other hysterics came to Freud in great pain demanding to be cured so that they could lead normal lives, most of the perverts Freud eventually treated, especially the fetishists, seldom wanted to change their predilections:

> In the last few years [the text is from 1927] I have had an opportunity of studying analytically a number of men whose object-choice was ruled by a fetish. One need not suppose that these persons had sought analysis on account of a fetish; the devotees of fetishes regard them as abnormalities, it is true, but only rarely as symptoms of illness; usually they are quite content with them and even extol the advantages they offer for erotic gratification. ("Fetishism" 214)

Perverts do not wish to become normal: often, they do not wish to become legal; if they do wish to become legal, they do not wish their transgressions to seem routinized, certainly not to themselves. When discussing the perversions in 1905, Freud noted laconically, "Disgust seems to be one of the forces which have led to a restriction of the sexual aim. [... Nevertheless, t]he sexual instinct in its strength enjoys overriding this disgust" (*Three Essays* 18). A queer theory sympathetic to the perversions may wish to describe a world that it has *no* intention of changing.

So before we feel the need to "further queer" these stories of desires that go beyond the normal, we had better clarify the relationship between the normal and the perverted, at least as sketched by Freud, to see what changes (if any) *he* wished to bring about by bringing their stories into public light. In 1905, the year he published his *Three Essays on the Theory of Sexuality*, his position is a theoretical one, whose goal is to expand—somewhat—the notion of the normal in sexuality. He had concluded that all humans in their infancy are polymorphously perverse, and that the clear difference between adult hysterics and adult perverts was that hysterics were sick from too much repression, whereas perverts were aberrant from not enough, or the wrong kind of, repression. While Freud was more aware than his readers that what he referred to as repression was separable from the social sanctions of his day, he nevertheless makes clear that social and especially parental sanctions operate as the principal factors in repression, however unconscious the parents are that they are transmitting these sanctions; therefore, a "politics of perversion" could well entail changing the sanctions around normality. Yet Freud does not confront those sanctions directly. If Freud wishes to bring about a change in how normality is defined, and thus if he wishes to be more radical than many of the perverts whom he eventually treats, nevertheless he also refrained from supporting the political movements of the fin de siècle (Ulrichs, Weininger) that hoped to reform the recent laws passed against one of the perversions in particular, homosexuality. Freud in 1905 had as yet no patients who were perverts, only hysterics: the 1905 essays, then, are theoretical in a double sense, with neither a political nor a therapeutic program behind it. If it sticks up for queers, it does so only in theory.

And yet the 1905 book does stick up for queers, albeit partially. Freud's belief in infantile polymorphous perversity required that he provide two stories: the rhetorical demonstration of how this infantile perversity could be so, and the various stories of how this polymorphous perversity either becomes or fails to become normal sexuality in the adult. Freud organized his demonstration of the theory of polymorphous infantile sexuality by means of the three essays, the first of which is the essay on the sexual perversions or "aberrations." Through a tight, elegantly brief text (which the author of the introduction to the Norton Edition, Steven Marcus, is correct to say expands "palimpsestically" over twenty years of revisions), Freud begins with a definition of normal sexuality that is too impossibly narrow, so that no normal reader could accept it: analogously to the tradition of Poe and Dostoevsky alluded to above, "normal" sexuality is imagined to have a purely utilitarian context, such that any "perverse" deviation would be a pleasure which could not lead to procreation. Freud's analysis of the perversions is designed to remind the normal reader time and again that many aspects of normal sex simply extend beyond that narrow definition. (He scores an especially large number of debater's points from the kiss, which he naughtily refers to as the union of the openings to two persons' digestive tracts.[5]) It turns out that Freud uses the various findings of the sexologists of his day to push home the point that the libido (what he limits himself here to calling "sexual instinct, as understood by the ancients") can be conceptualized independently of the objects to which it attaches, insofar as it is true that homosexuals or inverts cannot be distinguished from the rest of the population by any biological degeneracy, and to push home the point that almost every one of the "sexual aims" of perverts—the zones of the mouth and the anus, and so on, the activities of looking and being looked at, and so on,—can be understood as phases which the normal sexual subject has incorporated into part of his or her sexual behavior, or did so at one time in the past. Naturally, Freud finds all these perversions to be interesting in and of themselves, yet for the rhetorical purpose of his essay, the perverts have been introduced to help convince normal people that they, too, are just a little bit perverse, that if they are normal it is because they never got "fixated" on these earlier phases and because they have learned how to "integrate" these perverse impulses into a sexuality that gives primacy to the genital act. Queer theory departs from Freud for the most part by calling into question exactly how problematic the notions of fixation and especially integration are, how they recapitulate much of the force of normalization which Freud had taken from the unthinking, self-contradictory Victorian status quo of sexual normality.

For the second story I have alluded to above, Freud's third essay is his first sustained attempt to explain the numerous hurdles that the infant has to clear before he or she achieves normal sexuality. It is at this stage of the argument that Freud becomes something of a storyteller, though not a storyteller of the perverse, but of the normal. His first developed version of Oedipus, in *The Interpretation of Dreams* (1900), served only as one kind of story in that enormous text's multiple occasions for narration: the summaries of the history of dream interpretation, the many dreams recounted, the analyses of the dreams, as well as non-narrative topographic descriptions of the relationship between the conscious and the unconscious (descriptions that would get more and more narrative as successive revisions shifted from the function "the censorship" to something like an entity, "the superego"); with so many fireworks, the importance of the Oedipal story might have been lost. Here in the 1905 book it exists in splendid isolation, just as Freud is inventing in other books the new literary genre of the case history, that unusual cat-and-mouse game in which the analyst pursues a neurosis (and/or theoretical knowledge) hidden in the patient as a detective combs a city looking for the criminal (and/or reconstructing the scene of a crime). The story of the achievement of normality, then, makes an appearance in Freud's oeuvre at the same time as he narrativizes the story of the hysteric. The story that is deferred or suppressed, however, is any story of the pervert, whose diverse features are parceled out in a taxonomy of objects and aims in, perhaps, an attempt to imitate the taxonomies of natural scientists (Marcus in his introduction to the *Three Essays* finds many parallels with Darwin in the book) but who does not receive a narrative of his own. Indeed, such narratives as Freud had available are suppressed: with no pervert patients of his own yet, Freud is depending upon material by Havelock Ellis and Krafft-Ebing, which is predominantly case histories, however tendentiously composed.[6] Foucault was telescoping many years of fin-de-siècle sexology when he said that "The nineteenth-century homosexual became a personage, a past, a case history, and a childhood, in addition to being a type of life, a life form, and a morphology" (43); in 1905 homosexuality was a diagnosis and a character type, but not yet a life history for Freud.

So for Freud the pervert serves as the ground for the normal, in the form of polymorphous perversity, and also as the detours in which the libido might get trapped, fixated, as it maneuvers toward normal sexuality. Praised for its role as pointing us toward the origins of all sexualities, perversion is then reinscribed, not as a crime, but as an immaturity. Queer theorists interested in narratology such as Judith Roof or examining the *Bildungsroman* such as Jeffrey Nunokawa have recognized that there are parallels between a novel's need for an ending (what Roof calls heteronarrativity, the need for an ending to be productively other than its beginning) and the ideological pull toward narrative heterosexuality as the appropriate ending: the plot for every novel is the "marriage-plot," and same-sex passions, boarding-school crushes, and so on, are treated by family and novelist alike as "only a phase." Moreover, adult perverts can serve as foils for the heterosexual characters in a novel much as fools and comic figures serve as foils in Shakespeare, to reinforce the theme by showing the road one would of course never take. The metaphor of the road or path, basic to Freud's hydraulic metaphors for the libido and to almost all language of sexual development, is also a basic metaphor to describe forward movement in a narration.

Once perversity becomes perversion, thanks to the fin-de-siècle sexologists, and once perversion helps identify the pervert, then perverts can provide for normal people a theoretical reminder of what the normal mature person once was as an infant and a gamut of the different component parts of normal desire frozen and fixated into hieratic freakishness; and in the social life of the adult the pervert can serve as an interlude to threaten, very temporarily, the marriage plot. Normal people also have the privilege of ignoring perverts: even a tolerant Marxist like Valentín has never bothered to inform himself much about homosexuals: "I know very little about people with your type of inclination" (29). Turning the question around, one can also ask, what do normal people provide for perverts? Insofar as normality provides a master narrative, whether Freudian or social, the pervert gets a role to play. Not a particularly creative thinker, it is nevertheless the Marxist Valentín who labels Molina "the spider woman, that traps men in her web" (261), an image Molina decides immediately that he likes. The pervert also gets the thrill of transgression, the enjoyment of overriding socially sanctioned disgust when sexually aroused. The pervert does not have the privilege of being ignorant of the master narratives of normality, but in exchange he or she does become very well versed in reading these texts against the grain, catching the encoded meanings placed in them by other perverts or simply interpreting these texts differently than they were originally intended: the various effects of camp.

However, rejecting the privileged position initially offered for identification does not definitively solve the question of identification, the question of reading against the grain, because any narrative will offer subordinated positions for reader identification. Furthermore, textual desire and identification can spread itself flickeringly over many positions in a text. Like other deconstructive queer theorists, I am happy to read textual positions that do not line up entirely with any of the characters in a story. In *Kiss*, for example, it would be correct for a pessimistic theorist like Roof to point out that Valentín's morphine dream at the end reunites him mentally with his lover Marta, as the Spider Woman looks on, bestowing gifts but immobile (trapped?) at the center of the very webs that s/he spins; and that all this proves that the now-dead Molina was just an episode on the way to a young macho's getting in touch with his feminine side without losing his masculinity. However, it would be equally true to read the ending as a multiple refraction of many feminine figures in Valentín's dream (not just Marta and the Spider Woman but a naked island girl with whom Valentín has sex, and perhaps the voice of Valentín's mother, and even the island itself is described as being in the palm of a woman's hand), a dream in which many of the voices, including Marta, quote turns of phrases we associate with Molina, and that therefore Molina has succeeded in installing himself in Valentín's subconscious, supplanting any real female figures or even any of the basic fantasmatic figures of one's Imaginary.

Yet whereas there is something to be gained sometimes by pointing up the wrinkles in which textual desire insinuates part of one's reading libido, I nevertheless would not wish to be too subtle in my readings of some of my authors: here, too, I partly take my cue from Molina when Valentín asks him which of the characters in the panther movie he identifies with: "With Irena, what do you think? She's the heroine, dummy. Always with the heroine" (25). The act of identification can be more complex than Molina at this moment wishes to acknowledge, but it is a complexity that happens between a reader and a character, not between a reader and the spaces between characters. For this reason I hesitate somewhat to endorse the theoretical move made by some psychoanalytic queer theorists, especially Silverman, de Lauretis, and Garber, in taking up psychoanalytic theory as wielded by Laplanche and Pontalis and especially the way that these two Lacanians describe the primal scene and primal fantasies.[7] According to them, the self is invested not in the content of any particular actor in a fantasy sequence, but in the space of fantasizing itself, and in the movement between these characters. (One might recall Barthes's counterintuitive yet in the end persuasive argument in *Sade/Fourier/Loyola* that neither Sade nor the reader identifies with the libertines performing the acts described, but rather with the libertine who for any given evening arranges the tableaux.) My hesitation lies only in that, thus described, the space of fantasy can line up too easily with the space of fiction (Silverman uses the term fantasy to lead quickly to the phrase "dominant fiction," for instance), and I think that it is rather too neat that people who have trained themselves to read fiction choose the brand of psychoanalytic theory that equates fantasy with fiction.[8] Some of the risks of identifying with characters are obvious, of course:[9] identifying with characters can inadvertently give them a solidity, a reification, that they do not possess as words on a page or as textual constructs; it can tempt you into not just partisanship but also into the pathetic fallacy of trying to sound like the characters with whom you identify. This "overvaluation" of a character's position can lead to a relationship to the text that, interestingly enough, has some of the hallmarks of the fetishistic relationship (Freud used the word "overvaluation" to describe the fetishist's relation to his desired object as early as the *Three Essays*), what Freud called the "I know, but nevertheless"—I know that the woman is castrated, but nevertheless I endow her with power anyway. In *Kiss* the clearest example of the *mauvais foi* which comes from identification is the one highlighted by the movie version: Molina is so enchanted by the romance of one of his films that "he knows but nevertheless" does not care that the film is Nazi propaganda. One of the most important debates in contemporary popular cultural studies is, of course, the extent to which real audiences can actually read a narrative against the grain without being affected by its primary ideological purpose.

   If, in some ways, fetishism is the most privileged of the various narratives of the perverse I will be examining (because, as we shall see, the narrative Freud offers for it is so vividly bizarre, and because it thereby offers a position from which to critique Freud's definition of the perverse), in other ways homosexuality is best suited to serve as a warning to our perverts. A fetishist loves objects, a transvestite loves himself and the world when cross-dressed, masochists love pain and the subject positions which pain can produce, but only the homosexual loves the man who represents normality. (Not all homosexuals, of course, as Molina makes clear: "No, there's the other kind that fall in love with each other. But as for my friends and myself, we're one hundred percent female" (203; 207).) It may well be that all perverts love the normality against which they contrast themselves, but only the Spider Women allow themselves to fall into this trap so obviously.

THE LATIN AMERICAN PERVERSION: PAZ AND MACHISMO

> *[Valentín]—No, the man of the house and the woman of the house have to be equal with one another. If not, their relation becomes a form of exploitation.*
> *[Molina]—But then there's no kick to it.*
> *—Why?*
> *—Well, this is very intimate, but since you're asking about it . . . The kick is in the fact that when a man embraces you . . . you may feel a little bit frightened.*
> *—No, that's all wrong. Whoever put that idea into your head? It's absolutely wrong.*
> *—But that's the way I feel.*
>
> (*Kiss* 243; 246–7)

Is there a uniquely Latin American contribution to the narratives of the perverse? The question rankles, in part because it arises so naturally from the institutions and disciplines of the U.S. academy: one is tempted to say yes simply in order to guarantee one's position of expertise and uniqueness in discussing the narratives of the perverse in a Latin American context. But the question of the location of theory, one might even say the nationality of theory, is not trivial. As I have foregrounded, I will not relinquish a focus on the sexual in my project, and therefore my narratives of the perverse borrow heavily from the stories that Freud tells about the origins of the perversions as he understood them; yet his understanding came from studying with French neurologists, listening to Central European women patients, reading ancient Greek and Latin literature, and following accounts of British and other contemporary European anthropologists. Surely even a sexology of perversions, let alone a broader understanding of what it means to be perverse, would look suspiciously at this limited basis for analysis. Feminist analysis is the principal tool which other recent authors use (and which I too shall use) to critique Freud's methodology and actual conclusions about his narratives of the perverse, but it too made claims to universality which have had to be modified, both strategically and also theoretically, to take into account non-European stories about wayward bodies. We consult anthropologists and local intellectuals for such stories, perhaps. Yet virtually all Latin American intellectuals take their tools from Europe; and a search for a uniquely Latin American perversion should not presume that all moments of anthropological thinking are free either from a general Western bias or from a specifically psychoanalytic influence.

The psychoanalytic focus of my project comes out of a universalizing tradition that expects to find (indeed, in *Totem and Taboo*, claims to *have* found, and founds itself upon having found) Oedipus among the savages, and claims to discover laws of the unconscious which function in any psyche in any part of the world. The long unwinding of Freud's claims to transhistorical truth, his selective use of the anthropology of his day, and the use of Freud by the anthropologists of the next generation such as Levi-Strauss, need concern us only tangentially here.[10] But the importance of anthropology to discourses which make claims to tell the truth of Latin America, as persuasively asserted by González Echevarría,[11] inevitably draws us to the use of the incest taboo in the works of French structuralist Levi-Strauss, who founds the elementary structures of kinship on the exchange of women among male-defined kinship-groups. This more abstract version of Oedipus, in which one is prohibited from marrying any of the women in one's clan and that this prohibition is what defines one's clan, was subjected to a critique by Deleuze and Guattari in their *Anti-Oedipus*, and the critique was extended and brought back to the Oedipal family itself in Foucault's *History of Sexuality*: over the course of the eighteenth and nineteenth century, Western society was deploying a sexuality that was increasingly eroding the importance of family as a site of social control and subject formation, and so the incest taboo of the Oedipus complex served, paradoxically, as a reassurance to the family, a guarantee that, however flawed or perilous the development of the child in its care, it is the nuclear family that endows the child with its most profound subjectivity, that is, its sexuality (Foucault 119–31). And indeed, incest is an unusual taboo even in a contemporary world more skeptical of Freud but more dependent on pop psychology than ever: when it is between an adult and a preadolescent it is seen as the source of all the wounds and damages of that child's life, yet when it is an attraction between children of an equal age, it flies under the radar of pop psychological anxieties. This was not always true: what sometimes brought incest into visibility, into literature, was its usefulness for a Romantic/Gothic paradigm of the self's alienation from itself or from its idyllic childhood, or when the taboo between half-brother and half-sister maps on to other social taboos, principally racial ones.

All this is to say that the incest taboo is a taboo for conservatives, whether the recluse of the House of Usher or the uncannily passive brother and sister in Cortázar's "House Taken Over," whether the tormented Southern gentlemen of Faulknerian fiction or the tormented last living couple in Comala in Rulfo's *Pedro Páramo*. When in the hands of a liberal, as in John Sayles's border movie *Lone Star*, incest makes less sense: the white sheriff and his Chicana girlfriend realize that the abusive old sheriff is the father of both of them—a conclusion that emblematizes perfectly the inheritance of violence in Texas–Mexico interactions—but this fact suddenly stops their relationship dead in its tracks, and the movie reaches an abrupt and melancholy end. When in the hands of a conservative libertine, as in Mario Vargas Llosa's *Aunt Julia and the Scriptwriter, In Praise of the Stepmother*, and *The Notebooks of Don Rigoberto*, incest is a way to provoke some (but not too much) scandal, a way to stay true to the values of class and clan (as the younger partner, to learn or to replicate the values of class and clan) while not losing your claim to the outlaw status all twentieth-century writers need.

And yet the most important Latin American novel of the twentieth century—according to all recent literary histories—takes as one of its structuring principles the movement toward, away from, and eventually toward incest once again: Gabriel García Márquez's *One Hundred Years of Solitude*. If we accept the idea that Freud and Levi-Strauss are characteristically modern(ist) thinkers, and that therefore incest is a modern(ist) perversion par excellence, the structuring presence of incest in Rulfo, Vargas Llosa, early Cortázar, and especially García Márquez would reinforce the common argument that the novelists of the Boom should be considered "late modernists" rather than "post-modernists." García Márquez's title also directs us to a text which is the most likely candidate for our own search for a uniquely Latin American contribution to the narratives of the perverse, Octavio Paz's *The Labyrinth of Solitude* (1950) and his story about what *machismo* is and where it comes from.

The Labyrinth of Solitude subordinates its tale of perverse sexuality to the larger question of Mexicanness, a topic which circles around the concept signaled in the title, solitude. Paz's Mexican keeps himself more separate, more alone, than other alienated Western men. Otherwise incapable of opening himself either to his friends or to his wife or mother, he explodes into aggression or into communal festivals more violently than Euro-Americans do, because he is more in need of the release than they are. The essay is clearly indebted to a tradition of essays on national character that includes the Spanish Generation of 1898 and Ortega y Gasset and culminates for Paz in Samuel Ramos's *Profile of Man and Culture in Mexico* (1934); like Ramos's essay, it claims to use psychoanalysis to explain its main points (Ramos emphasizing Adlerian inferiority complexes, Paz focusing more on ambivalence toward parental figures); like Ramos's essay, it takes its point of departure from an underclass type. Ramos begins his essay describing the *pelado*, the blustering, wily urban peasant portrayed most often by the comic actor Cantinflas;[12] Paz begins his essay reacting to the *pachucos* he encountered in California in the 1940s, the gangs of Mexican-American youths, arrogant dandy outcasts from American culture who have not preserved (according to Paz) any authentic Mexican culture in their transplantation. Paz's emphasis on masks and authenticity is both a marker of mid-century existentialism and, no doubt, one of the causes of the essay's frequent presence in meditations on Chicano identity: furious with Paz for his negative portrayal of the *pachuco*, Arteaga (*Chicano Poetics*), Anzaldúa (*Borderlands/La Frontera*) and others are still too often caught up in debates of what constitutes an "authentic" Chicano for them to be able simply to ignore his analysis.

Paz's unease around the unorthodox hypermasculinity of the *pachuco* could itself be of interest to queer theory;[13] here, however, we are more interested in how Paz's claim that the Mexican male is "closed" to others affects Mexican sexuality and is itself supposedly caused by Mexico's colonial history. While occasionally this refusal to open oneself to the other is considered a trait both of Latin American women and of men (after all, the parched spinsters and widows, the cruel matriarchs of García Márquez endure their share of solitude), for Paz the binary of closed vs. open corresponds most directly to that of Mexican masculinity vs. femininity in the notorious, much-anthologized chapter "The Children of La Malinche," which provides us with not just a narrative but the précis of a historical novel of the perverse. The chapter establishes, through some sleight of hand, the position that all Mexicans consider themselves "hijos de la Chingada" (sons-of-bitches, literally "Sons of the Fucked Woman"—the chapter includes a three-page etymology of the various uses of the word *chingar*, to fuck or to screw over), and that the disrespect toward the maternal figure implicit in the phrase should be given equal weight in discussions of gender relations with the more obvious matriolatry of the Mexican male: "But the singularity of the Mexican resides, I believe, in his violent, sarcastic humiliation of the Mother and his no less violent affirmation of the Father" (103). Indeed, humiliating the traitorous mother overwhelms Paz's narrative: at first Paz identifies Mexico's Oedipal couple as the Conquistador and the raped Indian woman, but although sometimes the raped Indian woman is passive, submissive, and opened without the possibility of voice or agency, it becomes more relevant for Paz that the most interesting, most novelistic Indian woman of them all was by no means passive, but instead actively contributed to the downfall of Mesoamerican indigenous civilization: Malintzin, "Doña Marina," La Malinche, the Tlaxcalan Indian slave whom Cortés acquired in his first victory over a coastal Mayan tribe and who served him as an interpreter as he marched inland, made treaties with the Tlaxcalans and other unhappy subjects of the Aztec empire and (with La Malinche's aid) passed himself off as the reincarnation of the god Quetzalcóatl who was coming back to reclaim the throne from Moctezuma.

This story, set forth not just in the official histories of the Empire but in the vivid personal chronicle of the Conquest by one of Cortés's foot soldiers, owes much of its intelligibility to various cultural traditions and imperatives. The tradition of "Doña Marina" or the good Malinche who understands her providential role in Christian history harks back to the Moorish romance traditions of Golden Age Spain; the rhetoric around the bad Malinche cites stereotypes of the treacherous woman that go back to Spanish tales of the Muslim conquest of Christian Spain and ultimately to the misogynistic reading of Eve in Genesis.[14] The narrative makes room for other masculine positions besides that of Cortés: for instance, recent queer theory has connected the portrayal of the indecisive Moctezuma in these accounts to a broad imperial need to devirilize Indian males, even their most powerful representatives;[15] and Paz himself spends a certain amount of time imagining the position of Cuauhtémoc, the murdered son of Moctezuma whose martyrdom and iconology blends with Spanish traditions of the crucified Christ and pre-Columbian martyred gods so as to furnish future indigenist movements with a hero figure whose status is not grounded in the Conquest. However, despite her presence in the chapter's title, Paz does not extend his imagination as fully toward La Malinche as he does toward Cuauhtémoc. The tradition has spun a variety of motives for La Malinche's treason of her race—Did she share the theological illusion? Was it a sexual attraction? Was it merely a realpolitik ploy to free herself and her tribe from the Aztecs, a strategy that underestimated the Conquistadors' ability to extend their conquest across Mesoamerica?—but Paz himself is uninterested in her psychology or motivation. Perhaps this should come as no surprise: in a previous chapter he has declared that the Mexican woman has no will, can serve only as an idol or a symbol, and (following Romantic and Surrealist dogma) exercises power over the male imagination only as silence, as Enigma. Here, Paz invests much more energy examining the reaction of the son of La Malinche, the hijo de la Chingada, who expects his arrogant militarized father to abandon his Indian wife; while the son on the one hand creates a cult around his mother in the image of Guadalupe the Virgin, he also both expresses his contempt toward her in the aggression he practices against all other women and militarizes or closes himself up against all other men.

So Latin American men have a perversion peculiar to them, *machismo*; its main characteristics are a refusal to open up to the other and extreme ambivalence toward the mother and toward all women; and the narrative of its cause is an Oedipalized reading of all Western and pre-Columbian history culminating in the tragic fall of an Empire. Paz's fiction of the origins of machismo is so extraordinarily powerful that one must spend a certain amount of time criticizing it before it is safe to actually analyze the force of its power. It is something of an open question whether the book correctly assesses the status of myth in history;[16] we can clearly see how it manipulates the status of myth in historical argumentation. Paz, after all, is setting out to examine what he considers to be a historical entity, Mexican national character; he claims that it came into existence in 1519, underwent solidification (the Colonial era), denial and/or mystification (the liberal and Porfirian eras), renovation (the Revolution), and now stagnation. Paz is indeed comfortable declaring the existence, continuity, and vicissitudes of such entities over time: not only does he not avoid the metaphysical language of Being, he declares that the Mexican's national character flaw is that "he does not dare to be." A Mexican is only authentic when he declares himself to be an "hijo de la Chingada," when he accedes to the level of an archetype that has a specifically historical inflection: for better or for worse, authenticity and archetype mutually define each other. Read this way, Paz is not castigating his machista contemporaries for repeating the cruelties of hated Spanish ancestors but rather endowing cruel and sexist behavior with historical resonance: one is, fatally, most Mexican when one abuses one's wife. Again, the language of Being spoils another aspect of this analysis, the language of class and race: Paz rejects the notion that only the lower classes mistreat their women (although this is part and parcel of Paz's notorious dismissal of class, even on his own archetypal terms[17]) and denies that any Mexican considers himself of pure Creole heritage, yet he does so only to install permanently a racialized Oedipal couple within the Latin American himself.

It is a pity that the historical trappings of this version of Oedipus confer upon it a fatalistic promise of eternal repetition,[18] since otherwise it would serve as an interesting extension of the narratives of the perverse as they have been inherited from Freud. Freud famously assumed that the male infant's anger toward his parents would be jealousy toward the father for interrupting a perfectly symbiotic love between himself and his mother; only a later theorist such as Melanie Klein would analyze the child's ambivalence toward the mother, but even she did so on the grounds of the pre-Oedipal, in the mother's function as the breast, not as a figure in the family triangle. The Freudian infant son supposedly feels ambivalence toward the father when he is encouraged to be like him but is forbidden to possess the mother whom the father also desires. In Paz's historical-mythical costume drama, in contrast, the son feels he is being encouraged to be like a man who denigrates the mother he loves, which produces ambivalence toward both father and mother. Indeed, stripped of the historical resonances of Cortés and Malinche, the model sums up what most people understand to be the misogyny of sexual relations of patriarchy: perhaps it is not so surprising that a lesbian feminist such as Anzaldúa should include its imagery and historical fiction so prominently in her writings, nor that antifeminists should accuse her of exalting the woman-as-victim into an archetype. Nevertheless, I suggest that if authors are choosing to invoke Paz instead of, say, his contemporary Simone de Beauvoir for their analysis of how men cannot recognize women as their legitimate others, it is not because Paz has understood men's contempt for women better than de Beauvoir did, but rather because of his use of a story with recognizable characters to convey that analysis.

If the power of Paz's argument depends on his ability to tell a story using historical figures, perhaps we should counter with other stories, not with logical critiques of the relationship between myth and historical argumentation, but with countermyths. Arteaga, in "Heterotextual Negotiations," in *Chicano Poetics*, summarizes some authors who have done just that, examining other minor male characters from the period of the Conquest. The Conquistador Alvar Núñez Cabeza de Vaca lost his army and was adopted by Indians in what is now the American Southwest, becoming something of a shaman before he found his way back to New Spain; closer to the Malinche story, Arteaga examines the castaway Gonzalo Guerrero whom Cortés also discovered on the Mayan coast, but who lived happily and pacifically as an Indian with his native wife and who refused to join Cortés in his trek inland. Useful as they are, such counter-myths cannot draw on the energy of the Oedipal triangle in Paz's story. It might be more valuable to work further variations on Oedipus in Mexican or Latin American terms. For instance, it might be useful to complicate the relationship between race and gender in our mestizo Oedipus. After the first generations, the Inca Garcilasos and Guaman Pomas, miscegenation was not always white husband, brown wife but a rainbow of variations including the direct opposite. In the case of Mexico, the most visible of these pairings was Benito Juárez, the dark-skinned nineteenth-century liberal general and his light-skinned Italian wife, whose joint portrait hangs in the presidential palace[19] and whose Reform period is criticized fiercely by Paz as too hostile to religion and myths for a truly Mexican taste. But we might look closer to home for these mixed marriages: say, that of Paz himself, who emphasized in interviews that his paternal grandfather (although an intellectual in the service of that same Benito Juárez, indeed a historical novelist who twice took as his subject the tale of Cortés and la Malinche[20]) was a mestizo with very Indian features (Guibert, *Seven Voices* 17), his father a lawyer for the most "Indianist" of the Mexican revolutionaries, Emiliano Zapata (*Labyrinth* 313); whereas his mother was a first-generation Mexican whose parents were from Spain, his first wife Elena Garro a very light-skinned Mexican woman (and playwright and novelist in her own right), and his second wife a blonde Frenchwoman. The facets of machismo that would now stand out are somewhat different, a machismo in which violence and contempt toward women expresses the desire for revenge of decolonizing former peasants, not the shout of triumph of a Conquistador. If the Mexican man in the twentieth century feels ambivalence and self-contradiction, it may be because he has an ideology of indigenism but a social practice of *blanqueamiento*, "improving the race" or "marrying up."

Paz's first wife Elena Garro seemed to have accepted the mythology of the Malinche while also trying to free herself from it: besides the Pazian rewriting of Rulfo's *Pedro Páramo* in her 1963 novel *Recollections of Things to Come*,[21] her 1964 short story "It's the Tlaxcalans' Fault" is a nice proof that false consciousness doesn't always prevent true action. A housewife in 1960s Mexico City becomes convinced that she is also an Indian woman reliving the fall of Tenochtitlán, where she has betrayed her cousin/fiancé, possibly with a Cortés figure. Her psyche/Her mythical position having been coerced into the Malinche position, the protagonist in the present confides her visions to her (Indian) maid at the kitchen table, and then runs off into the night, presumably with her Aztec lover. The story is both conservative and radical, conservative because it looks back to the past and because the woman's escape is coded as a move from one man to another, radical because the new lover is ideologically progressive and, well, imaginary, more malleable to her desires than her real boorish modern husband.[22] Hardly a feminist even at the level of her Brazilian contemporary Clarice Lispector, Garro nevertheless parlays Paz's *méconnaissance* into a tale of a "treachery" that brings about the liberation of a woman.

But since Paz himself focuses on the son of the Malinche, it might be more useful to examine a novel by Paz's first literary son, Carlos Fuentes, his most *Labyrinth*-influenced *The Death of Artemio Cruz* (1962). The debt to Paz's essay is almost slavish at points, down to the novel's own three-page interlude featuring the verb *chingar*. But Fuentes has also inherited one of the main plots of the "Novel of the Mexican Revolution" in which a poor mestizo protagonist rises through ruthlessness to an important position in postrevolutionary society. Artemio, like Octavio Paz—yet *un*like the paradigm Paz described—"marries up," achieving social legitimacy partly by marrying a Spaniard's daughter in Puebla (Mexico's equivalent of Boston, a blue-blood city). If Garro found a way to "betray" Paz's paradigm from within, Fuentes finds a way to *recuperate* it from within: at night, in bed, mestizo Artemio and Creole Catalina become the Conquistador and the Chingada. "I let myself go," repeats Catalina every morning when she awakes (79, 86) but every evening she surrenders to him once again. "My God," she thinks to herself, "why can't I be the same woman by night as I am by day?" (81). By night she yields to passion, by day she recalls that he married her for her social position and money. The novel is a harsh criticism of Artemio and implicitly of an entire generations' immorality, but it is an immorality that comes from the man's machista anger at La Chingada, and the solution, says the omniscient narrator: "Let's kill her"—it is not clear whether he means that Mexican men should love women without the ghost of La Chingada, or whether Mexican men should face death and meaninglessness (the novel begins in the present at Artemio's deathbed) alone, without any women. If the latter, Mexican men like Fuentes are still using mythified history to justify contemporary sexuality, not to critique it; to shift the scene of sexual politics from the immediate social reality of Mexico to the mythical, mystified time of the Conquest.

But indeed Fuentes's reading of mythical Mexican machismo may have exceeded Paz and Fuentes's own needs. Remember that Paz's mother figure is ambivalent, split into a good and a bad figure. The good Mexican mother is also autochthonous, doubly so, a syncretistic mix of the Virgin Mary and the Aztec fertility goddess Tonantzin, the Virgin of Guadalupe. Paz considers her to be more passive than other Western figures of the good mother (even though, as he notes elsewhere, Guadalupe was the rallying cry of Mexican nationalism during the Wars of Independence). Likewise, Paz considers and deliberately rejects a more Western version of the bad mother:

> In contrast to Guadalupe, who is the Virgin Mother, the *Chingada* is the violated Mother. Neither in her nor in the Virgin do we find traces of the darker attributes of the great goddesses: the lasciviousness of Amaterasu and Aphrodite, the cruelty of Artemis and Astarte, the sinister magic of Circe or the bloodlust of Kali. (85)

Against such active figures of female evil, Paz implies, male machismo would not express itself with the disrespect and contempt it does toward la Chingada.[23] At the same time that he was creating Artemio and Catalina, Fuentes was also attributing the powers of the "great goddesses" to another Mexican woman in his much-anthologized short novel *Aura* (1963). This story, in which a young historian is seduced by a phantom girl into becoming the sexual slave of a witch, suggests that Mexican men, albeit in the fantastic mode that Fuentes's novella employs, can thrill to the lasciviousness and cruelty of a black magic Spider Woman just as easily as non-macho European men.

Occasionally in conversations with Latin Americans not from Mexico I hear the comment that machismo must be only a Mexican affair, since it does not apply where they come from. Since what a North American observer encounters as sexism is far more common throughout Latin America than in Europe or the United States, and yet a certain kind of machista misogyny is available in almost any sexist society, it might have been more accurate for those Latin Americans to say that Paz's *description* of machismo must be only a Mexican affair, a story that has grabbed the imagination of Mexican men, and many women, to describe a situation in which women blame themselves for their lack of agency or in which their agency seems limited to collaborating with a male outsider against the men of their family and tribe. If we look more generally at the relations between men and women in Latin America, we see far more instances of what Paz had called "the great goddesses," those fantastic versions of female power looming large in the male imagination, than Paz was willing to attribute, even among those Mexicans who were cleaving closely to Paz's line on the subject. In *Kiss of the Spider Woman*, Molina's sexual politics is hardly that of an enlightened woman—Valentín is the one who rebukes Molina for enjoying the subjected position and for claiming that a little fear of the man who embraces you is part of the kick, although of course Valentín also ignores the signs that Molina intends to sacrifice himself not for the cause but for Love—but in the fantasies that he spins out, Molina restores the power to the female figure that his "feminine masochism" prevents him from taking in real life.

EXIT THE SPIDER WOMAN

[Molina]:—And when the chorus number's finished, the stage gets left in total darkness until, up above, a light begins to rise like mist and the silhouette of some divine-looking woman, who's very tall, absolutely perfect, but still just a hazy outline, slowly emerges sharper and sharper, because she steps through layers and layers of hanging tulle, and you obviously get to see her more and more clearly,

wrapped in a silver lamé gown that fits her like a glove [como una vaina]. The most divine woman you can imagine. And she sings a song, first in French and afterwards in German.

(*Kiss* 50; 57)

Where is the most divine woman you can imagine in Freudian theory? What happens to her? What kinds of stories does she find herself in?

Freud wrote whole books about fathers elevated beyond the human: his work on *Group Psychology and the Analysis of the Ego* is his contribution to the theory of charisma (and a refinement of his theories of the superego) and in *Totem and Taboo* he tries to show that a primal horde of men killed their father and, panicked by guilt feelings, elevate the dead father into a totem figure who prevents the children from engaging in new rounds of incest. In both cases, of course, the Enlightenment Freud is not endorsing the behavior of insufficiently rational masses or primitives, but he nevertheless considers their errors to be natural: for Freud, fathers are much more likely to turn into gods and führers than mothers—or other women—are.[24] When an actual goddess appeared in a story, the novel *Gradiva* which he analyzed in 1909, Freud decided that she could stand in allegorically as the analyst—not, apparently, much of a mother, or woman, at all. Although quite patriarchal in his own life, at least Carl Jung enjoyed spinning his tales of animus and anima claiming to give equal time to the feminine principle, however conservatively defined. Yet one place where we do see the charismatic woman in Freud is in the narratives of the perversions. Although each of the following chapters examines one of these narrations of the perverse in greater detail, a brief glance at the fate of the Spider Woman in each of these stories will serve as an introduction to them.

This powerful charismatic woman does not appear in all these narrations in the same way, so it is a bit dismaying that Freud deals with her with such a similar theoretical ruthlessness in each case. In his essay on masochism, "A Child Is Being Beaten," Freud is most blatant: after examining the accounts of four women patients who are aroused at fantasies of watching a child being beaten, where Freud comes to the conclusion that this fantasy is the final formation in which a woman's father is beating rival siblings to show his love for her, or her father is beating her to show his love for her—but never admitting the possibility that beneath the repression she herself might be enjoying beating the child—, he moves on to his few male patients with similar fantasies, who tell him explicitly that it is their mothers who are beating them. Freud refuses to believe them and declares that underneath their mothers or mother substitutes, it is their fathers who are beating them. Given Freud's aggressiveness in voiding the mother from sadomasochistic scenarios, we will study such narratives in future chapters using Sacher-Masoch's *Venus in Furs*, especially as explicated by Gilles Deleuze in the highly charged atmosphere (for Latin American Boom literature) of Paris in the 1960s. Freud has no transvestism narrative per se, except that of the psychotic Doctor Schreber (who had to dress in his wife's clothing in order to attract dangerous alien rays up into his ass, thus rendering them harmless); I am rather inclined to think that if Marjorie Garber in *Vested Interests* is correct to argue that the figure of the transvestite is a mark of semiotic anxieties, productive of more semiotic anxieties, this may in part be because Freud never devoted extensive space to disseminating a narrative about transvestism, however much we would probably disagree with it now. We will be cobbling together a narrative about the transvestite from a variety of sources, including the writings of Severo Sarduy, the Cuban exile writer who attended Lacan's seminars in (where else?) the Paris of the 1960s. (It seems that our narrators of the perverse, inversely to Leni in Molina's Nazi movie, sing their theories first in German, and then afterward in French.)

The dominating mother is of course the cliché of Freudian stories of homosexual development: it is so well known that even Molina, as we have seen, has heard a version of it. For our purposes it is important to emphasize not just that Freud disapproves of the smothering mother who, together with the absent or unlovable father, destroys the possibility of normality for the infant boy, but also the corollary to this narrative which Freud advances in his essay on narcissism: when he grows up, the male homosexual takes over the position of the dominating mother, looking to find a younger man on whom he can shower affection as if he were loving his younger self. (Oscar Wilde on such theorizing: "All women grow up to become their mothers; that is their tragedy. No man ever does; that's his.") While the position of the dominant woman is permitted to remain, albeit as one corrosive to a son's masculinity, it seems to have been preserved almost as a placeholder for its eventual occupation by a male.

It is worthwhile to pause here, for an observation and for a admission. The observation is that we are losing some of the specificity of the Spider Woman as we look for her presence in the narratives of the perverse. Surely we are not just looking for power in these figures, or even some "female power" to be negotiated later against the more obvious maneuverings of male power, but rather we are looking for glamour, the charisma attributed to the leader in *Group Psychology*, the thing that sets Leni and the other movie heroines apart from Molina's poor ailing mother. Molina recounts no anecdotes in *Kiss* of watching movies with his mom, but because that scenario structures almost entirely Puig's first novel *Betrayed by Rita Hayworth* and because he has so often in interviews described this childhood scenario of daily visits to the small-town movie theater with his mother as a child (much of Suzanne Jill Levine's 2000 biography of Puig also recounts these memories), we might feel justified in saying that Molina does not necessarily look at Valentín or at other *men* with the eyes of his mother (although he might), but he does look at *women*, Leni and the other screen goddesses, with the eyes of his mother. The glamorous one is the cynosure, the object of all the gazes; it seems important to its role in homosexuality that it oscillate between a fantasmatic version of the mother and a fantasmatic source of the mother's admiration.

In that sense, of the various narratives of the perverse that I might privilege for this project, I return time and again to the narrative Freud offers for the fetishist, from a late (1927) essay that does not collapse the position of the desired woman into someone else, even though Freud, as in other narratives of the perverse that we have seen from him, will not take the woman at the valuation that the fetishist himself will. In Freud's story, the child who will become a fetishist discovers the mother's absence of a penis at a somewhat late moment, around the age of five or six when reason is rather developed, in a moment after an excited anticipation of seeing the mother's genitals. As usual in Freud, the child's intellectual revulsion at the mother's castration arises from a perceived threat to his own penis, not (say) an anger that a person as wonderful as his own mother should not have the social standing which having a phallus would guarantee. The trauma of discovery can lead to any of three outcomes: a shock one gets over quickly and another reason to avoid identifying with women as one consolidates a male heterosexual identity; a permanent aversion toward the female genitals, which leads one to a male homosexual identity; or an intellectual denial (not the same as repression) that she is castrated at all, along with a fixation on some chance object upon which one displaces the excitement and anticipation that one had been feeling toward the mother's genitals. These chance objects become the fetishes—shoes, underwear, hair or furry things, and so on. A savvy woman who knows how this sort of game is played might turn her entire body into a fetish in a silver lamé dress that fits like a glove (*como una vaina* in the original Spanish, "like a sheath," an even more explicit image of woman-fetish as penis/phallus), and her admiring entourage will continue to attribute glamour to her; "he knows, but neverthless" he will treat her as if she were phallic, powerful, and perhaps he will reinscribe her castratedness, her vulnerability in a man's world, on some other level of the plot and character: perhaps if she is kissed she will turn into a panther, or perhaps her husband's first wife is now a zombie sent to murder her, or maybe she is a drunk bolero singer in love with a man who doesn't love her back. She is no less admirable for all these vulnerabilities.

My admission is that I have had an admirable, glamorous model over the course of this chapter as I have been critically summarizing Freud: Puig himself. For one of the most truly eccentric, yet truly appropriate contributions to the polyphony of *Kiss* is a series of long footnotes to the text, which are the only components of the novel written in the third person (although there are some important moments of interior monologue, the rest of the novel is either dialogue without stage directions or transcripts of police reports) and whose purpose is to summarize what was accepted in 1975 on the left of the psychoanalytic community about the origins of homosexuality. These footnotes come into the text when Valentín admits, "I really know very little about people with your type of inclination," and appear at intervals through the center of the novel, finishing at about the point where Valentín agrees to have sex with Molina: coming into being at Valentín the rationalist's request, it seems appropriate that they end when his seduction is complete. In another sense these footnotes are designed as an affirmation of Molina's position: the only other kind of footnote is a long excerpt from the press kit summarizing the end of the pro-Nazi movie, and its primary purpose in the text is to show that Molina was correct when he claimed to have been impervious to the more outlandish propagandistic moments in the film, so it seems fair to read the other footnotes, too, as proof that Molina, though no intellectual, is in the right.[25]

It is not clear to me, however, whether Puig's footnotes themselves stay in the right. I said that the psychoanalysis footnotes are "written in the third person" instead of "written in Puig's own voice" because Puig has eliminated all the characteristics of a personal voice in these footnotes: they are another exercise in genre for him. They do have a strong narrative drive: roughly following an updated version of Freud's own narration in the 1905 *Three Essays* from the most biological to the most psychoanalytic explanation of homosexuality (and especially effeminate homosexuality—Puig is less interested in a taxonomy than in the story of Molina), the footnotes then go on roughly following the ideas of Herbert Marcuse on the relationship between sexuality and revolution.[26] In this story, put forward by Marcuse as early as 1955 in *Eros and Civilization*, homosexuality is one variation of polymorphous perversity, not to be valued particularly in itself, but not to be repressed either, and a proof that our society suffers from surplus repression; as Puig's footnote puts it, "Marcuse points out that the social function of the homosexual is analogous to that of the critical philosopher, since his very presence is a constant reminder of the repressed elements of society" (195; 199). By such statements as that, Puig hopes to put Valentín and Molina on equal footing as revolutionaries, one conscious, the other unconscious forces for change in society. And yet it is difficult to reconcile this with Molina's own disaffection from politics and lack of belief in change: indeed, the only role of a homosexual in Marcuse's understanding of contemporary society is to be a victim, someone for the left to rush to defend just as it defends other helpless and downtrodden peoples. Yet Puig seems curiously unaware that his summary of Marcuse reduces his main character to no more than a canary in a coal mine, and this penultimate footnote ends by suggesting that the ultimate value of homosexual liberation would be to liberate the feminine side of heterosexual men. In both cases, these positions start to resemble Judith Roof's pessimistic assessment of narrative closure bringing with it a "heteronormative" ideology: the success of a political movement will seem to depend on whether it improves the lot of the straight men of the world. The last long footnote returns to the notion of cross-gendered identification, of sissies and tomboys. Introduced by Fenichel, it summarizes a Danish woman, Dr. Anneli Taube, who suggests that effeminate boys' identification with their mothers (and with their mothers' submissiveness) may be eventually eliminated, as the mothers with whom these boys identify are reached by a feminism that will allow both them and their sons to stand up for themselves: "a submissive spirit, a conservative attitude, a love of peace at any cost, even the cost of perpetuating their own marginality" is not natural in women or in women-identified gay men, it is "proven not to be deliberate, but compulsive," and feminism will help liberate both women from "heterosexual bourgeois models for conduct" and gay men from "'bourgeois' models for homosexual conduct." Indeed, the footnotes end, "the subsequent formation of homosexual liberation fronts is one proof of that" (213–4; 211), that is, that the housewives that proto-gay children are imitating are less Betty Crocker and more Betty Friedan. On the one hand, these sentiments seem admirable, like Valentín's enjoining Molina not to let his lovers exploit him. But on the other hand, they also seem to be expressing the desire to do away with the effeminate homosexual altogether, not just (as the plot of the novel demonstrates) as a danger to himself as he sacrifices himself in a cause in which he does not believe because he feels fulfilled when sacrificing himself for a real man's ideology, but also as a sort of embarrassment to an otherwise progressive gay community.

Eventually I admitted that I was holding back one of the important narratives from the reader of this chapter; in interviews, Puig eventually admitted that, whereas all of the other footnotes are real authors, the last of them, the only woman, the Danish Dr. Anneli Taube, was Puig's own invention. He was somewhat coy about the revelation, like the layers of tulle which slowly make clear Leni's profile in the cabaret, dropping a hint or two in a 1977 interview with Ronald Christ and in personal interviews with Lucille Kerr (235, n. 40), and finally admitting it in an interview conducted in Germany in 1981, published in 1992 (Amícola 275). The invented authority was justified in terms of expediency: Puig says that he couldn't find someone who said precisely what he wanted to say, so he said it himself. Certainly one does not suspect this gesture of Borgesian irony, subverting a message by deriving it from an apocryphal text: rather, it is an attempt to increase the authority of one's statements by claiming a credential one does not have. It is also not Borgesian in that virtually all readers need to be alerted extratextually that this footnote source is not authentic. And surely Anneli Taube's hope, that homosexuals and leftists will free themselves together from two different but mutually reinforcing aspects of bourgeois oppression, belongs in this book, and belongs in this book *as a man impersonating a woman's voice.*

Other than his desire to support anti-machista relations between husbands and wives, one can't help but attribute this decision on the part of Puig as a final chance to take on a female persona, where one would least expect it, to choose once again to wield the phallus (she's a doctor!) *as a woman* instead of as a man. In that sense, one does not begrudge Puig the desire to do what his protagonist has been doing the whole length of the book, even if in doing so he ventriloquizes a discomfort with Molina's most basic identifications and life decisions. It is more appropriate to think of the sacrifice at the end of *Kiss of the Spider Woman* not in terms of killing the faggot in order that the revolution may come faster or in order that the young macho get in touch with his feminine self, but in order for the effeminate homosexual *storyteller* to achieve an apotheosis into the ever-vulnerable yet powerful fetishized woman, who may seem trapped by the stories she tells but on closer inspection feigns immobility the more fully to draw you into her web. Over the course of the rest of my book we see many other authors examine the possibilities of the phallic woman, the spider woman, as a model for escaping or deferring the compulsory heterosexuality (at times, the compulsory machismo) that is considered "normal" Latin American masculinity. These stories are still parasitic upon definitions of the normal—following the metaphor of the spider, perhaps it would be better to say that they are *predatory* upon the normal: a spider does not wish to see a change in the nature of flies, and authors work best when they know the expectations of the readers to be seduced. However, the stories of these authors are not used to help shore up a definition of normality; rather, they show a dangerous mobility within the contested terrain of masculinity which contrasts with the Freudian notion of "fixation"; and an unwillingness to accept the notions of "integration" and

"maturity" that subordinate some pleasures to others or force the abandon-
ment of certain erogenous zones or sites of pleasure.

This relationship to normality obtains even when what constitutes
normality in the literary tradition differs from standard psychological
realism. But "normal" sexuality may function to shore up the claims made
by such alternatives to psychological realism.

MAGICAL REALISM'S NORMALITY

*What astonished [the doctor] most, however, was the logic of the [old man's]
wings. They turned out to be so natural in that completely human organism that
he could not understand why other people did not have them.*

(García Márquez, "A Very Old Man with Enormous Wings,"
Innocent Erendira 18)

*... but at this point the housekeeper stops talking. And the [young bride] asks her
what's the matter, and the housekeeper tells her how there's a legend, which probably isn't true but just the same it scares her, and it's about the zombies. Zombies?
What are they? the girl asks her [...] And she explains that they're the dead people that witch doctors manage to revive before the corpses get cold, because the
witch doctors themselves are the ones who kill them, with a special poison they
prepare, and the living dead no longer possess any will of their own, and they obey
only the orders of the witch doctors.*

(*Kiss* 167)

If there is any book that can stand in our field as representative of both what
is unique and what is universal about the Latin American twentieth century
novel, that would have to be *One Hundred Years of Solitude* and the other magical realist stories of that era, such as "A Very Old Man With Enormous
Wings," quoted above. Its foundational place in Latin American letters inaugurated a reaction to contemporary realism, and to its immediate precursor the
deliberately dry Borgesian fantastic, to produce the kind of writing everybody
recognizes as Latin American. How does it achieve its naturalness, its normality, whereas a novel like *Kiss of the Spider Woman*, less than a decade later and
rigorously realistic after all, must traffic in the narratives of the perverse?

Unsurprisingly, a narrative of even magical normality founds itself in
Nature:

Many years later, as he faced the firing squad, Coronel Aureliano Buendía
was to remember that distant afternoon when his father took him to discover

ice. At that time Macondo was a village of twenty adobe houses, built on the
bank of a river of clear water that ran along a bed of polished stones, which
were white and enormous, like prehistoric eggs. The world was so recent that
many things lacked names, and in order to indicate them it was necessary to
point. (1)

The sexuality of its characters contribute to the novel's appeal, although not
differently from its other treatments of nature. Sexuality is elemental in the
novel, like the house, river, water, eggs, of the first sentences. The rural
ambience of Macondo combines with "the wonder of the New World" to
make the novel's attitude toward sexuality, like the rest of its folk wisdom,
not just palatable but surprising: from a distance the values of the novel are
conservative (though anti-clerical), nostalgic, and predictable, but while
reading it one feels like the people of Macondo looking at the objects
drawn to a magnet for the first time (again from the first paragraph):
"Things have a life of their own," the gypsy proclaimed with a harsh accent.
"It's simply a matter of waking up their souls" (2). The novel itself is a thing
with a life of its own, and the novel as a genre was given renewed life by the
Colombian "gypsy" who knew how to wake up its soul.

Sexuality is elemental in *One Hundred Years*, but that does not mean
that it is entirely unproblematic. Rather, its problem is the problem which,
according to Foucault, guarantees that sexuality remains within the bounds
of the family. For in this novel sexuality is shadowed by the fear of incest:
patriarch José Arcadio Buendía and his wife Úrsula are cousins, and her
pregnancies are haunted by the fear that she will bear a child with a pig's
tail. The novel really does end when this fear is borne out and Amaranta
Úrsula, one of the last two Buendías, dies in childbirth with a pig-tailed
stillborn child, the son of the other last Buendía (Amaranta Úrsula's
nephew), who deciphers the gypsy's manuscripts that predicted it, all as a
whirlwind blows the house and town away. That deciphering and cataclysm
has been rightly read as allusions to Borges in general and to Carpentier's
The Kingdom of This World in particular, the novel whose prologue is
canonically given as the source of the definition of magical realism, labeled
there "lo maravilloso real." But one need not wait until the last pages to see
Foucault's claims of the incest taboo in operation: if chapter 1 of *One
Hundred Years* introduced us to the natural nature of Macondo's first generation, chapter 2 brings us the natural nature of Oedipus in the next generation. After telling us of Úrsula's fears of incest and the tale of how they
left the coast to found Macondo in the interior, the narrative passes on to
the puberty of José Arcadio Jr. and Aureliano. José Arcadio Jr. is a "monumental adolescent," and his mother Úrsula, accidentally seeing him naked,

finds him to be "so well-equipped for life that he seemed abnormal" (25). One of the servants, the fortune-teller Pilar Ternera, reassures Úrsula that things will go well for her son, and then she seduces José Arcadio Jr., with the predictable Oedipal result: "He wanted to be with [Pilar] all the time, he wanted her to be his mother ..." (26); when they finally have sex in the dark of Pilar's house, "he tried to remember her face and found before him the face of Úrsula, confusedly aware that he was doing something that for a very long time he had wanted to do but that he imagined could really never be done" (28). Much of modernism, including this example of late modernism, depends on this reading of instinct as an unfulfillable demand to copulate with the mother, and of myth as the unfulfillable demand to return to an impossible origin.

Insofar as José Arcadio Jr. is associated more with the natural, even the primitive (he runs away from home with the gypsies and returns like a Levi-Straussian savage, tattooed all over including his "unusual masculinity" (93), and makes a living at first by raffling himself off to the prostitutes in a hypervirile "protomale" (95) manner that might recall the hypervirility of Paz's pachucos), his brother Aureliano rings the more sublimated changes on the themes of incest. As if following the dictates not of Freud directly but the Collége de Sociologie anthropological literary critic René Girard, Aureliano learns how to desire from listening to his elder brother's stories of lovemaking (30–1). Aureliano, however, does not fall in love with the maternal image, but rather with the image of a daughter: he first experiences love (without sex) when he is taken to the town brothel and meets the nameless granddaughter whom García Márquez will spin off into the separate novella *Innocent Eréndira* and who leaves town before Aureliano can consummate his passion for her; he then falls in love with the nine-year-old Remedios Moscote, whom he betrothes well before she reaches puberty (indeed, she isn't fully toilet trained), and who dies during pregnancy. In one of the false or illusory binary oppositions of this novel,[27] Aureliano begins by imitating his brother, then veers around to desiring an opposite, but while desiring daughterly innocence he nevertheless loses his virginity one evening to motherly experience, to the same Pilar Ternera who bore his brother a child, and who also bears him a child. Whether the model is Freud's Oedipal triangle or Girard's mimetic triangulated desire, whether the scene emphasizes titanic exuberance or titanic self-restraint, *One Hundred Years* seats desire—heterosexual desire—all in the family.

Given that so many of the novel's myths are ironized and so many binary oppositions are established only to be blurred, it is important to note that desire is virtually exclusively heterosexual in *One Hundred Years*, even as sexuality is completely detached both from the social (marriage, respectability) and from love (that genuine concern, whether Christian or existentialist, for the Other, a concern which conquers self-love or solitude). This understanding of sexuality as something independent of alliances and in need of being trained, within the family, toward a healthy mature love, is similarly modern and it too can be found in Foucault's reading of the history of sexuality. Sex is associated with fertility, as often extramarital as not: Aureliano Segundo never has children with the town's prostitute Petra Cotes, but their enthusiastic lovemaking brings about fantastic fertility in their livestock.

Sexuality, fertility, and (so very rarely) love are in that sense no different from the other elemental elements of *One Hundred Years*: they are partly detached from ordinary causation in order to fulfil the dictates of a poetic justice of the specific narrative trajectory of the rise and fall of a Latin American Founding Family as its guilt-driven energy and optimism drive it into Innocent America, only to breed stagnation, then incestuous self-destruction. The novel's poetics reinforces both profusion and despair: once detached from love, neither sex nor fertility nor family can conquer the solitude of the Buendías, and love and sexuality are fated to coincide only in the last incestuous passion; but seemingly every dead end of these detached fragments is explored in nearly infinite variation. Such, then, is the paradox of the centrality of *One Hundred Years* to the Latin American canon: it brings a literary tradition into maturity as it tells the story of a family that can either never grow up or grows up into an apocalyptic sterility.

No amount of humor or irony seems to have been able to dislodge the foundational gesture of primitivism from the genre of magical realism, certainly not for the European and North American reading public that devoured these novels and helped make magical realism the wedge that turned Comparative Literature into World Literature. Primitivism is the equivalent of an appeal to a natural heterosexuality in the developmental history of the individual: Alejo Carpentier's canonical 1949 prologue to *The Kingdom of This World* claims that Latin American historical fiction should be full of marvels because the Conquistadors, natives, and slaves lived in an age of Faith, and that most Latin Americans still do today; and Carpentier's essay, alluding to the "supermacho" of Jarry and the Surrealists, argues that heroic virility is characteristic of the non-European imagination. The primitive, like the instinctual, lives outside history: for the most part, the conventional literary historian and the psychoanalyst need not worry about its transmission through time.[28] After establishing a level of "true" instinct and primitivity, the theorist can then examine the vicissitudes that these forces undergo through development. These syncretisms will often be presented as grotesqueries and corruptions, both of the First and Third World value systems, such as Henri Christophe's faux-French court in *The Kingdom of This World* or the perpetual bacchanalia of the fat years of the banana company's occupation of Macondo and the Buendía household. In psychoanalytic narratives, as we have seen, instincts are expected to undergo vicissitudes on the road to a mature sexuality, but this theoretical difference with primitivism leaves plenty of room for the grotesqueries of the perversions when those stubborn drives resist integration and fixate on one or another zone or stage.

And yet we cannot do without psychoanalytic approaches altogether, for only they take into account the status of the interpreter of literature and his or her willingness to strongly read, even willfully misread, the texts of a tradition. The two epigraphs I have selected for this section point out two quite different projects for a "doctor" and his interaction with the "supernatural." In García Márquez's story of the very old man with enormous wings, the doctor's task is that of simple validation: he pronounces that the magical is also real ("the logic of the wings"); their mechanics are so natural that they can be said to threaten the definition of normality ("he could not understand why other people did not have them"); and then the doctor leaves the story. Since the other village interpreters interpret too much (the old man for them is an angel, or a dangerous fallen angel), and since the marvelous is itself inarticulate (the old man is tested in Latin and Hebrew, but knows neither; he stays with a village family for years, but is never taught Spanish), the man of learning who documents the marvelous is to be praised for his interpretive reticence. A literary critic facing the oddities of the magically real should likewise, according to García Márquez, document the presence of the imagination and then get out. Without affiliation, without influence, performing ironic miracles appropriate for ironic times (lepers who touched the old man were not cured, for instance, but sunflowers grew in their sores), the imagination swoops down upon us from above and leaves just as abruptly.

How different the practice of the witch doctor in Puig's creative retelling of the zombie movie. Hardly a minor character in the movie, the witch doctor is our heroine's principal antagonist: he is the husband of the housekeeper who is telling the heroine here about zombies; he is the man who forced the first wife of the heroine's husband to become his zombie sex slave; he has hypnotic powers; all along in disguise he has been the husband's majordomo on the Haitian plantation; he is French. Since he is the plantation majordomo and uses the zombies to work the fields, he is as much the Marxist Valentín's enemy as he is Molina's. Naturally, like Molina we identify primarily with the heroine in this tale; but as critics we also read the books of the dead, giving them a life for our own purposes and asking them to do work they would not do on their own. I am tempted to say that we as literary critics must have a certain amount of the witch doctor in us, perhaps especially at that moment when we hypnotize an artwork into surrendering its will to us, when we wish to satisfy our desires upon it even more than when we wish it to perform our work for us; but of course in our split identification between protagonist and antagonist we are happiest when in the end the artwork resists and even triumphs over us.

A critic who acknowledges his perverse desires and his ambivalences welcomes the desire, even the inconvenient or resistant desires, in the text. Rather, it is the normal author who must fend off and make abject the perverse possibilities of seductive writing, moving on to maturity as Dante moves past the adulterers and the sodomites (each associated with books and teaching). Let us return to García Márquez and Puig, looking at a somewhat uncanny moment in which the normal(ized) predicts and co-opts the energies of the perverse, where García Márquez narrates not just any decadence, but the sort of decadence that invokes the narratives of the perverse.

DROWNING IN THE PERFUMED MIRROR

[Molina]: She doesn't want to ever have to leave that house again, she feels so at home there, and she looks all around and the drapes are dark velvet to block the light out, and so to let the light in she draws them open and behind them there's another set of lacy curtains. Then you get to see the whole turn-of-the-century decor. She asks who picked out all the lovely things and I think he tells her how much his mother had to do with all that . . .

(*Kiss* 14–15)

Much has changed in the fashions of Western intellectual and literary history since Raymond Williams in 1958 could call the fin de siècle an "interregnum" (174–213) in thinking about culture and society. A committed Marxist humanist in England's heyday of labor politics, Williams would no doubt have been as impatient with fin-de-siècle interiors as Valentín is with Molina's descriptions. Valentín, who is a tolerably good psychoanalytic critic (and *Curse of the Cat People* is, after all, a real movie: Valentín is never closer to Puig himself then when he is a movie critic), reads the fiancé's apartment as a proof of the character's castration, a sexuality which is unthreatening because it remains in the sphere of the mother, and the conversation between him and Molina goes on from there. Williams, Valentín, and Molina are all in agreement that the fin de siècle is coded feminine, a space of the private and of the interior, a retreat from revolution and any other public activity.

The fin de siècle is always at least partly shadowed by decadence. When there is no female presence in the house, but the man takes on too great an enthusiasm for the art of home-making, even the great house of Macondo can become a site of decadence. Perhaps here the synecdoche is inappropriate, however, for although the fin de siècle appears often enough in García Márquez's writings, its recognizable signs never seem to quite touch the Macondo of *One Hundred Years of Solitude*.[29] Here the fin de siècle is both acknowledged and disavowed: Macondo and the Buendías absorb its energy, only to domesticate it and then phobically expel it; finally, a sort of textual uncanny puts "decadence" in this novel in a relationship to *Kiss of the Spider Woman*.

The signs of decadence are organized in the novel's penultimate position, just before the final catastrophe; since the schema of *One Hundred Years* follows more smoothly a rise-and-fall sequence, decadence need not be linked specifically to the 1880s and 1890s. Interestingly enough, it *is* associated with an "interregnum" of sorts: the matriarch Úrsula has died, and now the repressive Catholic Fernanda del Carpio dies too, leaving the Buendía household without a feminine presence for the first time; indeed, only the bastard grandson Aureliano Babilonia is left, slowly deciphering the parchments left by Melquíades the gypsy. Fernanda's two legitimate children, José Arcadio and Amaranta Úrsula, were in Europe at the time of their mother's death, and José Arcadio returns immediately in hopes of collecting the wealth his mother had lied in her letters to him about. José Arcadio too had been lying, and has abandoned religion (Fernanda had been preparing him to be a pope) to eke out a life of pleasure in Italy. As soon as José Arcadio arrives he orders his bastard nephew back to his room, and then creates to the best of his financial abilities a decadent interior in the Buendía house, which will last until his murder and Amaranta Úrsula's return, which in turn puts an end to the interregnum. García Márquez is quite explicit about the gender trouble at stake, introducing the adult José Arcadio as he returns home with "It was impossible to conceive of a man more like his mother" (370–1). For García Márquez, decadence is the activity of an arrogant yet not fully virile dandy in a woman's sphere.

He may be in America, but the furnishings of José Arcadio's decadence are purely European. At first he can barely afford it, restricting his "vest-pocket empire of worn, exotic clothing, false perfumes, and cheap jewelry" (373) to his dead sister Meme's boudoir and bathroom, and befriending the children of Macondo, inviting them to the house to play and to help him in his elaborate grooming rituals:

> The four oldest children, who wore short pants in spite of the fact that they were on the threshold of adolescence, busied themselves with José Arcadio's personal appearance. They would arrive earlier than the others and spend the morning shaving him, giving him massages with hot towels, cutting and polishing the nails on his hands and feet, and perfuming him with toilet water. On several occasions they would get into the pool to soap him from head to toe as he floated on his back thinking about Amaranta. Then they would dry him, powder his body, and dress him. One of the children, who had curly blond hair and eyes of pink glass like a rabbit, was accustomed to sleeping in the house. (377)

Curly blond hair and pink eyes imply both non-Latin-Americanness and unnaturalness in the pederastic scenario of the Roman bath which goes back through D'Annunzio and the Italian decadent popes all the way to Tiberius Caesar's "minnows." This scenario is exacerbated when José Arcadio discovers a long-lost treasure (originally hidden in a saint's statue, now buried underneath Úrsula's old bed); with this money he "convert[s] the house into a decadent paradise" (377–8), which develops into a full-blown orgy, set up entirely with imported goods "from the railroad station in crates marked with his name"; in the pool, now filled with champagne, "they jumped in en masse, swimming like birds flying through a sky gilded with bubbles, while José Arcadio floated on his back on the edge of the festivities, remembering Amaranta with his eyes open" (378).

Amaranta, José Arcadio's virgin spinster great-grand-aunt, is invoked in these two passages both to explain and to neutralize José Arcadio's perversion. José Arcadio grew up in a house run by three old women: old Úrsula "had instilled a fear of the world in him" as a child, but "the caresses of Amaranta in the bath and the pleasure of being powdered between the legs with a silk puff would release him from the terror" (375), while his mother Fernanda groomed him to be a future pope. A momma's boy from three sides, then, José Arcadio is explained as other Latin American failed masculinities from mid-century are explained; but insofar as he is still dreaming of Amaranta, José Arcadio and his desire remain heterosexual, remain all in the family. The European décor of the fin-de-siécle perverse is neither *in* Macondo nor really *of* Macondo, then; it is not surprising that, after the champagne orgy, José Arcadio takes an "ecclesiastical cat o' nine tails" and drives his minions out of the house, "because of the disgust and pity that he felt for himself in the emptiness of the saturnalia" (378). Well, yes, the saturnalia has been emptied by an author who claims that it is unrelated to its host's inner desires, an interiority which follows the path that (as

Foucault indicated) Freud and Levi-Strauss have laid out for him more than the old women of his tribe ever did.

The end of this decadent interlude brings about a tentative rapprochement between the "pervert" (failed fin-de-siécle masculinity) and the "normal" (solitary incestuous magical realism) once José Arcadio and Aureliano Babilonia again inhabit the house by themselves. Aureliano breaks his own reclusiveness to go to the pharmacist's to buy asthma medication for José Arcadio; José Arcadio discovers Aureliano's great erudition; and "[t]hat drawing together of two solitary people of the same blood was far from friendship, but it did allow them to bear up better under the unfathomable solitude that separated and united them at the same time" (380). Surely only a tendentious reading such as my own could see in this relationship a melancholy anticipation, from an author hostile to the perverse, of the relationship between Molina and Valentín in *Kiss*, as if that novel had already been written here in 1967, but by someone who never identifies "with the heroine, dummy," but rather only with the lonely, lovestruck Marxist. (In an inside joke, Aureliano meets a lovely girl in his trip to the pharmacist's— García Márquez met his own wife when she was a pharmacist's assistant.) Taking Aureliano's side over José Arcadio's, García Márquez sees to it that it is only the normal Aureliano, not the pervert José Arcadio, who is translating stories into the conversation between the two cellmates ("[José Arcadio's] attention was attracted by the rare wisdom and the inexplicable knowledge that his desolate kinsman had" (379)); hence he sees to it that these stories must come from the Borgesian esoteric realm of the English-language encyclopedia (which Aureliano has gone through "as if it were a novel" (379)) and from his mystical asceticism, not (as in the case of Puig) from popular culture of movies with glamorous heroines.

García Márquez will also not give José Arcadio the heroine-martyr's death that Puig gives Molina. Nevertheless, he seems to toy with the Puigian idea that the military still structures human relations despite the self-imposed prisons of the Buendía solitude. In the chapter's penultimate paragraph the last of the seventeen illegitimate children of General Aureliano Buendía suddenly appears on their doorstep, only to be gunned down with a Mauser shot to the forehead by his indefatigable pursuers. After that, in what García Márquez *is* willing to characterize as "such a rapid, methodical, and brutal action that it was like a military operation" (381), the four eldest children of the orgy scenes sneak back into the Buendía house, drown José Arcadio bathing in the pool, steal the hidden treasure, and escape. Magical realism, which so often has been said to serve an anticolonial or postcolonial logic of resistance to Western rationality, here serves the logic of a sexually normative poetic justice: as the decadent pervert sows, so shall he reap; having corrupted minors, these corrupt minors must do away with him. When Aureliano discovers José Arcadio floating on the "perfumed mirror" of the pool—those two heavily loaded words of the *modernista* vocabulary—, constant to Amaranta even beyond death, "[o]nly then did [Aureliano] begin to understand how much he had begun to love him" (381).

Expanding aggressively Freud's concept of melancholy, Judith Butler and other queer theorists have suggested that the unnamable "lost object" that the melancholic mourns is not so much a lost object as a lost possibility, the renunciation of the homosexual component of our originary polymorphous desire in order to operate within the homosexual matrix. Normality seems encyclopedic when one is in it; *One Hundred Years of Solitude* certainly seems infinite when one is reading it. Yet the emptiness of some characters' pursuits of pleasures, and the melancholy solitude of nearly all the characters, may not spring as much from the inaccessibility of the *forbidden* objects of incestuous desire (Amaranta; in the last chapter for Aureliano Babilonia, Amaranta Úrsula) as they do from the *foreclosed*, unacknowledgable objects of desire.

REENTER THE SPIDER WOMAN

> *It happened that in those days, among its other attractions, the wandering fairs of the Caribbean brought to the town the sad spectacle of the woman who had been turned into a spider for disobeying her parents. The admission price to see her was not only less than that of the angel, but they allowed people to ask all sorts of questions about her absurd condition, and examine her from front to back, so that no one could doubt the truth of the horror. She was a fearsome tarantula the size of a baby goat and with the head of a sad young girl. But what was most wrenching was not her nonsensical shape but rather the sincere affliction with which she told the details of her disgrace . . .*
>
> (García Márquez, "A Very Old Man")

The very old man with enormous wings is upstaged by a girl. García Márquez wishes to use this scene to contrast the inarticulate and ironic spectacles of magical realism with the didacticism and easy solutions of mass media spectacles, a distinction he probably does not see as gendered: in the gypsy brothels in *One Hundred Years*, for instance, the over-endowed but sexually anxious José Arcadio Jr. (Pilar has just announced to him that she is pregnant) passes "the crowd that was witnessing the sad spectacle of the man who was turned into a snake for having disobeyed his parents" (33). Mass media spectacles require clear and vivid motivations, such as the violation of parental prohibitions, and both the snake-man and the tarantula girl allow the crowd to interrogate them with an intimacy that García Márquez hopes his magical realist novel and short story collection keep at a distance. As with the penultimate chapter of *One Hundred Years of Solitude*, it is a pleasing coincidence that the story of the very old man with enormous wings, written seven years before Puig's novel, should feature a spider woman that makes vividly clear how Puig's concerns would be treated by the master of magical realism: García Márquez already imagines the moment when the mass reading public turns away from him and turns toward the woman who speaks their own language, and whose compulsive storytelling prevents her from generating any real Engima.

Nevertheless, sooner or later the magical realist wishes to speak in his own voice; what language will he use, and to whom?. The spider woman speaks good clear Spanish. Nobody, however, can understand the very old man (the priest tries out Latin and Hebrew, to no avail, and concludes that he therefore cannot be an angel); the author's best guess is that he is speaking Norwegian, since he looks Norwegian. A complicated play between the domestic and the foreign, the all-too-human and the supernatural, is at play in these national and linguistic markers. For our purpose, in which we examine the role that magical realism is supposed to play in the literary history of Latin America and in World Literature, the most interesting marker is the marking of the nationality of the audiences. The joke international audience for García Márquez is often the Pope: here the parish priest sends a letter to the Vatican asking for advice, but it gets lost in the Papal bureaucracy; in the proto-magical realist "Big Mama's Funeral" of 1962, the Pope himself hears of the death of Big Mama, remembers her from their mutual youth, and to divert attention from a local Italian scandal he decides to cross the Atlantic to attend her funeral. But García Márquez is equally capable of imagining a foreign audience as the validation of a Latin American magic: at the very end of his tender "The Handsomest Drowned Man in the World," the sad little fishing village that has reformed itself after a beautiful unknown male corpse washes ashore, cleaning and dressing his body, baptizing him Esteban and giving him a funeral at sea, vows that inspired by him it will rebuild their village:

> so that in the dawns of years to come the passengers of the great cruise ships will awaken suffocated by the odor of jazmine on the high sea, and the captain will have to come down from the forecastle in his dress uniform ... and pointing out the promontory of roses on the horizon of the Caribbean will say in fourteen languages, look over there, where the wind is now so gentle that it lingers to sleep beneath the beds, there, where the sun shines so

brightly that the sunflowers don't know which way to turn, yes, there, that's Esteban's home. (39)

If this story can be read in part as a utopian response to the death of Che Guevara the year before its publication (1968), the admirals of Caribbean cruise ships become the more complex audience of his 1982 Nobel Prize acceptance speech, "The Solitude of Latin America." Here the sympathetic European audience members are entreated to convince the cold warriors of East and West (especially the Reagan administration) that Latin America has a unique history, irreducible to Euro-American concepts: having won the right to an independent imagination, García Márquez argues, we should have the right to independent political structures. Perhaps it is no accident that the old man may be Norwegian, that Eréndira's young lover Ulysses is half-Dutch, that Gaston, the complaisant husband of the last Buendía Amaranta Ursula (he lets himself be led around by her on "a silk rope tied around his neck" (382) before he gallantly returns to Europe so that she can pursue her incestuous passion), is Belgian. In a world where the Indians are illiterate, the Yankees are exploiters, and the old Spaniards are repressive or too Catholic, García Márquez must pin his hopes for a reading public on the good North Europeans, as if anticipating the moment when he reads a speech to them in 1982.

It is in this sense, then, that magical realism as a term functions within two literary histories, although these histories are not fully dissoluble one from the other: in the history of World Literature and in the history of Latin American Literature. We can see its function in World Literature, that dream of Hegel's suitably updated to postimperial, neocolonial cultural globalization times, in the works of such prestigious writers as Harold Bloom, Frederic Jameson, and Franco Moretti. Although each in his own way shadows their enthusiasm with some sort of suspicion, each sees *One Hundred Years* (and, synecdochally, Third World Magical Realism) as the movement in World Literature which gets European letters out of the impasse of the 1960s, of the nonnarrative Joyce, the self-critical *nouveau roman*, the tragically nihilist Beckett: García Márquez is a return to storytelling and to a primitivist transparency of language (Moretti), a return to the national—perhaps more strictly, Pan-American—allegory and national subject which the post-national subjects of the First World can no longer write because they no longer need to (Jameson), a return to the near-Biblical wellsprings of imagination (Bloom). Insofar as the ideology that moves these assessments requires the corollary that Europe can't write 'em the way they do in the periphery—an argument with its roots in Carpentier's prologue to *The Kingdom of This World* and repeated with little variation in García

Márquez's 1982 Nobel Prize acceptance speech—the argument can serve as the foundation for certain claims we associate with the multiculturalism of the 1980s and 1990s, in which marginal groups (i.e., those not yet "disenchanted" by modernity) draw upon non-Western wisdom in order to talk back to the Empire. Aureliano Babilonia reads Melquiades's manuscripts first, but soon the boat captain will point out the roses and the sunflowers of Esteban's town.

So both Puig and García Márquez are aware of the international scene in their fictions that take place in Latin American prisons and small towns. It is only Puig's perversions, as opposed to the "native" Latin American perversions of incest and machismo, which banish him from the fin-de-siècle house of Latin American literature and into (no more than) the canon of World Literature. *One Hundred Years of Solitude* is fertile, and produces offspring and finds a lineage, although it is a jealous patriarch of letters: García Márquez has forbidden any movie to be made from the novel itself, even though he himself has been a scriptwriter and even though magical realism so clearly "belongs" to the cinema. In contrast, Puig's novel is an immigrant momma's boy, uncomfortable with if perhaps desirous of the macho works of the Latin American past, whose narratives of normality it needs, in order to find and revalorize the spider women one can find therein. Perhaps the story is capable of getting future momma's boys to identify with it,[30] but otherwise it feels as if it is to the side of metaphors of fertility, incapable of founding a tradition yet capable of reproducing itself narcissistically as play, as movie, as Broadway musical, a perversion of what a Great Book ought to do for Latin America's literary tradition as captured in Oedipal lineages. Yet it would be a strange critical decision to use *Kiss* to argue that critical interpretations should try to purge themselves of desires and points of strategic identification. Perhaps, as we shall see in my next chapter, before we abandon psychological metaphors in literary history altogether we should make more attempts to look beyond Oedipus when we do use them.

2. The Impenetrability and the Glory: Ellipsing Lezama Lima ∾

> "There's glory for you!" cried Humpty Dumpty.
> "I don't know what you mean by 'glory,'" said Alice.
> Humpty Dumpty smiled contemptuously. "Of course you don't—till I tell you. I meant, 'There's a nice knock-down argument for you!'"
> "But 'glory' doesn't mean 'a nice knock-down argument,'" said Alice.
> "When I use a word," Humpty Dumpty said, in rather a scornful tone, "it means exactly what I choose it to mean—neither more nor less."
> "The question is," said Alice, "whether you can make words mean so many different things."
> "The question is," said Humpty Dumpty, "which is to be master—that's all. [...] I can manage the whole lot of them! Impenetrability! That's what I say!"
>
> (*Alice Through the Looking-Glass*, 163)

STRETCHING THE CLOSED CIRCLE

Only the most obscure precursors can be chosen. That is to say, first, that a crass, unsubtle tradition is thrust upon us before we are of the age to choose; the vast majority of Americans gain our sense of a plot and a dénouement from the thousands of hours of television and trashy movies and good realist novels we go through before we turn, say, fifteen. Second, for gays and lesbians, the forces of compulsory heterosexuality hide from us the variety of our cultural tradition and impose upon us the few stereotypes available at any given historical moment: all gay men are Oscar Wilde and Federico García Lorca, none Edward Carpenter or Vicente Aleixandre. Twisting the connotations of the phrase a little further, however, we might say that only the most obscure precursors offer themselves up as "the chosen"; elitists often welcome the obscurity that protects them from the vulgar masses, and such elitist feelings characterizes the modernist matrix that helped socially construct the fin-de-siècle homosexual who is still with us today. Many a gay man makes a virtue of his status in the closet by reimagining it as a closet with a secret passageway into a gothic castle of ineffable fraternal mysteries. Indeed, so many factors conspire to make the fin-de-siècle gay man dwell in an alluring obscurity that obscurity can itself be the stereotype imposed upon us.

And so we who study the Latin American novel cannot choose but to choose José Lezama Lima, who himself seemed free only to choose among obscurities. We take with us to his massive novel *Paradiso*, published in full in 1966, all the conventions of a thousand trashy movies as well as a thousand good conventional novels. Because of the circulation in the 1960s of the central chapters and their graphic description of hetero- and homosexual acts,[1] because of the banning of the book in Franco's Spain, and because of the arguments in highbrow magazines at the time by Vargas Llosa and Rodríguez Monegal over how to "place" the book's sexuality,[2] we take with us the knowledge that *Paradiso* comes to us as a text about which we have no choice but to polemicize. Even before Senel Paz's 1991 short story, expanded into the 1993 movie *Fresa y chocolate*, we take with us *Paradiso*'s own sense of being an initiation rite: its first seven chapters are the painstakingly detailed genealogy of one family and its Stephen Dedalus, the portrait of an artist through his illustrious forebears; its next four chapters are a novel within a novel about that future poet José Cemí and his passionate friendship with two young men, Foción and Fronesis; and its final three chapters focus on José's relations with shaman and scholar Oppiano Licario, who spurs him on to regain part of his heritage and to accept his vocation as poet.[3] The elaborate hermeneutics needed to explicate some of Lezama's dense imagery and quirky metaphysics help reinforce the idea that to read Lezama well one must choose to enter a Delphic circle which one may not choose to leave.

Yet those who limit themselves to such explication from within of Lezama's ideas on homosexuality come to dauntingly negative conclusions. The first generation of authors of studies of *Paradiso* all argue that Lezama brings up homosexuality to show that it is a cul-de-sac.[4] In the novel's forty-page long conversation about the issue, Cemí and his two friends all agree that both poetry and gay sex partake of "hypertelia," activity that goes beyond or exceeds conventional ends; but when the openly gay friend Foción argues that it allows one to preserve a space of innocence, and cites dozens of mythologies to back this up, Cemí counters by calling such so-called innocence a closed space whose denizens are trapped in a wheeling circle of lust, the tail-swallowing serpent ouroboros, and proposes instead a more celibate androgyny beyond sexual activity.

Perhaps the best way to avoid succumbing to the fixity of the Delphic circle is to make an ellipse with two eccentric foci: not José Cemí, the stand-in for Lezama who never has an openly lustful thought in the whole novel, but first José Eugenio Cemí, the protagonist's father who dies (as did Lezama's father) when the son is nine, and then Eugenio Foción, the openly gay friend who triangulates the desire between Cemí Jr. and their perfect heterosexual friend Fronesis. Foción is not treated well by the plot mechanics of a novel that, when it strays from Lezama's own autobiography, ricochets from the conventions of trashy movies to genuinely brilliant, genuinely obscure allegory, and back again. After sexuality, we examine creativity. When the second point of an ellipse is infinitely far away, we have a parabola; when little Cemí's father is a ghost, the other point will be little José's uncle, who will give José lessons in literature. But before we can flesh out the two foci of our elliptical discourses, we should examine the first "gay" response to the novel, couched in terms of an eroticized, subversive use of language, in a bit more depth.

CODING SEX

In *Paradiso* José Lezama Lima does not speak my language. Or yours, of course, even if Spanish is your first and native language: even compared to other Cuban masters of neo-baroque idiolects such as the straight Alejo Carpentier or the gay Severo Sarduy, Lezama is far and away the man who speaks to himself out of himself, using a language whose sideways referentiality seems to preclude communication. Sometimes Lezama is merely difficult; in chapter II's vignettes from José Cemí's childhood, for instance, we hear of the deflowering of Martincillo, a young flute teacher, "so effeminate that even his quotations wore nail polish":

> One night he was at the house of a sculptor friend, who was showing him a model calash, when the rain began, accompanied by tropical lightning. Suddenly the Polynesian, disturbed by desire, began to dance in convulsions and spasms, his hair turning into phosphorescent tow. Pricked perhaps by distant sulphur from one of those lightning flashes, an earthworm escaped from his body and like a lance sank into the abstract Pre-Raphaelite. (25)

But at other times Lezama's language simply fails to communicate. Here the narrator interrupts a Chinese servant observing an orgy at the summer home of an employer of José Cemí's maternal grandfather:

> Golden Cruller or Grasshopper Tray was annoyed at that silent, slow, sweated oily round, beginning to emphasize the gesture over Two Obeisances and his procession of sentences. Rainshape, Cloudshape, Woodshape, time crisscrossed horizontal, vertical, and now time made for man. A vertical shape of time, that is buried, a shape acquired in flight and a shape that uses man as an intermediary, wiping him out afterwards. The breastplate of the tortoise and the arms of Achilles weigh down, that's why I'd rather see the fourth shape dissolve and reappear in the night of a motionless bird, because if it did not, the shadow would survive him as body and would tinge the wall with the chalk's tracks. (50–1)

One is tempted to say, with Alice upon hearing the Knave of Hearts' poem, "*I* don't believe there's an atom of meaning in it."

To be sure, the effect of such very long passages is double. On the one hand, we are tempted to create a nonnarrative means of appreciating the text. In this case, we might ignore the relationship of this passage to the orgy and think about the relationship between three and four, between a man using wooden objects while alive and being "wiped out" in a wooden coffin after death, and between the three shapes proffered and the praise of shapelessness, the fourth shape which cannot be seen because it reappears in the night (a preference to which we will return). On the other hand, the other effect of such passages is to reinforce the idea that there is indeed a piece of narrative happening "behind" those words, to which the author is denying us access; the signs have undergone an arbitrary shift.

At any rate, Lezama's movement from the merely difficult to the hopelessly opaque seems itself motivated by autobiography. Here is his father teaching him how to read:

> The father pointed at two small, square pictures on the right and left pages, with two captions: The Student and the Grindstone. […] His curiosity ran faster than the time it took him to distinguish between the two pictures, and when José Cemí's forefinger stopped on the picture of the grindstone, he heard his father say "Student." Thus a warped accommodation of gesture and voice caused him to believe that the student was the grindstone and the grindstone the student. Several days later his father asked him, "When you're older, do you want to be a student? [" "] What's a student?" and with the certainty of one whose visions have been proved, he answered, "A student is a wheel that gives off sparks and as the wheel picks up speed the sparks multiply until they light up the night." (135)

So to know what Lezama means you had to be there; and the sense the reader receives of a man writing in code, speaking only to himself where the words mean something quite precisely different from what they ought to mean, turns the image of Lezama, round, huge, condescending, not a little bombastic, into the Humpty Dumpty of Havana's sea wall Malecón, whose "impenetrability" is not nonsense but can only be properly explicated by the man himself, if he should so deign. My language, English, is that of Lewis Carroll, whose renegade sexuality found a compromise with the academic institutions of his day through a rigorous celibacy and the vigorous voyeurism of a new technology, photography. We shall have something to say of voyeurism later. The institutions of Lezama's youth, such as the University of Havana he ferociously parodies as "Upsalon" in *Paradiso*, were of course hostile to his gay sexuality; and in this excruciatingly autobiographical novel one ends up with the impression that, if we except an odd encounter on a Florida beach with a sixteen-year-old girl when he was himself no more than eight, the protagonist José Cemí is still a virgin on the novel's last page. On the other hand, Lezama freely banded together in the thirties and forties with heterodox Catholics and other aesthetes to produce a variety of literary magazines, including one titled *Nadie parecía*, the beginning of a Cuban catch phrase about gays, "Nadie parecía, pero todos lo eran" ("Nobody looked it, but everybody was one"). Such a climate of unofficial tolerance did not last, however, and the notoriously homophobic Castro regime under which *Paradiso* was finally published almost banned the book and forbade the reprinting of it in Cuba until quite recently.[5] Minor characters in the novel get thrown out of school or react violently when their hidden homosexuality is discovered, yet although the eerie serenity with which Lezama utters unintelligible paragraphs has analogies to the novel's plot, in which no one goes to jail or is arrested for being gay, we should not be fooled: *Paradiso* is no paradise for its gay characters and author, and certain strategies of displacement are operating in the text to get it past external and internalized censors.

We might invoke Lewis Carroll for another reason. Carroll's nonsense has been seen by Hélène Cixous and other French critics (Cixous 1982) as an exemplification of Freud's argument in *Jokes and the Unconscious* to the effect that puns and wordplay derive as much from hostility as other sorts of humor do, this time not directed at people but at the arbitrary rules of language itself. In Lacanian terms, the infant's entry into the preexistent symbolic order from a nonlinguistic babble is a subjugation to the Name of the Father. Enrico Mario Santí's essay "Parridiso" suggests that Lezama's notorious misspellings and random punctuations are an attempt to call into question the reliability of the rules of grammar, of the names of the father. Is it just slowness, then, that encourages the young José Cemí to trade the father's "student" for his "grindstone," that is, to mix up the namings of the father?

I have no doubt that to attribute Lezama's semantic strategies either to self-protection or to unconscious hostility seems to demean them, especially when the defenders of Lezama in his own generation emphasize Lezama's ingenuousness and the relation of his writing to Barthesian *écriture*. Julio Cortázar's brilliant "To Arrive at Lezama Lima" confronts Lezama's sexuality directly as one of the novel's themes but never says how it contributes to what he calls the novel's prelapsarian capacity for vision; indeed, he paints Lezama as a noble savage ("Lezama on his island rises in the morning with the joy of a pre-Adamite without the albatross necktie" (141)) to be contrasted with his own, fallen, sophistication. But if Cortázar stayed generally in an aesthetic of modernist primitivism to praise *Paradiso*, the linguistic richness of this text also fit nicely with the post-structuralist aesthetics of the late 1960s, exemplified best perhaps by an essay by Severo Sarduy, "Dispersion/False Notes/Homage to Lezama." Sarduy, affiliated to the Tel Quel movement and one of its best disseminators into Latin America, was also proud to be Lezama's disciple, referring to himself as Lezama's heir or disciple, choosing Lezama as his Obscure Precursor. Sarduy praises *Paradiso*'s excess, the rustle of its language, the signifiers confused with signifieds. Form is alluded to, indeed calls attention to itself, yet cannot provide meaning; for instance, there is a student riot against the Batista dictatorship at the beginning of chapter IX (by which point we have met José's friend Fronesis, and in which we will meet gay Foción; the debate on homosexuality also begins here); the riot is paralleled at the end of the chapter by José's vision of a bizarre anachronistic street parade:

> He did not know whether to walk home or to take a bus. Suddenly, amid the tumult of the fifes, he saw an enormous phallus advancing, surrounded by an aristocratic file of Roman ladies, which, with the gentle movements of the dance, they were depositing on the tumulus where the phallus was quivering as it advanced. The glans was a dry carnelian red. The rest of the knob was formed by leaves of spikenard painted white. The scandalous multiplications of solar reflections fell on the whitewash of the glans, devouring it in such a way that the conical carnelian casque seemed to be entering the houses or beating the cheeks of the women [. . .] The cart was drawn by Minoan bulls, their generative attributes made brick-red by the heat and the exertion. Astride the bulls, winged youths were dancing and anointing the horns, which were decorated with leaves and bees. (269–70)

In best Barthesian fashion, such outré moments cannot be recuperated fully either by realistic codes or any one nonrealistic code; and if it is an extended Baroque simile for something else, we are not sure what the tenor for that vehicle is. Unlike a doctrinaire version of Barthes, in which subtle negotiations *between* signs lead to jouissance, it is not just an undecidability in the relation of the riot to the parade that dizzies the reader but the illegibility of the parade itself, caused partly by "the scandalous multiplications of solar reflections," that makes one gape.

The Sarduyan/Barthesian tradition tends to stop at this point, accepting Lezama as a writerly writer whose style and theoretical statements posit a theory of signification that redeems the French error of championing the minimalism of the French nouveau roman. True as this is, we must go further; for this stance, by ignoring the plot of the novel and its surface reactionary ideology, leaves the ground open for allegorical readings affirming a repressive patriarchy.

PATRIARCHAL GLORY IN A WORLD WITHOUT PSYCHIATRISTS

How can *Paradiso* be a *parricidio*, an act of linguistic parricide, if it does not also question the patriarchy that we see in the autobiographical chapters of the text? An almost idolatrous regard for José Eugenio Cemí, the protagonist's father, reigns throughout the book. In a novel whose narrator takes clear sides as he narrates, we are expected to share the reverence for a father who humiliates his black servants, mocks his poor relations, bullies at times his inferiors, and shows no sympathy for the class-based resentments of the bandits his military unit is asked to wipe out, while his principal interactions with his son are full of errors at best and embarrassment and contempt at worst. Little José has asthma, and his impatient father almost kills him with an ice cube treatment; teaching José how to swim, he withdraws the finger José is holding onto, and the boy nearly drowns; he frightens José deeply by hiding behind a door and reciting a poem in which he pretends to be dead. At only one point does the narrator acknowledge that his description of Cemí Sr. might suggest that the author has not resolved some hostility: after recounting nightmares of the six-year-old boy, trapped in the prison his military engineer of a father helped build or in which his father becomes the waxen corpse of St. Flora or in which he carries his father's gun, the narrator applauds the way the family plays down such subconscious dreamwork:

> Rialta relayed the news to the Colonel to give him time to interpret it, to laugh and turn it into a joke, so that later an assortment of labyrinths would not be manufactured, [...] the headless dance of horrible complexes beginning then and there in front of a freckle-faced psychiatrist. (143)

It would be nice to think that such warnings are deliberate ironies, but, alas, the glory of the Colonel, its own nice knock-down argument, is always the master of interpretation for the narrative voice.[6]

The passage above is an instance of how Cemí's mother colludes with his father, and the family romance in the Cemí family certainly has none of the gendered hostility between the sexes seen in the young homosexuals in, say, Puig: little José does not identify with his mother except insofar as she too worships José's father. She is maternal in that overwhelming way that sons take for granted without feeling the need to imitate. Yet even Rialta's tolerance for her son's deviance has consequences. After José returns from the riots at the University safe and sound, Rialta gives him an astonishing speech, followed by an astonishing collusion between omniscient narrator and character:

> "I only asked for a word from the Father and the Holy Spirit, or from your dead father and the living spirit; no mother, when her son returns from danger, should say anything worthless to him. Listen to what I'm going to tell you: Don't reject danger and always try what is most difficult. There's a danger that confronts us in the form of substitution, there's also a danger that sick people seek out, a sterile danger, the danger without epiphany. But when a man throughout his days has tested what is most difficult, ... he knows that a day has been assigned to him in which he will be transfigured, and he will not see the fish inside the current but the fish in the starry basket of eternity... For me, the event, as I told you, your father's death, left me with no answer, but I've always dreamed, and those dreams will always be the root of my being alive, that it would be the profound cause of your testimony, of your seeking difficulty as transfiguration, of your answer. Some doubters will think that I never said these words, that you invented them, but when you give the answer and the testimony, you and I will know that I did say them and that I will say them as long as I live and that you will continue saying them after I have died."
>
> I know that these are the most beautiful words Cemí ever heard in his life after the ones he read in the Gospels and that he will never hear any others that will so decisively set him in motion .... (228)

Rialta gives her son the freedom to do whatever he needs to do to achieve "testimony," "transfiguration," and "answer," but only so long as this freedom is understood to honor his father. Despite the political context of this particular chapter, then, José knows that his way of honoring his father will be by becoming a poet and, eventually, an autobiographical novelist, reinterpreting his father's slights toward him with the same narrative voice that will brook no contradiction, as here.

The final proof that the maternal principle will not serve a refuge from patriarchal heteronormativity comes later in the chapter amidst the dizzying, wonderful, almost absurd displays of erudition about homosexuality in the debate between the three friends. Conducted entirely on the terrain of comparative mythology (Fronesis and Foción) and Thomism (Cemí), the debate covers the Presocratics, Plato, the Egyptians, and some theories of the evolution of fish, but not a word about the three youths' personal lives, until Cemí starts relating Aquinas to Augustine, then shifting abruptly to Homer:

> "There is a fraternal grace, . . . which may be characterized by a highly intemperate love of death, an appetite for enjoyment that excludes participation in the mystery of the Supreme Form. That's where deviations begin, because there will always be men who go through darkness to be able to participate in form, in light, but there will also be the insufficient ones, the ones who go through the light like madmen kissing Greek statues of discus throwers to drown themselves in the descending and cold darkness. . . . [E]very act must be pure, with no memory and no future unless the act takes place in the 'pernicious night' of the eleventh book of the Odyssey, where entangled Circe guides the descent into gloomy Hades. . . . To Tiresias, the man-woman-man, he makes the promise of a pit filled with black blood. Odysseus' mother is lost in the valley of the moaning shades; three times he goes forward to embrace her, but his mother flees until at last she tells him what she wants. 'Try to return to the light as soon as possible, observe these things and later describe them to your wife.'" Cemí paused, held back by the memory of his mother's words: Live in danger of obtaining the most difficult. . . . "'Don't stay in Hades,' she seems to be telling him, 'in spite of the excuse that you've come to the Lower World to find me; . . . don't gaze into the mirror of death to see me.'" (265–6)

At this point in the novel, Cemí's mother is alive, although Lezama did not publish these chapters until his own mother had died; it is uncanny to see Rialta permitting her son only the right sort of descent into the underworld, and only a temporary one at that, as a Homeric ghost.

The patriarchy's taboo on homosexuality, then, will not be stormed by Barthesian excess alone; moreover, the narrator conspires with the narrative to praise the father, although the selection of events keeps us doubtful; more still, the patriarchy keeps the psychiatrists at bay while being supported by the mother. Where can a reader reading as a gay man redeem this text? Oddly enough, first of all, in the portrait of José's father's own adolescence. Meeting his future wife Rialta and loving her seems almost an afterthought to the relationship the young Colonel wanted with her brother Alberto. Like a voyeur he peeped through the blinds at him, the view fragmented fetishistically, when they were both twelve:

> For him the newcomers became fragments of chance and mystery, sparks surrounding the blinds with a plane of massaged and divided light, his vision retaining fragments which he could not reconstruct in the totality of a body or a situation, so that they continued their caress with an undefined and floating voluptuousness. (72)

José Eugenio admired Alberto's public insouciance as he smoked on the street corner while his own grandmother was laying down castrating rules about José Eugenio's own money: The smoke becomes an impenetrable armor for Alberto:

> He acted as if an ancestral deity had thrown him into that neighborhood, recognizing situations and objects with a kind of memory as ancestral as it was erotic, which instantly befriended what was around him. ... He reached the tobacco stand on the corner and was soon wrapped in smoke like a diving suit, like a crossroads. The smoke dances around his head, as if he were being shaken by a wave perceived only by his underground memory. He shows his pride, although he does not much care whether he enters the cone of someone else's vision, in that first meeting with his own smoke ... The smoke surrounds him like a suit of armor, its burnished metal bound with the sea's congealed mist ... In his indifference in the restlessness of that corner where he stationed himself, [José Eugenio] saw how he was breaking up, like a statue that begins to show an old glove, into some of those moments that [Alberto] Olaya had shown to be hard, impenetrable, a sand soldier retouched by the mist of the coast with expressions, improvising the non-existent fuzz of a beard. (71–3)

In both the Spanish and the English the syntax blurs the difference between José Eugenio and Alberto, at the same moment that both of them are breaking up, and yet both of them are also impenetrable. Andrés's impenetrability is extended to José Sr. when they are at school and a student Fibo jabs everyone with his pen except the two of them:

> [José Eugenio asked Fibo,] "Why do you suppose that day we were the two who saved ourselves from Fibo's Malayan kris?"
>
> [Fibo answered,] "Olaya told me that you were his neighbor, and that if I jabbed you it would be the same as jabbing him. He seems to have a lot of regard for you."
>
> "I didn't think he was even aware that he was my neighbor. We've never spoken to each other. I'm glad you told me that." Cemí was overcome by an indecipherable joy. It was going to change his life like a lightning bolt. (80, 87–9)

Such emotions speak the language of love, if not of eroticism; and one assumes that some version of these stories was part of Lezama's family history. Yet where can he have gotten the idea of his father's behavior at night at boarding school, the one Lezama himself would later attend? The headmaster at dinner tosses little chunks of bread, "floury doves," to the students, who await in "near ecstasy." Then the students go to the communal showers:

> For a long time José Eugenio Cemí had retained a memory from his body, and on the thirty-fourth night it clarified itself, when a young man, the King of the Black Isles, moaned and raised his tunic, and confessed in the palace that he was a man from head to waist, but the rest of him was black marble. As he reached the peak of tension an electric wire running through him to fulfill surprise, in expectation of that flying floury speck, the sound of water mixed in with waiting seemed to [be] sequester[ed in or mixed into] the glory of those bodies dressed in towels like Oriental heretics and martyrs. Feeling the mixture of the taste and bodies, ... hidden also in the very sound of the water, engendered again in José Eugenio a tactile impression replacing the visual. This mingling of taste produced an infinite sexuality warmed by the memory of an impossible touch, which the body will blindly reconstruct in the distance and in the sound of cascades filtered by jail-like walls. One had to blind oneself in order to reconstruct the leaping bodies in a midnight cascade, in order to feel the tingling of sex, while the grace of lying in wait for a visible and immediate sexuality had simply brought him to waiting without possibility.... (85–6)

Associating gay sex with a germinative darkness, the fourth shape "in the night of a motionless bird" as the narrator prefers in his description of the orgy quoted earlier, is surprisingly absent from the longer debates about homosexuality later in the book. In order to reveal homosocial relations as homoerotic relations, Lezama literally turns out the lights, but makes it clear that if the patriarch wanted to have gay sex then gay sex is all right, an escape from Lezama's own temptation to mere voyeurism and from the tyranny of sight over the other senses, an escape from the social censor—ergo, sex in the closet; yet also sex free from the narcissism often attributed variously to gays and to the Lacanian mirror stage.

It is pleasing to conjecture that Lezama transferred some real lived experiences of his own to his father at this point in order to justify the sort of sex that José Jr. is never seen to have.[7] The passage in itself, speaking only of "an infinite sexuality warmed by the memory of an impossible touch," is of course obscure enough for a hostile reader to claim that no gay sex is happening at all; but I think it is enough of a victory for Lezama to speculate on his father's sexual life among men, thereby using sex as the experience which liberates the son from a dependence on family anecdote while perversely hewing to the language of hagiographic biography. Perhaps, however, Lezama really does go farther and inserts autobiography into biography; that is, perhaps he is describing here not an experience which might have happened to his father, but rather an experience which did happen to him. If so, then the impenetrable son has inserted himself into his impenetrable father's childhood and thereby into the "glory of bodies."

BAD GAY BLOOD AND WORSE HOMOPHOBIC PLOTTING

By taking a stance neither fully inside nor fully outside Lezama's Delphic circle of heirs and disciples, by second-guessing the judgments he makes on his autobiographical characters, I follow a hermeneutical strategy that *Paradiso* itself half-acknowledges elsewhere: " 'Saying bad things about absent friends is completely passé. It's better form to speak well, and let the listener read between the lines.... The truth is, I never know when I'm speaking good or ill about a person' " (289). The person who encourages us to read between the lines as *Paradiso* feigns to speak well about the absent father is not the authorial stand-in José Cemí, but Eugenio Foción, José Cemí's out gay friend and the antagonist in the middle chapters in the debate about homosexuality between Cemí, Foción, and Cemí's perfect friend Fronesis. One way to penetrate *Paradiso*'s impenetrability is to defend Foción's position in a novel that wants to discipline his revolt against the patriarchy by using the strategies of subliterary genres.

The generic status of the Cemí-Foción-Fronesis chapters have always been somewhat in doubt. Cortázar's important essay acknowledges that, like his poor punctuation and foreign spelling, Lezama's unconcern for traditional novelistic composition should be read as a sign of the novel(ist)'s innocence and insularity, and also a proof that a true poet is at work. While the arguments have occasionally been made that Lezama's idiosyncratic punctuation can stand in for an asthmatic prosody returning us to his theories of *pneuma* or inspiration, and that his misspellings can function as a reminder that we engage in a necessary, possibly creative mistranslation every time we incorporate another's concept (especially a foreign one), no such arguments have been made about Lezama's plotting and characterization. Criticism behaves as if there were no invention of characters or emplotment in the first eight autobiographical chapters; the final chapters more clearly follow the structure of a rite of passage, of the mutual, predestined encounter of master (Oppiano Licario), disciple (José Cemí), and vocation (poetry). And yet between these generic stabilities we are exposed to three chapters of Cemí's college years, seemingly all about homosexuality, introduced by scenes of revolutionary ferment. At the very least we should try to read these chapters, as Terry Castle and Judith Roof have recently done in lesbian narrative theory,[8] in terms of the possibilities which an author in a homophobic period will open up in the middle of her or his texts even though the ending of the book cleaves to a regnant heteronormativity.

Lezama's punctuation and spelling might be signs of a poetry which, it could be argued, stands higher than prose, but his characterization and plotting in these three chapters partakes of the conventions of melodrama. Lezama seems aware of this, but also displaces this awareness: after seeing Fronesis with his girlfriend Lucía (who is in a far more amorous mood than Fronesis is) earlier in the day, Cemí goes to the movies:

> They were showing a variation on the Isolde theme, brought within reach of the children of the century. The spirit of evil had been replaced by a shifty hunchback invidiously hidden in the wheat fields, the timid king by a shotgun-bearing simpleton who looked like a headless watchmaker.... In the end, with the lovers dead and the egalitarian trappings, the choice between good and evil had become pointless.
>
> ... Before focusing on the large screen facing him, [Cemí] adjusted his eyes by scanning the faces of the spectators.... There were Lucía and Fronesis in the eternal return of their postures: Lucía increasing the snake-like activity of her arms; Fronesis unmoving, his chiseled profile sharpening its contours like an ax ready to chop up the serpent....
>
> The projector was now running through a tempestuous darkness. Isolde runs off to the seashore; the bird flies off with the golden hair from her locks....
>
> Her back against the sand, her hands behind her neck, Isolde flexes her legs. She has shown her inner thighs for an instant, where the bird's gold thread has become a mane or a grass patch preened by an owl. The pink skin changes into a twisted peak.... (272–3)

Ennobled and condescended to in this comparison with Tristan et Iseult, heterosexual romantic love is the space of melodrama, occupied by the body of a woman in a novel which spends far more time examining the bodies of men. Fronesis is disgusted by this female body (perhaps no more than by Lucía's ardor in the public spaces of park bench or movie theater: still, later that evening when they are in bed together, "the abrasions in Isolde's crotch, its craggy hair and swallows' nests, rose up in his imagination again, with a different modality but an identical nausea" (287)).

Melodrama is fine for women and "the children of this century," but it can be dangerous to watch it: just at the moment when Cemí is relieved to see that Fronesis is spurning Lucía in the movie theater, he realizes that Foción is also staring at the lovers, without the shame that Cemí has already felt that he might get caught looking. As always (one might also say, as in Proust), the author acknowledges the sexual jealousy in Foción's stare while being unwilling to acknowledge the same in his author-substitute's. Cemí leaves the movie theater before he is caught looking, and indeed disavowal of responsibility for looking is a successful survival strategy in the novel: Fronesis was introduced to us at the end of chapter VIII when in their first conversation together he tells Cemí about the village idiot "Godofredo the Devil," who lost his reason and the use of his right eye while guiltily running from a scene in which he spied on the local priest and a married woman. Godofredo had been attracted to the woman but then turned her down, so there the voyeuristic dynamic was heterosexual. The homosexual will be brought more fully into the sphere of melodrama over the course of chapters X and XI.

Within the space of melodrama, characterization shifts its functions within the previous method of characterization that rules *Paradiso*: the genealogy. Eight chapters have shown us Cemí's genealogy in thorough detail, including the impenetrable ne'erdowell uncle Alberto, grand in his youth, but in his middle age an alcoholic neo-Baroque letter-writer who dies in a car accident during Cemí's own childhood. Bloodlines and uncles are the main sources of Fronesis and Foción's characters, too: but what one might call Lezama's "hagiographic realism" in the portrayal of Cemí's forebears, where the humdrum is narrated while elevating it to the poetical and cosmic, is abandoned in the case of Fronesis and Foción. Nothing is humdrum: each is treated to an almost fanciful genealogy. Fronesis, the tranquil heterosexual who is loved by Cemí and Foción for his ability to occupy the center of life, is the son of a travelling Cuban diplomat who fell in love with a Viennese showgirl from an aristocratic family; the showgirl really loved the notorious homosexual dancer Diaghilev, who had a passion for Fronesis's father which the father rejected. After bearing Fronesis, the showgirl abandoned the infant in order to return to the stage; Fronesis was reared by her conservative sister and by Fronesis's father, who married the sister and returned to Cuba. Foción's genealogy is equally lurid: two brothers growing up fell in love with the same woman; the one who marries her becomes a doctor, but the couple moves in with the brother, who is something of an alcoholic. She enters his room during one of the doctor's long absences and mounts him in his sleep; he ejaculates and promptly dies, in language that makes his heart attack seem almost a suicide. When the doctor returns, he goes mad—or rather, partially mad: for twenty years during the day he stays at home but thinks that the sitting room is a consultation room, and forces his wife to behave as if she were his nurse, as they examine and tend to imaginary patients; when each workday is over, he regains his sanity. Foción does not know which of the two men, the alcoholic or the madman, is his biological father.

The conclusions we are expected to draw from these narratives (really, genealogies) of the perverse are somewhat complex. Cemí interprets Fronesis's genealogy for us: Fronesis's mother gave him bad but noble blood, which corresponds to his temporary impotence with his girlfriend Lucía, and his conservative stepmother is Fronesis's true mother, just as heterosexuality is his true identity whether he is attracted to women or not. Foción, we find out, not only was married at seventeen but now he has a son, although the couple was publicly humiliated when the doctors discovered that after nine months of marriage his wife was still a virgin: Foción's homosexual initiation came later, at the hands of a much older journalist friend of the family, called in to help him conquer Foción's fear of female genitalia but with an agenda of his own. Ergo, Foción's parents gave him mad, alcoholic, promiscuous blood; given this list of Foción's weaknesses, the text seems to say, homosexuality is his true identity whether he is attracted to women or not (as he is in a bisexual episode in New York with an American brother and sister (341–7), where he is attracted to the sister first). The heterosexual nauseated by women's genitals, and the homosexual who is a father and occasionally a woman-chaser: Fronesis and Foción could serve as characters for a contemporary queer theory which hopes to undermine the epistemological assurances of the hetero/homo binary. If I do not pursue this line of thought enthusiastically, this is because melodrama and a rhetoric of good and bad blood provides the novel's epistemological assurances instead.

Following the logic of the closet, categories of sexuality are determined more by public behaviors than by private desires, and in this case the behaviors that signify categories are tranquility (heterosexuality, Fronesis) and agitation (homosexuality, Foción); to a lesser extent, and more in fantasy than in real social relations, tranquility is masculine and agitated desire is feminine (recall the "snake-like activity" of Lucía's arms around Fronesis in the movie house). Foción, as impenetrable in words as are his two debating friends, nevertheless is unmanned by his agitated actions. While Fronesis invents a stratagem to enjoy sex with his girlfriend and Cemí gets an office job, daydreams about poetic *ars combinatoria* and grieves the slow death of his grandmother, in chapter XI Foción's behavior becomes ever more feverish. In chapter X he cruised Havana and picked up a lover (the teenaged boy's red hair is an echo of "Godofredo the Devil's") who, Foción suicidally hopes, will rob and kill him; in chapter XI Cemí comes upon Foción in the last stages of drunkenness and despair, still with the teenager, making speeches about Anubis, "god of the anal way," and grieving his separation from Fronesis. The last words we hear from Foción in the novel as he pisses in his own chair on the patio of the bar are "The one thing that homosexuality always achieves, ha, ha, ha, ha, ha, is to avoid a greater evil, in my case, ha, ha, I didn't commit suicide, instead I think I've gone crazy, ha, ha, ha" (354). Cemí last sees Foción in the hospital in which Cemí's grandmother is dying. Foción is silently, obsessively circling a poplar tree in the yard of the mental ward: "Cemí suddenly realized that to Foción, the tree ... was Fronesis" (371).

CHALLENGING THE DOCTORS AND FREEING FOCIÓN

We cannot fully rescue Foción from the melodramatic logic by which homosexual desire is associated with masculinity envy, suicide, and madness. But just as I proposed a Focionesque over-reading of the author's portrait of his father as an overtly adored but surreptitiously hated tyrant, his impenetrability only breached by the glory of bodies in the dark transposed from Lezama's own adolescence, so too we may overread two other scenes in Foción's last chapter. The first double scene is about the tyranny of fathers, the second is about the flash of glory in the dark.

Up all night after telling Cemí about bisexual incestuous adventures in New York, Foción gets on a bus to visit Fronesis in the town of Santa Clara. Instead of finding Fronesis at the hotel café, he is accosted by Fronesis's father. " 'I've come to meet you,' he said with deadly dryness. 'I've come to tell you that I don't want you to see my son any more' " (349). The father's brief comments (he will speak only three times in the exchange) are shocking, in part, because they are at the very limits of Lezama's idiosyncratic speech: mothers, servants, schoolchildren, peasants all have their words elevated and reconstituted by Lezama's narrator, but this paternal challenge comes to us undiluted. At first rattled into speaking equally plainly for about half a sentence (" 'I am sorry to have met you' "), Foción contests Dr. Fronesis in his dialect of Lezama's language, moving from a declaration of his right to see Fronesis to an accusation of the father's impropriety (intercepting his son's letters) to, finally, a sweeping denunciation in typically Lezamesque prose—a prose which up to this point has been incapable of criticizing fathers. The father's crime? Turning down Diaghilev's sexual advances, and the spiritual growth it would have given him.

Is this denunciation a mirage of our overidentification with Foción's position? It depends on what you think of the narrator's intervention before Foción's final tirade:

> [Dr. Fronesis] had expected to find a whining hyena and instead what crossed his path was a lithe animal that accepted combat. Foción's stand, in the face of such a difficult situation, was gaining ground in the subconscious. The father guessed that his son's friend was no mere knave, he might even be a pervert, but now he understood, a little too late, that his son could not have a friend who wasn't a man, who even from a position of disadvantage continued to look him straight in the eye. (349)

Although the narrator is less ambiguous than in the scene quoted earlier defending his mother's defense of his poetic vocation, he is hardly mouthing the patriolatry we have seen before in *Paradiso*.

Our sense of the extent of Lezama's sympathies with Foción also depend on what one thinks of the content of Foción's final denunciation:

> "You hindered your own fate and I am unaware to what extent you have adapted to that frustration, when you ran away from Diaghilev and when you ran away from Diaghilev's pursuer. It is at least excusable that a man who harbors a lifelong frustration wants to stop the plant from flowering, but it becomes more difficult to understand that he wants his own son to sink into the nothingness and the mortal tedium of a provincial pedagogue. Perhaps you don't need me to tell you that your son will prolong a destiny which has stagnated in you. You are not unaware, and therefore you are continuing a lie dictated by your own frustration, to 'save your son,' when what that does is drive him towards a solution that may be tragic or at least hurtful, which you are living in now, tranquil, poisonous fury which Gide called the *soif étanchée.* . . . " (350)

The language of generational dooms, in which the frustration of the father is being visited upon the son, is of a piece with the rhetoric of genealogies we have seen before in the novel: Cemí must complete in words his father's interrupted glory, Foción must fulfill his twinned fathers' curses of alcoholism and madness, and now, Foción argues, Fronesis must reciprocate the homosexual love his father denied himself. The genealogical logic once again is used not to exclude the sterile homosexual (who in this novel has an offstage child, anyway), but to implicate the fathers in homosexual desire and to defend gay desire in the present. Note also, however, that the denunciation goes beyond this motif to include an attack on Fronesis's own characteristic virtue, the "tranquility" hitherto associated with an enviable masculinity but now resignified as a "tranquil, poisonous fury" or (in noted homosexual André Gide's words) a *soif étanchée*, a stanched or stagnant thirst. It is a rare but crucial moment in which Lezama acknowledges a possible dissatisfaction with a Goethean integrity of centered masculinity.

Foción's triumph is short-lived. The father walks out on him; Foción's "mad scene" in the patio of the Havana bar follows immediately; more to the point, this scene of confronting the paternal tyrant is "continued" later when Fronesis confronts his father, and in it any ground Foción gained for his friend is lost. The son's position is strongest when the vocabulary is that of onanism and libertinage, of scattering seed and sowing wild oats (Fronesis is himself one of the wild oats his father sowed, after all): " 'sometimes the seed has to be propelled by the wind, because a breed cannot be guided like a kite' " (364). Lezama's constant equation of word with semen through the theological concept of the *logos spermatikos* brings Fronesis's position in line with the novel's masculinist aesthetics. But if the battle is unequal this time, it is partly because Dr. Fronesis carefully sees to it that his wife is present—another mother collaborating with the father against the son's desire—, and also because Fronesis will not challenge his father's *qué dirán* approach to homosexual attribution: " 'And what disturbs me most of all is that even at Upsalón the most malicious people are convinced that you're not a homosexual, and that you're basically making fun of [Foción]' " (365). The reader never sees an erotic component to Fronesis's feelings either, but Fronesis never does declare the nature of his friendship with Foción, or his investment in homosexuality as a subject of speculation. Fronesis's father can thus take the high ground: a *real* homosexual love would be fate, but this is trivial and without depth. The conversation has been detoured from exactly how real the desires of the father were. The final detour comes from the stepmother: "it is not a problem of destiny, of future; it is, on the contrary, a return to the past. Ricardo has felt desires to go in search of his mother" (368), and a trip to Europe to find his lost biological mother is agreed upon. The scene ends in a reconciliation and triple embrace, as Fronesis is thinking that this solution was wisely anticipated by, not imposed upon, his father: the patriarchy, defied for a time, is vindicated in the mind of the future patriarch. At least, however, Fronesis has admitted that his "tranquility" was premature, and that a father's authority should be challenged directly. It is a pity that the "real homosexual" is forgotten in the scene of reconciliation to whose "development" (denied by Fronesis's father) he has contributed.

Let us give Foción the attention that Ricardo Fronesis denies him, in two paragraphs before and after the death of Cemí's grandmother during a thunderstorm. Before the thunderstorm, Foción seemed enthralled, not just to the deep rooted poplar tree that is Fronesis, but also to the circle:

> [Cemí] saw a young man in a white uniform describing circles incessantly around the poplar, whose size was owed to its well-tended roots. It was Foción. He went round and round in his circles, as if the poplar were his God and his destiny. "From the time he gets up," said an attendant who passed Cemí, "until he goes to bed, he walks around the tree. Rain and sun have no effect on his circling and recircling of that trunk." Foción stopped for an instant to pick up a pebble and put it in his pocket. He had a dried-out look that went well with his thinness; the sun, while he followed his circle, passed energy into him deeper than his skin, and afterwards night, in a motionlessness that went to the farthest reaches of his soundings, brought a golden proportion to the scattering of what had been accumulated. His disordered mind functioned in the body of a devotee of what the day poured out and what the night absorbed. He opened up the enormous quantity of circles accrued during the day into spirals, submerged and silent as nighttime gathered him in. But in that devotion to day and night, Cemí suddenly realized that to Foción, the tree irrigated by his incessant, maddened rounds was Fronesis. (371)

The passage prevents us from direct access to Foción's mind, although Cemí's confidence in his interpretation of the situation is typical for the novel. Typical, too, is the presentation of extra information, in a poetic register: the passing attendant claims that the sun has no effect on his circling, but Cemí knows that the sun, and the cycle of day and night, are affecting Foción's body favorably. On the banal level that suggests an inclusion of Foción into the world of hagiographic realism we saw in the earliest chapters, Lezama seems to think that physical activity and adjustment to natural rhythms help to cure alcoholism-aggravated madness. Yet of course the passage is also suggesting that the physical health of Foción's body is not touching his disordered mind. What is striking about this suggestion, however, is that the language cannot quite decide how its main metaphors, light/darkness and circles/spirals, are to function. The passage seems to say that both are good: the day gives energy and the night absorbs it; the circle is a symbol of order, the spiral a symbol of release. Yet we know that the circle is a symbol of the tail-swallowing ouroboros, the sterility of the homosexual, in the earlier debate; and the scar of "Godofredo the Devil's" blind eye is a "pink spiral" (214) (mad Godofredo's walks also "describe immense implacable circles, with the radii zigzagging like bolts of lightning" (219)). Committed as Lezama is to exorcising Foción from Fronesis's life (he is after all a rival to Cemí for Fronesis's friendship), he denies Foción's—and his own—theories of the "germinative darkness" we have seen elsewhere in the book: Foción is to get his deeper energy from the sun and nowhere else, he is no longer even one of "the insufficient ones, the ones who go through the light like madmen kissing Greek statues of discus throwers to drown themselves in the descending and cold darkness" (265), let alone an adolescent achieving glory with bodies in the dark. But in this passage the "motionlessness" of the night also allows Foción finally to accede to the language of Goethean centeredness that his feminine agitation (and his daytime incessant circlings) had otherwise denied him.

Lezama permits himself, at the end of the chapter, an ending of supreme ambiguity, which nevertheless succeeds in using virtually every trope in the novella of Foción, Cemí, and Fronesis so far:

> [Soon after his grandmother's death], Cemí, moving along the same terrace from which he had watched Foción's rounds, looked for the tree. The biblical emblems of the night on which his grandmother was dying were intended for him. A lightning bolt had pulled up its roots, removing its flesh with its giddy fire. A bench, sunk in the ground, held up the entire length of the blackened trunk as if a hot iron had crossed over to mark it. With the tree's death, its guardian had disappeared. Cemí looked around with uneasy caution. The lightning that had destroyed the tree had freed Foción from his adoration of circular eternity. (372)

Cautious sexless Cemí, a better voyeur than a protagonist, receives a Biblical emblem while Foción receives freedom. For Cemí it is another elimination of a possibility of carnal desire (the "flesh" of the tree that is Fronesis), an elimination which coincides with a maternal figure's passing into the underworld. For Fronesis-as-tree, the tree's uprooting suggests that desire is stronger than Fronesis's own roots; the poplar was "well-tended," but because of his illegitimacy and bad (if noble) biological mother Foción's own roots were dangerously weak; the lightning bolt suggests that it may not be a desire to strengthen his roots after all, but a desire to know the glory in the dark, that made the poplar reach up to the thunderclouds. In what way has Foción been freed from his adoration of circular eternity? The most obvious reading is that Foción was also killed by the lightning bolt—the violence of the tree upon the bench implies that. Another reading, in which Foción survives the thunderstorm, would indicate that Foción has been cured of his homosexuality. At the very least it suggests that Foción has been cured of his madness and his obsession with Fronesis.

The novel *Paradiso* is in the end about José Cemí, and we can certainly say that the lightning bolt "cures" *the novel* of its obsession with homosexuality, which disappears for the final chapters. Lezama's posthumous incomplete sequel to *Paradiso*, however, flouts most of the likely possibilities presented above for the fate of Foción: in *Oppiano Licario* (1977)we learn that Foción did not die, and that he is once again obsessed with the phallus and with Fronesis. The unstable allegory that is José Lezama Lima's relationship with (the illusion of) centered masculinity, his desire demonized into a figure who is capable of confronting tyrannical fathers before being punished with madness, was simply not resolved by his becoming a patriarchal (closeted-)gay poet, and had to spill over beyond the *Kunstlerroman* form.

As we move from thinking about sexuality in *Paradiso* to thinking about creativity, Cemí's father will move infinitely far, a ghost who does not speak, producing a parabola, not an ellipse. For the second focus of this artist's parable, then, let us look not just at our fathers, but also at our bachelor uncles.

THE AVUNCULATE

Of the many attacks launched against Freudian theory in the last three decades, surely the most sweeping is Michel Foucault's *History of Sexuality*, which is best remembered for its argument that the psychoanalytic method is no more than an extension and refunctioning of the Counter-Reformation tactic of the confessional; this new use of an old method allows psychoanalysis to take its place among the many social practices whose purpose is not to repress sexuality but to incite it in order to manage it, reinforcing the institutions in which the practices take place: the boarding school, the doctor's office, the vice squad desk at the police office. But Foucault goes on to argue that psychoanalysis in the fin-de-siècle served another function as well, with relation to the family. When one's most important self-definition came from whom one married and the alliances into which one's marriage entered oneself and one's own, the family was a naturally meaningful unit; but as the secret definition of oneself became one's sexuality—the host of conscious and unconscious desires imputed to oneself by various social discourses—it became more difficult to see the importance of one's family to this self-definition. For Foucault, one of the paradoxes of Freud's impact on the European sense of self is that, while psychoanalysis is one of the forces that eroded the importance of the family on the one hand, on the other hand it returned to the family the influence it took away. Freud's invention of the Oedipus complex reinstates the predominance of the family in the center of one's self-formation. Foucault is characteristically sarcastic on this point:

> The guarantee that one would find the parents–children relationship at the root of everyone's sexuality made it possible—even when everything seemed

> to point to the reverse process—to keep the deployment of sexuality coupled
> to the system of alliance. [...] Parents, do not be afraid to bring your
> children to analysis: it will teach them that in any case it is you whom they
> love. Children, you really shouldn't complain that you are not orphans, that
> you always rediscover in your innermost selves your Object-Mother or
> the sovereign sign of your Father: it is through them that you gain access to
> desire. (113)

Since only by falling in love with his mother and entering into a competitive rivalry with his father can the male child learn to be a happy mature adult, the importance of the family has been preserved.

But not of the whole family. The Freudian regime of sexuality makes all one's family alliances of less theoretical importance, granted; but these people, some of whom may live in the house with you, do not go away for all that. The elegance of the Oedipal triangle also makes these other inhabitants of the house disappear, on a theoretical level—but not, perhaps, on the level of incitement and implantation of sexuality for any individual case (and we are all individual cases). Most of us read Freud's case histories and are slightly agog at the reductions and simplifications which the triangular elegance of Freud's theories require. It turns out that even the Viennese fin-de-siècle household had its governess, its stepbrothers, its family friend, its old nurse, the children of its servants: Freud's case histories oscillate between providing stories about them as part of his analysands' original narratives, and sweeping them away to place upon the center stage none but the mother and the father in the child's unconscious.

While a long, broad, and not always subtle attack upon Freud has been carried out for the last thirty years on many fronts, a more focused attack on the Oedipal triangle as a theoretical support of structural psychoanalysis critiques its use by the Lacanian school. According to Judith Butler, in a series of books from *Gender Trouble* (1990) through *Bodies That Matter* (1993) through *Antigone's Choice* (1999), Lacan forecloses the possibility of a primary homosexual desire; the heterosexual matrix upon which he maps the play between desire—essentially for difference—and identification—essentially with the same—precludes the possibility of any desire for the same. One or other of the lovers must take the masculine position, one must take the feminine position, whatever the biological equipment of the people involved. Some of the most interesting queer writers in the Latin American tradition, such as Lezama's disciple Sarduy, find the gymnastics necessary to map themselves and their desires onto Lacan's heterosexual matrix to be exhilarating, and much can be made of Lacan's concept of a "third term," by which one neither *is* the phallus (the feminine position) nor *wields* the phallus (the masculine position), but *seems* to be the phallus; we will return to Sarduy in a later chapter. But here I emphasize that this third position hardly exhausts the possibilities available to complicate, or perhaps even eventually dissolve, the Oedipal triangle.

The most vigorous solution I know to the problem of eliminating, via expanding, Lacanian thematics comes in Eve Sedgwick's critique of previous deconstructive readings of Oscar Wilde's *The Importance of Being Earnest*, a play which notoriously ends by discovering that orphan Jack, who pretended in the city to be named Ernest, turns out to have been christened after his father, Ernest, after all. Sedgwick acknowledges that deconstructive readings succeed in proving that the desire to have the father's name is absurd, but these readings unintentionally reinforce this desire if they give the impression that this is the only affiliative game in town:

> Forget the Name of the Father.
> Forget the Name of the Father!
>   Why can't that, which is after all what these characters do for the first seventy-four seventy-fifths of *The Importance of Being Earnest*, be said to constitute its imperative—that, rather than the final forced march of the play's amnesiac farce into the glare-lighted, barbed-wire Oedipal holding pen of the very last page?
>   ... I suggest, or I suggest the play suggests: Forget the Name of the Father. Think about your uncles and aunts. ("Tales of the Avunculate" 58–9)

Sedgwick's essay focuses on the familial and affective warmth which uncles and aunts can provide, and the way they humanize one's own parents: "having aunts and uncles ... means perceiving your parents as somebody's sibs—not, that is, as alternately abject and omnipotent links in a chain of compulsion and replication that invariably leads to *you*; but rather as elements in a varied, contingent, recalcitrant but re-forming seriality" (63). She also notes that "thinking about your uncles and aunts" can and should be carried out on a theoretical level: as the art historian and early queer theorist Craig Owens reminded her, the same mid-century structural anthropologists we saw in our previous chapter trying to generalize the incest taboo to all societies were very conscious that the relationship between uncle (especially the mother's brother) and nephew was of far greater importance in these societies than in our own.

Sedgwick's argument emphasizes more the *example* of the bachelor uncles and the spinster aunts, the non-procreative adults in the child's everyday interactions, as potential paths for the child's libido to imitate. A cursory glance at the representations of these figures, especially the spinster aunts, in Latin American literature reveals that what Sedgwick presents as an opportunity for identifications may actually be experienced by the child as a threat: as long as *una mujer decente* may not have a home of her own until she marries, the home of one's brother or father will no doubt be perceived as a cage and a punishment, both to herself and to the daughters of the house; even the usually hard-headed Angeles Mastretta cannot avoid the tone of a fairy tale at times in her wonderful collection of tales of "liberated aunts" in *Mujeres de ojos grandes*.[9] Where, then, can we hope to find a model in Latin American literature of a positive avunculate, the position from which an alternative to the father's sexuality and procreation can be established, and one that might also help us sketch out a parable/parabola of creativity?

LEÇONS DE L'ABÎME DE MON ONCLE: *PARADISO*

I want to consider another passage so significant that Lezama could have placed it, like a blazing light, at the head of all that follows:

Enfin, mon oncle me tirant par le collet, j'arrivai près de la boule.
"Regards, me dit-il, et regards bien! il faut prendre des *leçons* d'abîme!"

Jules Verne, Voyage au centre de la terre [Then, my uncle dragging me by the neck, I reached the crater. "Look," he told me, "and look well! One must take one's lessons from the abyss!"]

(Julio Cortázar, "To Reach Lezama Lima" 84)

The avunculate takes pride of place in chapter VII of *Paradiso*, where it suggests a direct link between the uncle and writing as a hermetic, decadent vocation.

The placing of this chapter is relevant to the discussion. Chapter VI has just presented the death of José Cemí's father, victim of the influenza epidemic of 1919 while in Florida with his family on a military mission. The chapter opens with the widow Rialta's family, scraping by humbly on government pensions, having moved in with her mother, also a widow, little José's grandmother Augusta Olaya. The only man of the house is Rialta's brother Alberto, little José's only uncle by blood, a man in his late thirties. We have already seen Alberto as a teenager cloaking himself in impenetrable smoke on a Havana street corner, spied upon from his house by an adolescent Cemí Sr. when they were schoolmates. There would be every reason to believe that he would be the man of the house and the new paterfamilias for the Olayas and for his widowed sister; in an old letter we will read in this chapter, he signed his name, "Alberto, *rex puer*" or child king. Yet Alberto, either consciously or through incompetence, rejects the position of the paterfamilias. The avunculate, then, does not seek patriarchal power, and cannot exercise it even if such power is thrust upon it.

The first scene of chapter VII involves an embarrassing incident: Uncle Alberto is drunk before lunch, once again on a street corner, harassing people who pass by the house. When he pounds on all the doors to be let in, his sister runs to her room in tears, and his mother Augusta stages a confrontation: "José Cemí came out of the first room and saw his uncle, his face red and his eyes furrowed by small red fibers like angry serpents" (159). With little José as the eyewitness, the narrator relates doña Augusta's rebukes to her son for not helping support the family's straitened circumstances, and a teary Alberto accepts the money she doles out to him in silence. Whereas the narrator interprets for us doña Augusta's thoughts and strategizing ("She [...] took out the folded bills which she had prepared in advance to put an end to the scene, and laid them on the arm of the chair" (159)), he leaves Alberto in a double silence, neither speaking nor spoken for.

There follows a passage essential for most readings of the text. Rialta, upset by "the first disturbance of her life since the death of her husband" (160), joins her three children in the patio of the house and, while the four of them play jacks together, the presence of the ghost of the dead father becomes apparent to them in a charmed circle. The rule of the father, albeit sublimated, provides a shelter against the instabilities of the rule of the matriarch and the incursions of the uncle. A third rule for avuncular creativity: as was suggested in my previous chapter, the contribution of the perverse and the eccentric will not be able to undo or supplant the patriarchy to which it contributes, at least not for the true believers.

What eventually follows is one of the novel's most famous set pieces, doña Augusta's Creole banquet, celebrated both in the movie *Strawberry and Chocolate* and in the Senel Paz story that was its basis. It is the space of the mother and the grandmother. Nevertheless, Lezama convokes the banquet's guests through an emphasis on uncles. Demetrio, doña Augusta's brother and hence Rialta and Alberto's uncle, arrives with the news that Augusta's daughter and son-in-law, Leticia and Santurce, are intending to drop in this afternoon for an extended visit. Lezama interrupts the narration to describe great-uncle Demetrio's new prosperity. He had been a failure of a dentist in Havana, and only achieved economic stability when he went out to the province of The Isle of Pines and married down, letting himself be courted by a pool hall attendant named Blanquita who was herself something of a matriarch ("Over the islanders Blanquita exercised a universal monarchy of kindness" (164)), and she predicted a prosperity for themselves as a couple in Havana which she then helped bring about. Demetrio's presence at the banquet is as a mediator. He is best at coaxing good moods out of his nephew Alberto and his nephew-in-law Santurce, a financially comfortable doctor who is portrayed as pompous and bristly. The next lesson of the avunculate, then: there are tedious uncles (Santurce) and minor ones (Demetrio) amidst the truly influential ones (Alberto). At this point, perhaps unexpectedly, Alberto returns, impeccably dressed, sufficiently sober, and ready to take part in his mother's banquet.

We have not yet seen Alberto perform his function for José as poet; but Lezama retards the action of this scene still further, with a three-page digression on the function that Alberto performs for the matriarchy:

> Alberto Olaya's reaction to the magnet of family demonism was especially Cuban. He would be freely, reverentially surrounded. Sometimes the whole family would hang on a single point: trying to guess what would be nice for Alberto. For the family dynasty of the Cemís and the Olayas, the small diabolic dose of Alberto was more than enough. The family watched over and cared for that little devil cat as if he were the end of a classical and robust development, characterized by smiling good sense and allied to the river of time in which that ark floated with alliances intertwined at the roots. Except for certain small features, Uncle Alberto formed an inaccessible and invisible part of this lustrous family tapestry, as if to receive the caress of the generations. (166)

(In the revised 1988 edition, the "gata" of the devil cat has become the "gota" or drop of the diabolic dose, and, perhaps, the drop of a liquid ally to the river of time; more relevantly for our project, rather than a mere "end" of a classical and robust development, in the original Alberto is the "contrapeso" or counterweight to the main tradition.) It is surely no accident that here we return to the notion that Alberto, as he had been as an adolescent, is impenetrable ("inaccessible and invisible") by the omniscient narrator, just as he had been impenetrable as a boy for his neighbor and future brother-in-law Cemí. But the passage also shows that, for Lezama, the family requires the demonism that Alberto contributes to it (Blanquita the ex-poolhall attendant, it turns out, is no more than a "feigned demonism" (166) in contrast). Indeed, it is not just any family member but the mother who engages in this conflict with the scapegrace:

> The first combat takes place between the mother and the demons who assault the family castle at its weakest tower. This son represents the ultimate sacrifice of reason, and the ultimate mystery. Thus, in the end, a mother may have wanted, in spite of her snood of irrepressible kindness, to be judged demonic too. (167)

This passage strives to make generalizations about the human character of a sort we recognize as Proustian, so it is fitting that it segues into two descriptions, first of the mother's desire to share the faults of her beloved son, but then of this same desire between "friends who would delight in the same eros" (167); equally fittingly, these friends cement their demonic tendencies by confessing, one to the other, crimes committed against grandmothers. It is ultimately more typical of Lezama than Proust that the crimes these two passionate friends should confess to should both be imaginary crimes, "affected by melancholy drunkenness": much as José Cemí never actually has sex in this novel and no overt criticism of the patriarchy can be made, nobody ever commits real crimes against the matriarchy either. But we have learned two more lessons about the avunculate: it is a decadent branch of a noble trunk, but one condoned, rationalized (however irrationally) by the matriarchal interregnum; and while it is "especially Cuban," it makes at least some claims to universal application.

This world of women is itself a sort of literary discourse, less monumental, more pragmatic, more gossipy. It is possible to speculate about the desire of the uncle more freely than to speculate about the desire of the patriarch, just as he is permitted to have bad moods when the patriarch is not:

> Alberto's sisters [...] along with his nieces and nephew, José Cemí and his sisters [...], also had their fabulous kingdom for the strolls of the household demon. His sisters saw in him the archetype of elegant manhood, the chosen one, the daring one, gallant, disdainful. At one remove in the family environment, the nieces and nephews had an indirect version. Like a medieval hero's, his herald arrived preceded by oral tradition, by the things that had been said about him in a low voice, about his moments of terrible rage, about the suppliant women who were bemoaning his indifference and rejection. It was said that one of the Colonel's sisters once fell in love with him, working herself up to the most prudish hysteria, weeping for every moment that Alberto was unattainable to her or gave her one more proof that her dreams would never be fulfilled. (168)

Lezama seems oblivious, in his chivalric metaphor, that uncle Alberto would fulfill the role of the dragon better than he would St. George. As we have seen in the novel's passages referring to Fronesis and his girlfriend Lucía, Lezama surrounds the men whom he himself finds attractive with women who are agitated in demonstrative enthusiasm for them. It is certainly very common, as here, to associate female discourse with "oral tradition" (and in other parts of *Paradiso* Lezama praises his grandmother and mother's contribution to his writing as the presence of the voice and, in the case of his grandmother Augusta, as a constant creative coining of and variation on Castilian adages and other oral folk wisdom). It should not be surprising to see this female oral world being contrasted with a scene of male written art.

This is the context, then, in which the scene of instruction begins. With his nephew Alberto in the room with them, great-uncle Demetrio reads a letter written to him by Alberto to entertain him while Demetrio was stuck in the Isle of Pines. Alberto seems to be irritated by the performance of "something [...] so insignificant as his letter" (169), and the first paragraph's supposed lewdness clears the room of all the female audience (its last phrase is, "Plenitud, desnudos orifican," which Rabassa translates "Fullness, naked people making gold"); it seems to be about fish, birds and marine plants, but everyone behaves as if it is really about prostitutes. Demetrio sets the scene for the rest of the letter:

> Demetrio was grateful for their withdrawal, as it kept him from having to leave half of it out. He said to Cemí: "Come close so you can hear what your Uncle Alberto wrote, and you'll become acquainted with him and his special ebullience. This is the first time you'll hear language made into nature, with all its artifices of allusion and loving pedantry. When I was on the island, what joy I had receiving his letters! When I was away, it brought back years when I, much older, studied with him. His mocking pedantry hides a tenderness that makes me weep [...]" (169)

Demetrio's emphasis here is on the hidden tenderness between nephew and uncle (and Alberto is still hiding his emotions as he hears his own letter performed); the emotion is well hidden, because there is no term of endearment, no speaking of emotions, in the entire three-page verbal display that is the letter. As with the other scene of instruction, here between grand-uncle and grand-nephew rather than between father and son, you had to be there. Just as you had to have the story of the misreading of grindstone and student to understand José's definition of student, so too here you had to be told that this is a letter of tenderness, for its language does not convey that it is: as with the act of reading, the context determines the emotional affect that we attribute to the act of writing. Our grand-uncles tell us what our uncles meant by their writings. It certainly had the effect on Cemí that Barthes and Sarduy would have approved of:

> At first, Cemí showed no reaction. His eyes didn't light up, he didn't lean forward in his chair. But something fundamental had happened to him. As if he had been struck by a harpoon of clarity, the family idea of Alberto's demonism [was erased in him (se le borró)]. What remained of Alberto in his letter to the dentist was the same sign that his vibration gave to his arrival, his laughter, his farewell, his manner of speaking and writing. [...]

Cemí felt as if he had suddenly risen up into a chamber where what was said would follow an inexorable path to his ears. When he first drew his chair closer to Demetrio's, he thought he was going to hear a secret. As he listened to the succession of the names of submarine tribes, his memory not only brought forth his class in secondary school where he studied fish, but the words themselves rose up, lured up out of their own territory, artificially grouped, and their joyous movement was invisible and ineffable as it penetrated his dark channels. (171–2)

Cemí seems to learn, first, not to betray emotion at the pleasure he is feeling, as Alberto is not betraying emotion in the text or at the recitation of the text: the impassivity of the dandy is another characteristic of the legacy of the avunculate for Lezama. Second, the matriarchal definition of the decadent uncle is erased, making it possible for the uncle's behavior to be reinterpreted.[10] Third, in accordance with the tradition of considering Lezama to be all about, and only about, the eroticization of language in the materiality of the sign, we see here the "words themselves" rise up as if they were fish. But we must also take into account the metaphor of the "harpoon of clarity" which strikes Cemí. Once again, the concept of being influenced by someone else involves an impenetrable older man penetrating a younger man or boy; but the harpoon implies that it is Cemí, not the prostitutes (of whichever gender), who has taken the position of the fish, who is being speared by the seduction of the uncle.

Lezama clearly liked to keep his father's personality separate from his uncle's. Insofar as these personalities became linked to a symbolic theory, the father must be upright, silent, central, always morally in the right, and (despite a homoerotically active adolescence) sexually conservative; the uncle must be decadent, associated with speech and with writing, marginal, morally wayward, and sexually libertine. The father must be redeemed from any hint of sexual libertinage, even (especially) if that means taking away from him the ability to write about sex and to employ neo-Baroque tropes: Vitier points out in the 1988 edition that Lezama in an interview claimed that this scene was inspired by a letter sent, not from Lezama's uncle to a grand-uncle, but from Lezama's own father the Colonel to his brother-in-law, Lezama's scapegrace uncle (170, n. 1). Of course the uncle must be redeemed, too: after a chess game with his boring brother-in-law Santurce, in which each captured chess piece contains a piece of paper from which Alberto pretends to read aloud witty aphorisms; after the great Creole supper, to which he contributes brilliant philosophic conversation and which is haunted by a great omen of death; after a conversation with Dr. Santurce, who tells him that doña Augusta has a cancerous tumor; after getting into a brawl outside in a bar and in the plaza with a Mexican guitarist, another omen of death: after all these events Alberto weeps at the police station while thinking of his dead brother-in-law the Colonel, and asks the police to free not just himself but also the Mexican guitarist. While being driven home by another policeman, listening to another anecdote about his brother-in-law and listening to another Mexican guitarist, Alberto and the policeman are abruptly hit by a train and die instantly, fulfilling all the omens.[11] I omit a close analysis of the chess game and the dinner purely for brevity's sake, since they also contain lessons from the abyss of one's seductive and impenetrable uncle. But if I am also hurrying through Alberto's repentance, redemption, and death, it is partly because something rings false in them: they are not scenes between uncle and nephew, and the narrator has already told us that the uncle's function is to be "inasible e invisible"; as a result, the scenes in which we have direct access to the uncle's (penitent, sentimental) consciousness must be deemed spurious. It is not in Alberto's character to be redeemed, only in the omniscient narrator's character to desire to redeem him. As Lezama famously liked to say about one of his heterodox Catholic opinions, there is a hell, but it is empty; he sees to it that both father and uncle, by different paths, have been granted paradise.

Now that Lezama is in danger of becoming no more than a poster on the wall of other phallocentric gay Cubans, we might wish to emphasize not just the figure of the man who fantasized about his father's sexuality while he obeyed the prohibitions of his mother, but the figures of two of that man's creations. The first, the avowed homosexual, is neurotic, rebarbative and often narrow in his loving, to be sure, but he uses what remains of his male privilege to look the patriarchy straight in the eye. When that fictional character is freed from his adoration of circular eternity, he might continue to study the circle, becoming a wheel that gives off sparks which as they multiply light up the night; but he might also investigate the joys (as in Hocquenghem) of his own anus ("the path of the god Anubis") without the obsession with the other's phallus; or (as in Sarduy) the joys of a neo-Baroque ellipse; or (as in the starry nights of that perverse heterosexual Van Gogh) the joys of spirals in the dark; or the joys of the lightning bolt itself, like the King of the Black Isles in José Cemí Sr.'s school days, "an electric wire running through him to fulfill surprise," an energy no longer imagined to come solely from the sun or from the closet, but also from the interaction of penetrable narrators and inglorious genealogies. The second figure is also a decadent ruin, whose arrogance and demonism is covertly approved of by the matriarchy and whose commitment to writing sexuality forms a literary chain between uncles and nephews, silencing while supposedly revering the patriarch.[12]

Only the most obscure precursors can be chosen. Yet it has turned out that there were more choices to make within Lezama's *Paradiso* than were first apparent, provided we are willing to rearrange the features of José Eugenio Cemí Sr. as an adolescent, and Eugenio Foción, and the decadent Uncle Alberto. There's a nice knock-down argument for you, as Humpty Dumpty meant to say to Alice; or, as he said after Alice protested that she did not think a person's face would look nice if their features were rearranged, "Wait till you've tried."

3. The Moving Target of Fixated Desire: Felisberto's Paper Dolls ∽

Our narratives of the perverse have up until this point shown little enthusiasm for the psychoanalytical narrative broadly construed. We started at the end, with Puig in the 1970s. Molina's populist understanding of homosexuality, in which it is the product of a doting mother and a distant father, is indeed bolstered by the novel's roughly pro-Freud footnotes; but Freud is not sufficiently liberatory for the novelist's sexual politics and must be completed by Puig in drag as a Danish psycho-analyst; meanwhile, the events in the narrative of Molina and Valentín in their jail cell seem at times to consciously mock the earnest left-Freud argument in the footnotes. When we look back some forty years to the generation in which the middle classes began to accept a Freudian vocabulary for describing their sexuality, we confront *Paradiso* and Lezama's utter hostility to the Freudian project, although this hostility arises precisely because Lezama has no desire to free himself, his protagonist, or his island from patriarchal erotics or poetics. The period of Oedipal struggle in which the son would like to kill the father, or fears that the father would like to kill him, is very plainly expressed in this novel but just as plainly denied. Whatever we think of Lezama's portrayal of the father–son relationship in *Paradiso*, however, the novel refuses to accept the idea of paternal castration or maternal smothering as the origin of male homosexuality. Lezama takes himself and his sexuality as a norm and refuses to consider them perversions at all. All Lezama's male characters, whether publicly gay or straight, interact homoerotically with other men, especially during adolescence, and all of them are gynophobic; if their blood is weak they cannot maintain sexually productive marriages, if their blood is strong they either conquer their distaste for female genitalia, or they choose to go beyond procreation into the "hypertelic" vocation of making art.

Against a figure of such titanic self-confidence as Lezama, we now turn to his contemporary, the Uruguayan Felisberto Hernández (1902–64), an author whose tentative, self-reflective texts are almost as inviting to psychoanalytic discourse as Lezama's texts are hostile to it.[1] Although the most anthologized of his works, the novella *Las Hortensias* (*The Daisy Dolls*, 1949[2]), is a third person narration, virtually all of the rest of his oeuvre is written in the first person, and his first successful piece of writing was a nonfiction memoir of his piano teacher, *Por los tiempos de Clemente Colling* [In the Times of Clemente Colling] (1942), as is the shorter 1943 *El caballo perdido* [The Stray Horse], also about one of his piano teachers; one of his longer pieces, *Las tierras de la memoria* [The Lands of Memory] (written mostly in 1944–45 and published posthumously), is also autobiographical, as is his posthumously published collection of observations *Diario de un sinvergüenza* [Diary of a Shameless Man]; and all of these pieces speak directly about the eccentric desires and impulses that the author recalls, whether he acted upon them or not. Felisberto (he is seldom referred to by his ordinary last name, although to refer to him only by his first name is perhaps a mark of the slightly deprecatory familiarity many readers feel toward him) for much of the rest of his oeuvre engaged in a first-person fictional practice that seems to be the stuff of which psychoanalytic sessions are made: expressions of frustrations, anxieties, inadequacies; compensatory fantasies; self-protective and self-revealing moves of every kind. Indeed, his more ambitious pieces thematize the psychoanalytic scene in various ways: Horacio the protagonist of *Las Hortensias* examines private tableaux of life-size dolls as if he were interpreting his own dreams; the biographer-narrator of "The Flooded House" rows his fat employer the widow Margarita in a boat while she tells him the story of her life, her love, and her obsession with water. If Michel Foucault is correct to say that the works of Freud and the practice of psychoanalysis have inaugurated a new configuration for confessional discourse in society, Felisberto is certainly an author who seems to ask us to read his fictions confessionally.

And yet it is useful to run the comparison both ways. That is to say, rather than merely reading Felisberto's fictional confessions to show that Felisberto "was" a fetishist and a voyeur, and that any of his textual effects not in strict adherence to the Freudian narrative are either irrelevant to some clinical definition or his attempts to conceal his similarity to that definition, I prefer to read these narratives as contributions to a theory of fetishism and voyeurism above and beyond Freud's thinking about perversions. Felisberto may be a better "theorist" than Freud himself.[3] Participating in the aesthetic of the various avant-garde movements, Felisberto theorizes a fragmented, constantly mobile subjectivity that pursues pleasure in subtly mobile forms.

He is far more open-minded than Freud is about the dynamics of some of Freud's key terms, such as disavowal and the maternal phallus. Felisberto's fictions, down to the level of details of style, always remain conscious of the need for mediation, and his favored protagonists do not always respond well to demands for immediacy. Such a privileging of mediation gives hints of the relation between the Freudian fetish and Marxist theories of commodity fetishism.

Yet, as we shall also see, Freud may have insights, not so much into the Felisbertian fetishist's psychology as a psychology, but into his psychology as a narrative, as a coherent story with a beginning, a series of reversals, and a satisfying dénouement. Ironically, if Felisberto is at times a better theorist than Freud, the latter will at times turn out to be a better storyteller than the former.

OVERVALUATION AND SETTLING FOR LESS

I entered a café which was near a church, I sat down at a table in the back and I thought about my life. I knew how to isolate the hours of happiness and wrap myself up in them; first I would steal with my eyes some neglected thing from the street or the interior of houses and later I would take it into my solitude. I took such great pleasure from dwelling on it that if people had known, they would have hated me.

("El cocodrilo" III: 75; my translation)

[Horacio] took a pair of opera glasses out of his pocket and tried to focus them on his wife's face.
"I'd love to know if the shadows under your eyes are also plants."
She realized he had been to his desk to fetch the opera glasses, and decided to humor him. He saw a glass dome, which turned out to be a bottle. So he put down the opera glasses and poured himself some more wine from France.

(177/ II; 178)

The first quotation above, although from one of his later stories, is typical of Felisberto's oeuvre in describing an adversarial relationship between the subject who aims for pleasure and the person who provides the object of pleasure. On the one hand, this characterizing of the desiring position as thief or spy or burglar indicates how far Felisberto's desire is from the mutual satisfaction of needs in an environment of warm communication and commitment to mutual growth (i.e., love), and it gives some aid and comfort to those psychoanalytic theorists who wish to preserve the pejorative connotations of the word "perversion" to mean, in Robert J. Stoller's phrase, "the erotic form of hatred."[4] On the other hand, the mechanism by which Felisberto fears he will be punished for stealing the sights he snatches from the street does not include a father figure, and it is surprising how seldom in Felisberto's oeuvre it is a male authority figure that puts to an end the protagonist's perverse desire.[5] It is much more common for the women themselves to threaten to curtail or to cut off access to male pleasure. In the initial position of *Las Hortensias*, as we can see from the other quotation above, Horacio's wife María can seem to be his playmate and his equal, foiling his theft of spying or burglary on her own. (It is tempting to correlate this lack of a triangular structure of desire with Uruguay's more liberal political system: Felisberto himself was married and divorced four times.) The woman in Felisberto is an object, but never an object trafficked between men; rather, she is an object with an alluring but also frustrating independence.

The possibility that a man cannot fully enjoy the object of his desire is the central defining motive in Sigmund Freud's first attempt to define fetishism; indeed, it is so important to his understanding of fetishism that it unbalances his entire taxonomic project. We return to Freud's *Three Essays* of 1905. The subject of the first essay, the sexual aberrations, is eventually put into a logical and narrative relationship to normal sexuality: most if not all the sexual perversions are components of polymorphous perversity which have been available since infancy (essay 2) and have somehow not been repressed or integrated into normality through a successful Oedipal complex (essay 3). Our various perverts—homosexuals, fetishists, sadists, masochists, transvestites—are precisely equal to Shakespearean foils and other minor characters in a complex narrative, included in order to provide an enlightening contrast with the protagonist, His Majesty the Normal Adult.

Freud thinks it will be useful to divide, for the purpose of exposition, all the sexual aberrations into two groups, those which err in the choice of an object (bestiality, homosexuality), and those which err in the sexual aims (voyeurism, anal eroticism), and confidently places all sexual perversions into each box. But it is not a taxonomic desire but also a didactic purpose which organizes the essay. The goal of describing the aberrations of object choice is to demonstrate that sexual libido exists independently of the objects that it chooses: there is no essential difference between the libido used to desire beautiful women and the one used to desire beautiful men, or prepubescent girls, or animals: the libido does not love its object because it judges that it is beautiful: it judges the object beautiful because it loves it: "It seems probable that the sexual instinct is in the first instance independent of its object; nor is its origin likely to be due to its object's attractions" (14).

Having established the concept of libido to his satisfaction, Freud builds the next section, on object aim, on the concepts that will prove essential to his branding people as perverts: *extension* and *fixation*. The voyeur and the fetishist are both enjoying, indeed exclusively eroticizing, components of the libido which should only be preliminary to the main sexual event. These preliminary parts of the story are overvalued by the pervert, who then settles for less than full genital eroticism. Too much, and then not enough, as Freud tries to formulate it:

> For there are certain intermediate relations to the sexual object, such as touching and looking at it, which lie on the road toward copulation and are recognized as being preliminary sexual aims. [...] Perversions are sexual activites which either (a) extend, in an anatomical sense, beyond the regions of the body that are designed for sexual union, or (b) linger over the intermediate relations to the sexual object which should normally be traversed rapidly on the path toward the final sexual aim. (15–16)

That is to say, the libido goes too far, eroticizing more than just the genitals of the beloved, or it does not go far enough, preserving too feverishly the preliminary or infantile pleasures that others traverse rapidly on the road to normality. The metaphor of a path or road, which the protagonist The Libido must take, is one of Freud's most basic metaphors, like the economic or the hydraulic, and is invoked throughout the *Three Essays* in particular; it seems particularly appropriate when one examines the stories of Felisberto, so often structured as the tale of a flâneur through the streets of small towns or walking through rituals structured as underground tunnels or a sequence of department store windows, always tempted to pause, to linger, to lose the way to a normal home. The notion of extension, which could conceivably work into a sort of odd pansexual theory of further development (as if to say, achieving genital orgasm with a partner is a worthwhile skill that should nevertheless be *extended* into eroticizing the entire body of the other), quickly drops out of the text as such, and the second meaning consolidates into one of the two terms Freud most often uses to conceal moral censure under the guise of pure description, *fixation*:

> In the majority of instances the pathological character in a perversion is found to lie not in the *content* of the new sexual aim but in its relationship to the normal. If a perversion, instead of appearing merely *alongside* the normal sexual aim and object [...], ousts them completely and takes their place

in *all* circumstances—if in short, a perversion has the characteristics of exclusiveness and fixation—then we shall usually be justified in regarding it as a pathological symptom. (27; italics Freud's)

We will not be surprised, given the common use of the term, that fetishism is tightly associated with the notion of fixation.

But fetishism is also associated with the dropping out of the notion of extension. The mini-narrative that Freud gives us of the fetishist is that he is the person who engages in the characteristic activity of all of us who are doomed to desire, an overvaluation of the object we desire. While this supposedly involves a general overestimation of the beloved as a person, Freud also claims that it involves a sort of "geographic" overestimation as well: not just the rest of the body that has such an appealing warmth and wetness in its middle, but also that body's clothes and hair and any other unique characteristics, can be overinvested in, overvalued. Freud sets himself the problems of explaining why the libido retreats from the "normal" part of the overvalued object and pools in the supposedly peripherally exciting parts of the object once beloved in its entirety. Typically, he will attribute this change to a threat of castration.

But one of the effects of this plausible, if multistep narrative (desire, overvaluation/extension, castration threat, regression onto a peripheral part of the original desired object, fixation/fetishization of that nongenital part), is that it eliminates the possibility of a simpler narrative, in which the subject desires some nongenital object from the very beginning. Freud simply cannot believe that the sexual libido could function biologically that way. There can be no originary perverse desire: the fetishist is not permitted the luxury of desiring what he desires because he desires it, but only desiring what he desires because he has had to abandon some other more normal object of desire. It is perhaps a pleasant thought exercise, to imagine that some people, from the onset of their libidos, would be constituted to be aroused by fur, others by the smell of sweaty, dirty feet, and so on; Felisberto's oeuvre, full of "raros" and "ex-céntricos" who are quite aware of how unusual their desires are, provide an interesting gallery of fictional characters on which to test a Freudian theory of overvaluation.

These experiments take place in what José Pedro Díaz and others call Felisberto's third period, after his fragmentary "primeras invenciones" and his 1940–44 experiments in autobiography. In those two periods Felisberto reflected on an abiding discrepancy between his interest in some objects which produced unexpected feelings and thoughts, and the interest most people took in such objects. After 1944 he will dramatize this discrepancy in a handful of major stories, "The Balcony," "Except Julia," "The Usher,"

"The Flooded House," and of course, *Las Hortensias*; in four of these stories Felisberto (or an omniscient narrator) recounts the encounter with the obsessive fetishist and is not the fetishist himself.

Felisberto's female obsessives—the girl in love with her own balcony; the fat widow being rowed about her flooded house thinking of her dead husband; even *Las Hortensias*'s María in her own relationship to the Hortensia doll—have idealized but not overtly erotic relationships to their overvalued objects. It is his male obsessives who achieve the more directly fetishistic behavior. The main organs of erotic possession of the overvalued object are the eyes and hands, and at least to that extent Felisberto accepts the general lines of the Freudian scenario in these thought experiments. In the story "Except Julia," the protagonist owns a farm with a tunnel, in which he hires servants to set up an elaborate series of tactile enigmas. When the narrator is invited to participate in these rituals of touching and deciphering in the dark, he feels pleasure localized in his hands. Well beyond Freud's usual formulations, the Felisbertian narrator understands that there is an originary pleasure in the sense of touch, linked with the adult's pleasure in interpreting or deciphering the object being touched in the dark. Freud insists that such strong pleasures have a sexual component, and that the psyche must be trained to integrate these strong pleasures into the consummated sexual act; the tunnel owner refuses to integrate these pleasures. However, the Felisbertian narrator sees this pleasure as a threat, not so much to the integration of the sexual act, but to the integration of self:

> Then I fingered some tasseled material, and suddenly I realized it was a pair of gloves. I wondered what the gloves meant to my hands: the surprise, I decided, was for them, not for me. When I touched a piece of glass, I suspected that the hands wanted to try on the gloves. I was about to humor them, but held back, like a father who doesn't want to indulge his daughters' every whim. Then I began to suspect something else: my friend was too far advanced in that world of hands, perhaps encouraging an instinct for independence in them that allowed them to develop too much a life of their own. (100; II, 105)

The simile of a father and his two capricious daughters implies the tension between love and insubordination that will be literalized in the rest of the short story: the tunnel owner has fallen in love with one of the women hired to kneel in the tunnel, Julia, who talks back to him and breaks other rules of the tunnel ritual. When he decides he wants to marry her, she puts as a condition that he stop the ritual altogether. Yet this passage is also typically Felisbertian, not just for its comic yet just simile, but also because the Felisbertian narrator asks himself about the meaning of the object for him,

and tentatively concludes this intellectual quest with a notion of the fragmented self that goes beyond the Freudian notion of a fragmented psyche.

In that sense, gloves, fur, female dolls behind glass, and so on, can never
be inherently desirable for Freud the way they can be for Felisberto, but
must always be a substitute for something more closely attached to the
erogenous zones. Indeed, the section on fetishism in Freud's *Three Essays*
acknowledges from the very beginning that were it not for the narrative
pressed into service to describe it, to call fetishism a deviation of the sexual
aim would be a misnomer:

> From the point of view of classification, we should no doubt have mentioned
> this highly interesting group of aberrations of the sexual instinct [i.e.,
> fetishism] among the sexual deviations in respect of the sexual *object*. But we
> have postponed their mention till we could become acquainted with the fac-
> tor of sexual overvaluation, on which these phenomena, being connected
> with an abandonment of the sexual aim, are dependent. (19)

Rather than accepting the possibility that the concept of erogenous zones
which he is developing in this very essay should be expanded beyond the
various orifices (mouth, anus, genitalia) to include in theory anything to
which an infant could cathect libidinal energy, Freud closes down this possibility and declares that any other object of libidinal interest is merely a
"substitute" for the normal object, access to which has been too successfully
forbidden to the desiring infant.

So too, previous psychoanalytic readings of Felisberto and his protagonists
have portrayed him as a timid man who did not fall in love with so many
women because of their differences, or because he had many, perhaps contradictory, desiring impulses, but because each woman was an (eventually
unsatisfying) substitute for a previous woman—of course, his mother—and
they have even found a recurring scenario in his writings, the moment when
a character throws himself under the skirts of a large woman or in which,
while he lies upon the ground, she trails her dress over his face.[6] Of the major
stories, this scenario is most literally represented in "The Usher," and this
story is a good example of how fair Felisberto plays in testing our sympathy
for the fetishist. An impoverished young man who works as a movie usher
develops an uncanny ability to shine beams of light from his eyes. Rather
than using it for any more public or lucrative purpose, he sneaks into the private chambers of a rich man's house at night and, lying on the floor, casts his
eyes upon the beautiful objects in the glass cases. But the rich man's daughter is a somnambulist carrying a candelabra, and the usher has chosen a spot
on the floor that turns out to be on her regular sleepwalking path.

The narrative contraption that brings about this overvalued scenario is simultaneously voyeuristic and, with the manically ritual positioning of usher, floor, woman, and dress, fetishistic; in this case, at least, it seems correct to consider the ritual to be the expression of a fixation. Felisberto seems sufficiently sure that we the readers will try to achieve some distance from this narrator that he presents this story to us in the first person, unlike the third person of *Las Hortensias* or the setup of the other major fictions in which the narrator listens critically but empathetically to the fetishist's or obsessive's confession. The scenario continues for many evenings; and yet our poor young protagonist (because he is young?) refuses to continue settling for less. He seems satisfied enough in his dreams, where he appears simultaneously one night as a woolly dog resting on the sleepwalker's wedding dress and also as a member of the congregation. Rather, while wandering through the city the next day, he comes upon her awake, arm in arm with a man of her class who wears a cap; she does not recognize the usher and he stalks them. That night, he decides to bring a cap with him to the mansion, and as she approaches he tosses his cap at her. She starts; the candelabra falls to the ground; she collapses; he stares at her, his eye-beams now becoming a doubly uncanny X-ray vision; the majordomo and the girl's father come running and light the ordinary lights; amidst the threats, posturings and implausible explanations, the usher thinks, "I felt that nothing in my life would make sense to anyone else" (85; II, 91). So, egged on by the spectacle of daylight normality' the usher abandoned his fetishistic, voyeuristic settling-for-less, and forgot the "threats of castration" (his poverty, his solitariness) that block his access to the desired woman. Playing fair to our (Freudian) sense of normal erotics, Felisberto tells a story in which a character's originary desire (to see) is overextended, retreats (due to poverty), and becomes fixated into a fetishistic scenario.

The Freudian fetish narrative, then, is a legitimate way to approach Felisberto's *oeuvre*. Nevertheless, we might also decide to do otherwise than collude in a search for an originary scene and a normalized desire, and focus instead upon a story such as *Las Hortensias*, which suggests a centrifugal, rather than centripetal logic, in which one scenario gives way to another scenario after another—a man, in love with his wife, casts his imagination over tableaux of life-size dolls who enact scenes; then he commissions a life-size doll of the wife; he falls in love with that doll; then he has it made anatomically correct; then he is unfaithful to it with another life-size doll; then he cheats on it with a doll owned by someone else; then he cheats on that doll with a totally different make of life-size doll, and then with still another make of doll. Furthermore, an unsuccessful centripetal solution is offered twice, albeit abruptly and without Horacio's consent: twice his wife tries to bring his attention back to herself, substituting herself for the last of the adulterous dolls and then joining the dolls in one of the tableaux, yet both interventions drive her husband into agitation and finally madness. The wrong sort of move to the origin drives him to the wrong sort of flight.

It might be worthwhile, therefore, to examine two competing narratives around the fetish before going further into the psychoanalytic one. As with the Freudian narratives, we will encounter an argument about overvaluation and a narrative involving a fixation, a thwarted path of normality. And although it moves us more into history than psychology, it continues the concealed moral censure of the fetishist we have also seen in the Freudian tradition, a censuring that Felisberto, that unworthy thief of eccentric pleasures, cannot bring himself fully to protest.

THE I-DOLLS OF THE MARKETPLACE

> *[María reads in the newspaper]: "La Primavera, our smartest department store, will be presenting a new collection on its top floor. We understand some of the models sporting the latest fashion will be Hortensias. [...] One more example of the alarming rate at which this new version of Original Sin—to which we have already referred in our columns—is spreading among us."*
>
> (*Las Hortensias* 216; II, 218)

The word "fetish" did not originate in psychoanalysis but comes rather from the history of anthropology.[7] Portuguese and other traders brought back from Africa little statues of African gods that the Portuguese called *feitichos*, "something made" or handiwork, which the natives claimed had magic powers in and of themselves. As God among Christian thinkers in the nineteenth century was becoming more and more abstract, at least among Enlightenment thinkers, the ability to believe that there was a continuity between the statue of a being with power, and that power, was attributed to merely a Savage's mind. Much of the exciting history of the discipline of anthropology in the twentieth century is rethinking this automatic scorn or deprecation involved in the imperial process of grabbing objects from the Third World and using them to describe supposedly universal concepts really only pertaining to the First.

We can see the parallels between the narrative of Freud's 1905 essay on the sexual aberrations and this Enlightenment narrative, in which every day and every way the World-Spirit becomes a little more rational and the gods become a little less material and local, and in which those immature civilizations who do not travel this "inevitable" path are deemed to have fixated on an early stage in their development, overvaluing certain objects they have happened to encounter in their history. As in Freud (and as in popular thinking), the religious fetishist cuts a rather comic figure, not dangerous but small: he ought to know better—we know better—but he doesn't. Even more clearly than in Freud we can see a horror of the material in the Enlightenment's characterization of the fetish. And more prominently than in Freud's story there figures the glamour or aura that the fetish-object holds for the fetishist: one of the most important anthropological contributors to recent thought on the fetish, Michael Taussig, frequently cites the work of Walter Benjamin on the aura and the premodern artwork to suggest that representations really do participate in the power of the objects they represent.[8] Such skepticism toward Enlightenment religious imperialism is at least one dissenting voice against the consensus that fetishisms of all kinds are backward fixations.

Nevertheless, the Enlightenment narrative and its morality persists in unexpected places. One specific but fascinating hangover from an era which saw the fetish as a false god worshiped by ignorant fools for its borrowed, surely nonexistent magic is the Marxist notion of the commodity fetish. In a short but suggestive passage of *Capital* Marx said that the products on the shelves of your local department store had been cut off by the production and distribution process from any trace of the people who had produced them, and certainly from the social relations between the people who produced, distributed, and sold them. No one wants to think of underpaid coffee bean pickers while sipping a cappuccino. When as a consumer you walk through the mall with that bulge in your pocket until the right tie or CD makes love to you, then you have reduced the producer-to-consumer relationship to a commodity-to-consumer relationship, and this proves that you're a savage. Indeed, Marx goes further and says that all human relations are mediated by money in a capitalist society, so that your romantic relationship to your toys becomes more and more the template for your relationship to your girlfriend, essentially the relationship between a client and the prostitute he chooses.

This economic critique involving justice and a Hegelian recognition of the Other became by the post–World War I period a bridge between Marx and Freud. In the hands of a whole range of Frankfurt School thinkers, Marcuse, Fromm, Adorno, and of course Benjamin, the concept of commodity fetishism became a psychological as well as an economic concept to explain how modernity works, how the modern subject is constituted. It has proven to be a dauntingly durable connection between mid-century sexual conformism and (leftist) politics and ethics. The Kantian-Aquinan principle that no person should be treated like an object by another person, reinforced by this Marxist (also Christian, also Romantic) principle that the cash nexus should not mediate human relations, poses a formidable consensus against not just fetishism but any sexual experimentation that might be "freely" chosen as a consumer freely chooses between financially available options. If in this chapter I am defending fetishists, it still remains to be seen how I can keep from falling into the trap of throwing out too much Marxism with my defense.[9] Certainly, queer theory as an academic practice with a recognizable label has sometimes split into factions around the pros and cons of consumer culture.[10] It is a mark of the imaginative energy (and bizarrerie) of *Las Hortensias* that a text authored by a writer who showed no interest in social justice (and who became quite reactionary in the last decades of his life) and almost no interest in theory—in his well-known "How Not to Explain My Stories" Felisberto claims that for him to write stories "ruled by some theory of consciousness" would be extremely distressing (3; II, 175)—should nevertheless possibly contribute to the debate over commodity fetishism and its discontents.

And indeed Felisberto's contribution to such a debate is, first, to leave open for further discussion all three of these discursive threads, the psychoanalytical, the anthropological, and the socio-economic. Naturally at first the novella directs us toward the desires of a private man and his eccentric domestic pastimes. While any reader would recognize that the humor of the first few chapters lies in Horacio's attempts to manufacture and make material the scenarios that incite his thoughts and desires, we tend to read the opening chapters as being about desire and how it works within the psyche. Such thoughts as pass through Horacio's mind include a straightforward belief in the power of the dolls:

> Until recently Horacio had kept the store that had been making his fortune. Alone, after closing time every day, he liked to wander through the shadowy rooms, reviewing the dolls in the show windows. [...] One way or another, the dolls had their secrets. Although the window dresser knew how to display each of them to her best advantage, at the last moment she always added a touch of her own. (185; II, 186)

"Magical thinking," no doubt, according to an orthodox Freudian or Marxist, a minimal residue of unenlightened thinking. But on closer inspection we can see that Felisberto has created a narrative, here in this passage and elsewhere, that is not so much domestic and private but domesticated and privatized. Horacio *retires* from his activities in the public sphere, just as he literally *retira*, withdraws, the dolls from a previous public circulation, and his first theories about the dolls, formulated after he has sent his employees home and he wanders among the mannequins alone, involve the dolls' absorption of the envious glances of the passersby. This socioeconomic perspective, only implicit in the earlier chapters, accelerates as the novel progresses. The latter chapters of the text open up the issue of how objects become charged with desires, in a way that no longer encourages us to look backward into the past of the fetishist or transcendentally into metempsychosis, but sideways into the strategies of the culture. After four leisurely chapters taking place in Horacio's home, a "black house" near a noisy factory (the source of Horacio's income) with its private doll theater and a garden for walks and parties that are spied upon by neighbors full of (inaccurate) gossip, the novella's second half gains speed and moves out of the domestic space over which Horacio has such control. The following six chapters include scenes in one of the city's hotels, to which both Horacio and María have gone separately, after Horacio's perversion has been found out; any domesticity or control Horacio may find there is undermined by his awareness that the hotel used to be a brothel, and by a fire that occurs in a house across the street. María will then go to a cousin's house, also a domestic space, of course; but there she and the cousin will discover, in the public space of the newspaper, that the dollmaker Facundo is advertising Hortensia dolls for sale to other lonely men or unsatisfied husbands. Meanwhile, Horacio's mania is moving still more centrifugally, and after sleeping with one of Facundo's dolls that does not resemble his wife (the servants call it "the spy"), he bribes the servant in a house Facundo has told him of so that he can sneak into that house, take that man's Hortensia doll out, and enjoy an adulterous afternoon with her. The experience is disillusioning—Horacio takes no real pleasure in adultery, in invading the space of another man or of taking an Hortensia out to the unpredictable space of nature (he is excessively annoyed by a toad that watches them, for instance)—and returns to María and promises to mend his ways. Alas, Horacio's libido has not really returned to his legitimate spouse and space. He is irritated by María's own attempts at substitution (she has bought a black cat, but for Horacio "The cat, instead of adding to her appeal, cheapened her" (223; II, 225)), and goes out to his old department store La Primavera to pick out another Hortensia doll and set her up in a house of assignations as his new mistress. In the novel's most elaborate set piece, Horacio returns again to La Primavera, where the department store is displaying a variety of scenes, while crowds mill about fascinated by the knowledge that some of the dolls enacting these tableaux are anatomically correct. Besides the movement out to a public space, the story has moved out to a (fictional) national legend that some of the Hortensias are enacting, "the madwoman of the lake," and out to the cultural exoticism entailed by Horacio's fascination with one of the "Negress" Hortensias. What is at stake in the novella, then, goes beyond fetishism as the private theater of an eccentric wealthy individual, to the various plausible scenarios in which social desires circulate.

Yet a recounting of the novella's plot is somewhat misleading if it tempts us into a purely social analysis. To be told that the story moves to a hotel that used to be a brothel, to a department store's window displays, to the scenario of a national legend, and to an apartment house in which bourgeois men install their mistresses, might mislead the reader into thinking that Felisberto's antimodern dislike of consumerism allows him to espouse a feminist attack on men who objectify women, akin to that of an enlightenment feminist film theorist such as Laura Mulvey.[11] It is undeniable that these scenes are designed to wear down and chasten a protagonist who had thought to protect himself through bourgeois strategies from the consequences of his own desires. However, they are not merely satire, merely moralistic. Felisberto hopes that some sort of mystery or enigma continues to inhere in these dolls, despite the comic absurdity which his narrative sends his protagonist through. In the legend of the Madwoman of the Lake which Felisberto has invented for the department store scene, for instance, the ladies who come to visit the lake ask the Lady questions, but she gets up and walks around the edge of the lake: "The ladies, thinking that she was going to answer the question or show them some secret, followed her. But the lonely woman only went round and round the lake" (226; II, 229). A story without a proper ending, the legend is still supposedly worth dramatizing, the doll still lures the gaze, and, more relevantly, lures the reader into some kind of interpretation.

A flight from the interpreter suggests a movement forward; a historical legend suggests a movement backward, to the past, to origins. The interpretive search for the origin of the fetish, which Freud later in his career will pursue with gusto, may not really be useful. The fetishist himself will certainly ask why it is that he is so attracted to what attracts him, but *Las Hortensias* implies that he may ask this question more because it is inherently pleasurable to ask questions, rather than because these questions need to be answered.

THE HIDDEN MEANING OF A DESIRABLE OBJECT

> *When he was alone again in the darkness of the bedroom, his mind throbbing with the noise of the machines, he thought of the warning signs* [presagios] *he had been receiving. He was like a tangled wire that kept intercepting calls and portents meant for others. But this time all the signals had been aimed at him.*
>
> (*Las Hortensias* 183; II, 184)

The protagonist Horacio of *Las Hortensias*, at first sight, would seem to be on a double quest. He is searching for the object of his desires, and pursues the satisfaction of his desires no matter how comical or humiliating a position this puts him in. But he is also on an epistemological or semiotic quest, a search to figure out the meaning of his desires, to figure out and analyze what is so desirable in the objects of his desires. In his 1927 essay "Fetishism," Freud declares that telling the pervert what it is he seeks in the objects of his fixation will not cure him, but at least Freud promises that the search for the meaning of a desire will produce an answer, albeit a small, almost trivial answer. Irritatingly and yet tantalizingly, Felisberto does not promise an answer, yet he also suggests that the meaning of a desire might be grand or global or ghostly.

In its early chapters, *Las Hortensias* spends a good deal of time examining the pursuit of meaning in desirable objects, that is, the desire to interpret. The most visible and comic scenes of interpretation are of course Horacio's private doll theater scenes: private in one sense, but in another sense a group production of the dollmaker Facundo, the *muchachos* who come up with the scenarios, and the pianist Walter, to say nothing of the dolls themselves. Horacio interprets these scenes partly the way a spectator enjoys a silent movie or a drama critic interprets a play, but mostly the way an amateur Freudian interprets his own dreams or a Rorschach blot, in which he hopes to divine his own mood by virtue of comparing the "objective" meaning of the tableaux, as offered by the *muchachos*, with his own guesses.

Of course, in regular Freudian theory any kind of ink blot or free association can serve for projections. In *Las Hortensias*, however, some objects are already more suitable for this interpretive game than others—namely, female dolls behind glass. The novella is entertainingly incoherent on the reason that Horacio values the dolls the way that he does. Sometimes Horacio theorizes that it all has to do with his childhood, and the text occasionally provides a vignette from a childhood of parents who died young or the sight of a bloody wax-colored corpse to explain his phobias and manias, fears which are soothed by the company of women, animate or inanimate. Sometimes Horacio makes claims about the metaphysical or socio-economic world, such as that Hortensia has the soul of María's dead mother. As we have seen, Horacio believes that the dolls are capable of inspiring desire because they have stored up all the envious looks of the women who have looked at them in the shop windows. That passage continues:

> One way or another, the dolls had their secrets. Although the window dresser knew how to display each of them to her best advantage, at the last moment she always added a touch of her own. It was then that he started to think that the dolls were full of portents (*presagios*). Day and night they basked in

covetous looks and those looks nested and hatched in the air. Sometimes they settled on the dolls' faces like clouds over a landscape, shadowing and blurring their expression, and at other times they reflected back on some poor girl innocently happening by, who was tainted by their original covetousness (*aquella primera codicia*). Then the dolls were like creatures in a trance, on unknown missions, or lending themselves to evil designs. (185; II, 186–7)

We have followed for a while this half-metaphysical, half-socio-economic interpretation, whose search for origins ("aquella primera codicia") seems equally close to Marx and to the Bible. (Recall that the moralizing newspaper which María reads referred to the anatomically correct Hortensias as that "new version of Original Sin.") But it is more important to emphasize that no one of Horacio's theories are proven right, while many are incompatible with one another. (The omniscient narrator flatly contradicts Horacio's *presagios* about María's imminent death, for instance.) To favor one interpretation over the others, then, is a judgment on our part, out of keeping with Felisberto's desire to retain the enigma of women and objects.

The *presagios* themselves are a variation of a very Felisbertian theme, the object that produces an unexpected impression. In this variation, the impression is a *presagio*, a prediction about the future that might be narrative ("'Hold me, for María is dying" (183; II, 184)) or lyric (indicating or bringing about a change in mood). In *Las Hortensias*'s early scenes in the doll theater, the narrative is generally visual and the lyric is generally auditory or musical: much has been made by critics of the noises from Horacio's factory, which in the novella's first sentence get into the black house's shrubbery and combine with the piano playing and other noises of the house to contribute to the power of the dolls. The theme of obscure *presagios* begins with the noises:

> He listened for the hum of the machines and the sounds of the piano. At first they reached him in what seemed like watery murmurs, as if he were wearing a diver's helmet. Then he woke up and realized some of the sounds were trying to tell him something [. . .]. But when he tried to concentrate on the sounds, they scattered like frightened mice. (178; II, 179–80)

The will to interpret, the compulsion to interpret, is a symptom, then, of whatever disease Horacio suffers from. Furthermore, although Felisberto distinguishes between the impassive enablers to these interpretations (Facundo, the *muchachos*) and the fevered interpreters themselves, he would nevertheless not distinguish between the diseased interpreters and the healthy ones, between the patients and the analysts. He would certainly be suspicious of the insistence on returning all interpretations to the childhood of the dreamer or patient, and suspicious of the reductive act and the self-confident tone of Freud in the paragraph leading up to his fetish narrative:

> In all the cases the meaning and the purpose of the fetish turned out under analysis to be the same. It revealed itself so unequivocally and seemed to me so categorical that I should expect the same solution in all cases of fetishism. When I now disclose that the fetish is a penis-substitute I shall certainly arouse disappointment: so I hasten to add that it is not a substitute for any chance penis, but for a particular quite special penis that had been extremely important in early childhood but was afterwards lost. That is to say: it should normally have been given up, but the purpose of the fetish precisely is to preserve it from being lost. To put it plainly: the fetish is a substitute for the woman's (mother's) phallus which the little boy once believed in and does not wish to forgo—we know why. (214–15)

Freud reduces and simplifies by saying that the similarity lies in the objects, whose special meaning is always that they represent that desirable fiction, the maternal phallus. Felisberto on the other hand wishes to argue that the great reductive simplicity of the fetishist lies in his similar attitude to so many objects, each one, however different, crying out to be interpreted as a *presagio*, as having a special meaning for him. The similarity lies within the subject, as one of his faculties, the capacity to see/touch/interpret, becomes erotically independent and dominates all other aspects of his life. Freud claims condescendingly to know how to read a fetishist; Felisberto suggests that being a fetishist is all about reading in a certain way.

INTERLUDE: READING LIKE A FETISHIST

He opened the drawer and read ...

(*Las Hortensias* 179; II, 180)

As I suggested in my first chapter on *Kiss of the Spider Woman*, I am experimenting in this book with an interpretive strategy of selective overidentification (identifying "always with the heroine, dummy," says Molina). The repeated figures of the weak masculine, the paper doll, and the strong if vulnerable feminine, the spider woman, reappear sympathetically whenever possible. In a more generalizable sense, I proposed to myself to read these books, and the history of Latin American narrative, as a homosexual, as a fetishist, as a masochistic man or like a sadistic woman, as a transvestite. As the essays have taken shape, the project of individual chapters have mutated somewhat, so that in the Lezama chapter the identification flows into the abject or effeminate homosexual only (Foción, Uncle Alberto). But here in this chapter on Felisberto Hernández, I assure you that I am reading like a fetishist.

This is a dubious claim, and a claim of dubious worth. The first claim of this sort, in a most seductive text, was allusive rather than declarative, toward the end of Roland Barthes's *The Pleasure of the Text:*

> We can imagine a typology of the pleasures of reading—or the readers of pleasure; it would not be sociological, for pleasure is not an attribute of either product or production; it could only be psychoanalytic, linking the reading neurosis to the hallucinated form of the text. The fetishist would be matched up with the divided-up text, the singling out of quotations, formulae, turns of phrase, with the pleasure of the word. The obsessive would experience the voluptuous release of the letter, of secondary, discontinuous languages, of metalanguages.... A paranoiac would consume or produce complicated texts, stories developed like arguments, constructions posited like games, like secret constraints. As for the hysteric (so contrary to the obsessive), he would be the one who takes the text *for ready money*, who joins in the bottomless, truthless comedy of language, who is no longer the subject of any critical scrutiny and *throws himself* across the text (which is quite different from projecting himself into it). (63; italics Barthes's)

Barthes's flirtatious, unstable descriptions of perverse reader-relations replicate the deliberately unstable distinctions between *plaisir* and *jouissance*, and between book and text, in his essay. Like these relationships, the relationship between normal and perverse reader-relations is partly determined by the text, mostly by the reader. Some writers choose to write texts for a perverse *jouissance*. However, a willful reader of a "normal" book can also refuse the criteria of normality offered by the book and read it for a perverse pleasure against the grain. In a third and final possibility, a critical willful reader of "normal" books can contrast a book's will-toward-normality with the moments in which the semiotic excess of language parasitically inhabits and subverts that normality.

For Barthes, then, the analogy between perversion in bodily and readerly desire is virtually perfect. Yet Barthes never identifies when, if ever, he had been reading like a hysteric, a paranoid, a fetishist; nevertheless, his deft characterizations, at the end of this brief book, suggest that we could not only read like a pervert but that others would know when we were reading like one. Ironically, it is one of Barthes's most loyal explicators in the Anglo-American academy, Jonathan Culler, who in 1982 undertook a critique of "reading as a woman," which is supposed to be extendable to any identitarian reading practice (such as "reading as a fetishist"). Subtending each of the various feminist interpretive projects from Woolf through Showalter through the French feminists, Culler plausibly claims, is an appeal to a shared experience that really is itself in need of further interpretation: every woman who reads as a woman realizes that she used to read like a man, and that it was only by revalorizing experiences that she had been trained to ignore, and praised for ignoring, that she eventually learned how to read as a woman. In his clearheaded deconstructive way Culler targets the notion of unmediated experience, much as the Continental left critiqued the Anglo-American left (especially Raymond Williams) for depending too heavily on "lived experience," and Culler sympathetically but critically compares the consciousness-raising groups of early feminism with the Marxist's need to root out "false consciousness" in the proletariat. Both feminism and Marxism produce the "experience" on which they claim to ground their critiques of everyday interpretation. To read *as* a woman, Culler concludes, is really to read *like* a feminist woman, that is, to follow protocols of reading within an evolving paradigm of feminist understandings of the way women live, work, and read.

Analogously, to read as a fetishist could well imply to read like a consciousness-raised fetishist: to cast off the habits of normalized reading and accept (more or less) the identity of fetishist but without the stigma attached to it; to describe neutrally (or to celebrate) the pleasures you experience while reading the texts that make you burn with ardor, or which trigger in you the search for the hidden meaning in the desirable object. All of the phenomenology of the fetishist, as we have so far seen him in Felisberto or understood him in his informal taxonomy, could then be pressed into use to describe the reading experience: the isolation brought about by realizing that one's desire is eccentric; the impulse to accept the idea that one is overvaluing the object of one's desire; the temptation to enjoy the object in a secretive fashion; the conviction that the object has a secret meaning; and the fragmentation of the subject that ensues as a certain part of the self pursues the (secret meaning of the) object independently of the other faculties of the mind.

Culler's interpretation of the task to read as a woman finds a use for a certain sort of sociology, insofar as eavesdropping on the (mediated) ways that real women actually read is part of what a critic who wants to read like a feminist should do, as a resource for expanding or altering the evolving paradigm of what it means to read as a woman. Certainly it would be interesting to try an equivalent sociological project. Shall we go out into the world and ask people, first, if they are fetishists, and second, how they read when they read as fetishists? There are now such things as fetish communities, groups of people who identify as such, along the lines of the gay rights movement.[12] While it would be useful to ask such people how they read, their willingness to band together suggests that their responses will not tell us anything about all fetishists, but only about the sort of fetishists who congregate in groups. I don't want to posit an essential loneliness in the fetishist (as was routinely posited in the mid-century "homosexual"), although I do wish to hold on to the notion that a fetishist develops an ardent relationship to an object or an aspect of a person, not to the person herself or himself. Rather, I would like to emphasize that feminism, with its roots in the Enlightenment and Western socialisms and with a mandate to represent half the world's population, has a project around which a paradigm can evolve. "Fetishism-ism" should expect a wider gap between its vanguard and its mere practitioners, and work through the possibility that once it becomes conscious of itself as such it has thereby mutated into something else.

Sociologists of course have a variety of ways to study elusive, libertarian, and reclusive populations. We could study what they buy. Or at any rate, we could see what people try, with whatever success, to sell them. In many ways, *Las Hortensias* is a fable about fetishism in a consumer society (*as* consumer society), a topic to which I shall return. For now I would merely say that it is still necessary to interpret what it is that the fetishist is buying when he goes shopping (we are still, like the fetishist himself, seeking the hidden meaning of the desirable object). We might also be suspicious of the high-low cultural prejudices through which, as in Robert Stoller's interesting 1985 analysis of transvestite pulp fiction, one argues that the lowbrow form of art is the unguarded or unmasked version of a supposedly identical desire that appears merely sublimated and disguised in its high-cultural form.

The final caveat about a sociological approach to fetishistic reading practices springs from fetishism's relationship to the Freudian idea of polymorphous perversity. Just as many of us no longer demand the tight integration of all sexual components into genital "maturity" in our sexual lives but hope that our innate polymorphous perversity is preserved into adulthood, so too we hope that everybody is always already somewhat "reading as a fetishist," and that the full-time, one-object-only fetishist is only part of the story of fetishistic reading practices (especially since, as we have already seen in *Las Hortensias*, a "full-time fetishist" can actually transfer this supposedly fixated desire onto a varied sequence of objects). Likewise, in a way that the Culler of 1982 would perhaps have approved, queer theory expanded the notion of "reading as a gay man (or lesbian)" beyond the identitarian practices of the full-time gay-identified gay or lesbian-identified lesbian so that we can now assess the homoerotic effects of texts produced and consumed outside the sex ghettoes.

For all these reasons, then, the difficulties involved in this project, especially in the (for some) paradoxical notions of a fetish community, a fetish market, and the full-time fetishist identity, suggest why an anarchistic, solipsist reader such as Barthes would never have been so *vulgaire* as to base his flirtatious typology of perverse reading pleasures on a sociology. Insofar as we recognize the meanings of the words he uses, it is because he bases his descriptions on psychoanalytic discourse (the typology "could only be psychoanalytic"), and while thirty years and more of studies of psychoanalysis have thickened the context of this discourse, so that we know more of the pre-Freudian history of the perversions, we have the autobiographies and biographies of the Wolf Man, Anna O., and Dora, and we are conscious of the broader canvas of fin-de-siècle Vienna, it is still nevertheless the case that Freud's own writings are a crucial part of this discourse, and even our disagreements with Freud remain textual (and post-Freudian, rather than non- or anti-Freudian).

Still, Barthes has described just the tip of the iceberg when he says that the fetishistic reader "would be matched up with the divided-up text, the singling out of quotations, formulae, turns of phrase, with the pleasure of the word." On the one hand, this focus on the cut and the segment is very Tel Quel in its high-modernist aesthetics of interruption: Sarduy, Sollers, Robbe-Grillet write for people who want to read that way, but there are other aspects of the fetishist which also find their way into the practices and pleasures of reading (principally, as we will see, Freud's account of disavowal and the maternal phallus). On the other hand (although this is implicit in the passage: of his four perverts, only the hysteric in his willed naïveté disqualifies himself from the possibility of a sophisticated collaboration with the powers that be), Barthes's fetishistic readers are already part of the academic institution. The only "normal" writers about books are for the most part outside academia, producing newspaper reviews and useful manuals and other general-readership literary histories; all the rest of us are paid to be fetishists, obsessives, and paranoiacs, and to teach our students to read *that way* too. We may indeed produce knowledge about our texts or the world this way, but when we do so we are also producing for ourselves a pleasure in mastery, the desire for which is what Foucault in his introduction to *The History of Sexuality* critiques as the will-toward-knowledge, the *vouloir-savoir*, a will which is by no means without erotic cathexis and which combines with the other perverse reading pleasures alluded to by Barthes. Felisberto is a very interesting guide to the tension in our fetishistic reading practices between the desire for mastery, to appropriate and enjoy the enigmatic object, and an equal and opposite desire, a will-toward-ignorance, the preservation of enigma in the desirable (textual) object.

As we revise Freud on fetishism, first on the theme of fixation and, next, on the theme of the maternal phallus, we must acknowledge that part of our goal is to bring his notion of fetishism not just in line with the representations in our texts (the full-time literary fetishists like Felisberto or, say, Bruno Schulz, or Surrealist artists like Bellmer or Delvaux; the fetishist passages in otherwise straight authors, Apuleius on hair or Pushkin on feet), but that part of our goal is also to cast some light on our academic practices of reading. If we get a pleasure when we read as a fetishist that Freud cannot account for, we must consider revising Freud to suit ourselves too.

HONORING AND DEFILING THE PHALLIC MOTHER

[Horacio:] "After all, she was only a doll."

[María:] "Was! You sound as if she were dead. [...] And you think that dismissing her this way [will comfort me]?"

(*Las Hortensias* 188; II, 190)

[Clemente Colling said that his father] "was a great, very distinguished man;" his mother, "a very vulgar woman, a washerwoman." And immediately he would add, "I took after my father."

I did not want to admit, nor would I have acknowledged, that the high opinion [ilusión] *that I had of Colling could suffer setbacks. During those instants—like the one in which he spoke scornfully of his mother—there occurred to me things that I would rather not have remembered.*

(*Por_los_tiempos de Clemente Colling* I, 170; my translation)

In one of his autobiographical texts, the thirteen-year-old Felisberto's hero worship of his piano teacher Clemente Colling permits him to ignore most of the old maestro's eccentricities, but he takes great pains to explain that this blind Frenchman's negative comments about his mother were the hardest to look past of all. We might think about the agonistics involved in the son who watches the humiliation and rape of the mother in Octavio Paz's psychohistoric melodrama of Cortés and Malinche; in contrast, here the son registers but then refuses the father's negative judgment of the mother, and indeed it becomes one of the ways that Felisberto can see this father-figure independently. This passage is typical of Felisberto's presumption in favor of the mother, but atypical in the presence of all three points of the

Oedipal triangle. In that sense, Felisberto was out of step with the times, for Freud's narrative of normality, the Oedipal complex, was vivid, and it was soon accepted by entire generations of writers and thinkers. It is an origin story in an age that sought for truth and meaning in origins. Eventually, Freud proposed a vivid origin tale for one of the perversions. His 1927 essay "Fetishism" contains elements of the bizarre that keep it from being as immediately plausible as the Oedipal triangle and that subject it more easily to critique than Oedipus, but which align interestingly with the elements of the bizarre with which Felisberto's *Las Hortensias* provides us in its portrait of a fetishist.

The origin tale of the fetishist is as follows: the child, with great anticipation, gets the opportunity to see his mother naked, only to discover, horrified, that she has no penis and jumps to the conclusion that his own penis is threatened by this. Some little boys get over it; some little boys build their aversion to the female genitals into their homosexuality; some little boys, however, split their consciousness in a way different from the repression characteristic of the Oedipal complex. Instead, they perform a disavowal:

> It is not true that the child emerges from his experience of seeing the female parts with the unchanged belief in the woman having a phallus. He retains this belief but he also gives it up; during the conflict between the deadweight of the unwelcome perception and the force of the opposite wish, a compromise is constructed such as is only possible in the realm of unconscious modes of thought—by the primary processes. In the world of psychical reality the woman still has a penis after all, but this penis is no longer the same as it once was. Something else has taken its place, has been appointed its successor, so to speak, and now absorbed all the interest which formerly belonged to the penis. (216)

So disavowal requires a substitution, and Freud goes on to say that the object which the young fetishist substitutes for the missing maternal penis is probably a chance object near the site of the terrifying discovery:

> When the fetish comes to life, so to speak, some process has been suddenly interrupted—it reminds one of the abrupt halt made by memory in traumatic amnesias. In the case of the fetish, too, interest is held up at a certain point—what is probably the last impression received before the uncanny traumatic one is preserved as a fetish. Thus the foot or shoe ... (217)

So a fetish is a commemoration of the excitement one felt in front of the not-yet-castrated mother, preserved in disavowal despite consciously knowing otherwise, the commemoration a link formed almost if not perhaps entirely by chance.

Despite its bizarre implausibility, theorists of the fetish in literature have found Freud's text to be useful in a variety of ways. I have already mentioned that, for better or worse, this is a tale in which Freud takes up once again his favored theme of a threat of castration, but that this time there is no father present to make the threat: it is the object itself, or the mother herself, who induces the castration anxiety. It is tempting to take this story of Freud's and contrast it with the well-known fable of Lacan's mirror stage. As if she were as smooth and objectified as a mirror, the mother in the Freudian fetish-narrative is completely passive while the son is making his unwelcome discoveries: the trauma is visual and psychic, not physical, as if Freud's little boy was already in a reverential mood toward the statue of a goddess, or a life-size doll. (For its emphasis on visuality, I find this essay to be as useful as the Wolf Man essay's remarks on the primal scene for an examination of the Freudian dynamics of voyeurism.) Under these circumstances, then, it is hardly surprising that the male fetishist blames the object/mother for producing his anxiety, rather than blaming a father (or variations on the father, such as patriarchal society). Moralizing critics of the fetishist will emphasize the concealed anger which the fetishist expresses toward the woman even in his worship of some detachable part of her; a more political criticism, as I hope to sketch, hopes to show how social forces are concealed from the little fetishist himself by the scenario.

Freud, however, analyzes still another sort of concealment, and uses the fetishist's overvaluation as a chance to elaborate on the possibility of a double consciousness, disavowal, different from either denial or repression, summed up in the phrase, "I know, and yet, all the same ..." This phrase means both, "I know that the shoe [or whatever] is not the woman's genitals, and yet it will arouse me all the same," and, "I know that woman is castrated, and yet I will behave as if she has a phallus all the same." This provisional theory of Freud's suggests a close relationship between fetishism and irony, in which the speaker maintains *even for himself* a double, contradictory, or disavowable discourse.[13] The fetish, we might say, is the counterpart to Freud's other contribution to literary theory, the uncanny.[14] Typically for Freud, both the uncanny and the fetish-narrative imply that reality is hostile and threatening. In the uncanny narrative, pre-Oedipal and feminine objects (das Heimische) become uncannily monstrous (das Unheimliche), just as a pretty girl turns out to be a mechanical doll in Hoffmann's "The Sand-Man," the subject of Freud's analysis; in the fetish-narrative, the flawed, once-desirable feminine maternal, its flaw abruptly discovered, becomes repaired in the fetishist's fantasy at a point where he *can* separate reality from fantasy, just as a pretty wife is knowingly rejected in favor of anatomically correct dolls in *Las Hortensias*. In "The Sand-Man," mad Nathanael identifies the dollmaker Coppelius as the castrating man who humiliated his father and burned his family's house down; in *Las Hortensias*, the status of Facundo the dollmaker, visible in Felisberto's fetish-narrative but not in Freud's, remains for us to discuss.

On these general terms, the fetish-narrative is very reminiscent of feminist complaints about the idealization of women as no more than a strategy to conceal male misogyny, often from the man himself. Possibly the most elaborated—and most knowledgeably (anti-)Freudian—use of the fetish-narrative to drive this point home is Marcia Ian's 1993 *Remembering the Phallic Mother*, which argues cogently that psychoanalysis is no more than another discourse of European literary modernism, a movement characterized by a great ambivalence toward women; these discourses produced fantasies of both a giving self-sufficient mother and a self-sufficient autonomous aesthetic object.[15] For Ian, these fantasies are always bad and fetishism is always used as a negative term.

Ian's polemic tone of a prosecuting attorney energizes her text, but it could be argued that Freud's fetish-narrative would be better critiqued from a perspective that does not presume that all fetishists are misogynistically lost to the ruses of phallogocentrism. Ian makes much of other slips (especially by Lacan) in which the penis is equated with the phallus: let us begin there. Freud says that the erotic trauma of the little boy occurs when he abruptly discovers that the woman is castrated, has no penis, a discovery which the child (implausibly, I think[16]) takes as a threat to his own penis. How might the argument work out differently if the abrupt discovery is that the woman has no *phallus*, that is, that his mother does not have the *social* or *symbolic* standing which he is certain that she deserves? A child's protest that his mother ought to have the power that, until a traumatic event has occurred to shake his faith, he was confident that she did indeed have, might just as likely split a child's consciousness in a way that is similar to Freud's notion of disavowal. (And, since we are no longer looking for a substitute for the maternal *penis*, we are capable of seeing this substitute for the maternal phallus not just in a small part-object but also possibly in another woman altogether: a next-door neighbor, or a life-sized doll version of the disappointing woman.) It is true that such a disavowal also probably leads to a conservative sexual politics, just in the sense that disavowal leaves intact the consensual belief that women "really" have no power in society.

The fetishists whom Freud characterized omitted the agent of female castration (since women lack penises by nature): if we follow that aspect of the scenario, symbolic castration remains an anxiety-producing fact of life. Indeed, an act of violence upon one's mother without a visible culprit would indeed produce the timidity and defensiveness in the character of the male fetishists, whether rich or poor, who protagonize Felisberto's stories.[17] But the fetish then becomes a monument to a power that women ought to have in the world but do not, and a continued eroticization of some of the accoutrements of the powerful woman becomes a mode of celebrating the (always vulnerable) feminine principle, as the traumatized child understands it rudimentarily. Insofar as it is produced by a trauma, it is indeed prone to repetition compulsions and unclear thinking. But these inchoate emotions around the monument to an unjust action toward one's mother can be turned into account for a real feminism.

Almost exactly like the "shine on the nose," which is the first of Freud's examples of a fetish, a glamour that his fetishist can see but no one else can, *Las Hortensias*'s Horacio can see something in the women and dolls he is attracted to which others cannot see. Of his wife, Horacio thinks, "To strip her of Hortensia would be like stripping an artist of her art. Hortensia was not only part of her being but her most charming self" (189; II, 191). Although María clearly represents domestic comfort for him, he also respects, or thinks he respects, her creativity: the games she plays with Hortensia for Horacio, and the surprises she plays on him using the doll in the early chapters, are proofs of her creativity for him, and in that sense María's "charm" is Hortensia; she supplements María as Culture supplements Nature, as a fiction of the feminine-maternal phallus might supplement a woman whose subordination to domestic rounds can be as irritating as it is comforting. In one way María's surprises are the opposite of the *presagios* and other poetic thoughts which are characteristic of the doll fetishes: they are not produced in the eerie, thrilling space and time of ritual. (The least threatening of the surprises take place during the social ritual of Hortensia's second birthday party—although by then Horacio has also decided to end the evening by stabbing Hortensia, a pretext for returning it to the dollmaker's for, ahem, repairs; naturally, the stabbing is also an act of aggression against María.) This eerie ritual space is obsessively private for Horacio, and it may be partly why he does not wish to share the doll with his wife even while ostensibly declaring it to be the most interesting thing about her. Horacio's process of transferring his love from María to Hortensia marks the creation of a fetish, of abstracting from a desirable woman what you find desirable in her and taking it away from her so that you can have your own fantasy life with it. And yet, as always, Horacio does not attribute this creation to himself but to the object, or to the noises of the machine: one night in the garden he tries to kiss María over Hortensia, and is stuck by a needle accidentally left in the doll: "Almost at once he heard the machines pounding, no doubt to warn him against kissing María through Hortensia" (192; II, 193). So the surprises that María arranges by means of Hortensia are her attempts to be poetic, and Horacio, like Marcia Ian's Anglo-American poets, responds by "arguing" that true poetry is self-sufficient and comes from nowhere. Whereas Horacio elaborates a theory in which the dolls are in some sense alive yet are nevertheless not fully conscious of the *codicias* and *presagios* that they help to transmit, María's surprises are marks of her conscious creativity as a social subject. The surprises are not, like the *presagios*, from nowhere; they are from María.

After all, one of the most attractive aspects of Felisberto's oeuvre to women and feminist readers is his understanding that women are as likely to be subjects as men. (How appalling that this should be enough to set Felisberto apart, not just from Freud, but from the male Rioplatense authors of his generation: Onetti, Borges, Sábato all have literary strategies to make women invisible or have them appear only as objects of male desire.) In *Las Hortensias*, María is clearly humoring her husband's whims, ceding to him his room of doll tableaux. Yet she is a participant in the innocent games with Hortensia and is more creative with her "surprises" than Horacio is fully comfortable with: his habit of writing up her surprises in a log-book commemorates them, but also reappropriates them: "Although he was the only one to read the notebook, he signed each entry with his name, Horacio, in large letters and heavy ink" (181). Horacio's entries take a little of María's subjectivity away from these small shocks to his system which he says he appreciates but seems also to want to ward off. María's subjectivity, like anyone else's, can be subordinated to conventions: she has much invested in the rights and responsibilities of wifehood, and a more Romantic notion of the self is conventionalized by the book of poems that she is reading at her cousin's while angry at Horacio, a book which gives her some unexpected insights into the world but which mostly reinforces a stereotype of herself as sensitive soul—a stereotype which, she hopes, will help bring her husband back but which also is a stereotype-*for*-Horacio: "And one morning she decided: 'I would like Horacio to know I'm walking alone among trees with a book in my hand'" (215; II, 217). María returns; but she remains flexible as a person to the shifts in her marriage, whereas her husband stiffens step by step into a pure object. Really, to tell the story of *Las Hortensias* from María's point of view is to see Felisberto's mid-century ethics of love and relationships as consisting just as much of Simone de Beauvoir as Jean-Paul Sartre: love should be the encounter between two subjects who freely commit to be subjects-for-one-another, and the woman should—and can—resist the social expectations to become merely the object for the male subject.

We have said from the start of this project that our narrators of the perverse demonstrate not just perversion but perversity, that is, a stubborn refusal to abide by the normalities that they actually believe in, Poe's "Imp of the Perverse" as well as nonnormative sexuality, so we should not be surprised that Felisberto's male characters understand the rules of a sexual/ ethical game which they will not, cannot play honestly, or that the novella expresses a right for women to play creatively which nevertheless contributes to the male protagonist's madness. But Felisberto goes further in the rest of his oeuvre than talking a better game than his characters play. Insofar as he genuinely believes you have to be a little crazy to be creative— or, to rephrase it in the language of subject/object ethics and erotics, insofar as he believes that creativity involves the subject letting a distracted consciousness play in a mediated way on certain objects, if necessary objectifying the person the subject claims to love—Felisberto is willing to invent crazy-creative women as well as men. Women are, deliberately or inadvertently, spoilsports of fetishistic behavior in "Except Julia" and *Las Hortensias*; but María engages in some fetishizing strategies of her own with the doll that looks like her, and in "The Balcony" and "The Flooded House" the women are the subjects of the obsessive animistic thinking which, in the end, is the precondition for creativity for Felisberto. María's enthusiasm for the poems she reads is described in terms almost identical to what Felisberto uses for his creative male fetishists: "it was if someone had left a door open by chance, suddenly revealing what was inside. Then, for a moment, it seemed to her the wallpaper, the folding screen, even the washbowl with its nickel-plated taps also understood the poems" (214–15; II, 217). A generation of feminist critic-novelists will pay Felisberto Hernández the ambivalent compliment of letting him be the avant-garde author who can tempt them to rethink creativity and desire together, before going on to formulate relations between men and women which are not quite so bizarre in their post-existentialist, post-humanist eroticization of the object.[18]

But Felisberto's fetishes question the easy distinction in matters of creativity and erotics between subject and object. (Freud is famous for questioning the Enlightenment notion of the subject; however, he problematizes the object only insofar as the mind fantasizes or scotomizes or introjects the images of objects.) We might go so far as to say that objects can have agency in Felisberto, that they can be as alluring as people can be, and that therefore an entire field of sexual and general ethics opens up, in which a subject's relationship to another subject can no longer be summed up by the injunction not to treat the subject like an object, nor can it be presumed that an object is a pure instrumentality, to be used however one wills.[19]

Still, we feel that Horacio is incapable of thinking through this new fetishistic ethics. We could whimsically say that Felisberto hasn't given

Horacio the courage of his erotic convictions. He not only betrays María with Hortensia, but also, facing his human loneliness and the capacity of dolls to be indifferent to human mortality, he returns to his wife and thus betrays Hortensia with María. María is a package deal of tenderness and jealousy, creativity and conventionality: as a result, Horacio only has two choices, either to abjure his fantasy life or to pursue it furtively without his wife. At no time does he seriously consider including his wife in these fantastic pursuits. What separates the fetishist from the normal married couple's ritual couplings is not ritual—they both engage in rituals—nor in the fixation on a scenario—the fetishist experiments with variations on the scenario that arouses him, until it possibly becomes quite a different scenario—. It is, first, the eccentricity of his ritual, which makes it unlikely for him to find a partner in these games; and second, the solitariness of his pursuit, which, in Horacio's case, encourages him to hire employees to set scenarios and, rather than altering the object or scenario in consultation with the others who are experimenting with the scenario, to merely trade in the objects and procure new ones. The rules which are laid down by the other great fetishist in Felisberto's short stories, the man in "Except Julia" who has a tunnel on his farm and girls and employees who have specific, limited, and silent roles to play in the ritual, indicate that the fetishist's scenario can evolve through internal rules of its own or through the desires of the fetishist, but at all costs he tries to ward off the participation of others as subjects. In that story, the woman who demands the right to be treated as a subject is the spoilsport. In *Las Hortensias*, an individual with such habits of desire is particularly vulnerable to the ailments of modernity and modern society: alienation, individualism as narcissism, and—of course— commodity fetishism.

To that extent, then, our general thoughts on how fetishism might express solidarity with a "fantasized" phallic mother, rather than a defense against the disappointing or threatening object that is the "real" castrated mother, is only of limited use in our reading of Felisberto's *Las Hortensias*. Felisberto's Horacio clearly prefers silence and immobility in the female objects he treasures. Indeed, most of the traumas in the novella occur not because Horacio discovers his women to be castrated, but because his living wife María retains her subjectivity; when María crosses the line and starts substituting herself for the doll who is Horacio's mistress and then for one of the dolls in the tableau, Horacio goes mad. Felisberto suggests that women's mere subjectivity can threaten a man of a fetishistic type, a position that most of us as feminists are willing to entertain even though it does not square with Freud's fetishist narrative, dependent as it is on equating the penis with the phallus. According to Freud, because the mother does not have a phallus, the panicked child gives her a phantom phallus, the fetish. However, when she shows herself to have independence, that is, to wield the phallus on her own (an event Freud cannot admit), the adult male panics again.

In the context of Latin American *machismo*, then, Horacio's weak masculinity is perhaps less censurable, but it is not innocent. Felisberto knows enough to create an air of self-criticism or comic satire around his protagonist's confession, at the party celebrating Hortensia's second birthday, of the emotions the tableaux inspire in him:

> "If you wouldn't mind telling us what you feel watching the scenes," said one of the boys, "I think we could all learn something." [...]
>
> "It's very difficult to put into words, but I'll try ... if you promise meantime to ask me no more questions and to be satisfied with anything I care to say. [...]
>
> "When I look at a scene ... [...] (It's very important to see the dolls through a glass, because that gives them the quality of memories.; [...] when I look at a scene, it's like catching a woman in the act of remembering an important moment in her life, a bit—if you'll forgive the expression—as if I were opening a crack in her skull. When I get hold of the memory, it's like stealing one of her undergarments: I can use it to imagine the most intimate things and I might even say it feels like a defilement. In a way, it's as if the memory were in a dead person and I were picking a corpse, hoping the memory will stir in it ..." He let his voice trail off [...]
>
> The boys were also silent. One of them thought of emptying his glass of wine at a swallow and all the others imitated him. (195–6; 197–8)

Here Felisberto gives to Horacio all the violence toward *images* of women that we are accustomed to see in machismo's treatment of real women. Indeed, Horacio considers the gaze to be so phallic that he has little obsessive strategies to avoid being looked at, even by himself (the mirrors in the house must be veiled; he will eventually wear a mask and gloves). This basically voyeuristic passage also combines elements of fetishism, as we have seen throughout, insofar as seeing this woman's memory is described as robbing an "undergarment," also insofar as the still tableau is cut from a longer narrative just as Barthes's "psychoanalytic" taxonomy of fetishistic reading pleasure would suggest. Barthes would be less interested in how Horacio restores narratives to these tableaux, and Horacio's claim, "I deduce many things," is still another mark that the fetishist's pleasure is always also an intellectual, interpretive pleasure. Yet as the passage moves on to the extraction of memories from.a corpse, we must conclude that, despite his many genuine moments of tenderness toward María and toward various dolls, Horacio does seem to be as resentful of the women he adores as the more pessimistic reading of the fetishist tends to suggest. The embarrassment of the *muchachos*—they are, after all, the enablers of this rapist of fictional women—is expressed comically enough, and Felisberto achieves a necessary distance from the fetishist/voyeur's position even in a story with an omniscient narrator who refuses to pass overt judgment on his character.

Nevertheless, on a level of style, Felisberto's narrative voice displays an empathy for the fetishistic world view, for the disavowal that preserves the excitement in a world of strong women he wishes both to honor and defile.

A PRETTY DOLL IS LIKE A SIMILE (CHANGING THE SUBJECT WITHOUT CHANGING THE OBJECT)

Our central focus of attention in Felisberto's *oeuvre, Las Hortensias*, is exceptional for being a third-person point-of-view fiction, and we have already begun remarking on the function of the third person in a fetishistic fiction: the disavowal that is the mark of a split consciousness, that makes an obeisance to the reality principle while remaining aroused by the powerful phantom woman, splits the story into the character who has the feelings and the omniscient narrator who tells of the character. The distance between these two positions in Felisberto is not as far as it would be in a more moralistic writer. *Las Hortensias*'s omniscient narrator does not even offer the mild criticisms of the fetishist that the narrator makes in "Except Julia." In the novella, it will be the task of María, reinforced by her cousin Pradera, to be the spokesperson for the normal heart (a "normality" which requires Pradera to steal María's volume of poetry when she is outraged against María's husband). Most censorious of all is the third person, not of the omniscient narrator, but of Horacio himself in his depressed state: "Or he described his actions as if he were watching someone else: 'Look at him, poor idiot—there he is opening a drawer, unstopping the inkpot. Let's see how long he has left'" (218; II, 220). Censure and depression prefigure the novella's dénouement. But if the (implicitly censorious) third-person perspective of *Las Hortensias* is atypical, in another sense *Las Hortensias* is completely typical of Felisberto's corpus: the constant recourse to figurative language, especially the simile.

Figurative language is, in a sense, what writing is all about in Felisberto: life is about experiencing unexpected ideas and feelings, and art is about expressing their discrepancy from everyday or normal feelings.[20] We have seen, in "Except Julia" in the simile of one's hands as willful daughters, how these ideas and feelings can often express a fragmented sense of the perceiver's self. Felisberto's similes have an analogous effect on the objects (or persons) he perceives. Let us take a passage, also a moment of self-censure, from *Las Hortensias* to see how figurative language works in this third-person story. Horacio, who has begun planning to have sex with the soon-to-be anatomically correct Hortensia, looks at his wife María:

> He let his eyes dwell on her face, and with them his thoughts, going over each of her features as if reviewing every corner of a place he had visited daily through many long happy years. Then, breaking away, he went and sat in the little parlor to think about what had just happened. [...] Her face had been like a peaceful landscape, with a bit of golden evening glow on one cheek, the other shaded by the small mound of her nose. He had thought of all the good left in the innocence of the world and the habit of love, and the tenderness with which he always came back to her face after his adventures with the dolls. But in time,[...] her face and all its features would be devastated [...]
>
> So he had stood there, gazing at a spot of sun on his coat sleeve. As he withdrew his arm, the spot had shifted, like a taint, to her dress. Then, heading for the little parlor, he had felt his twisted insides lump and sag, like dead weights. Now he sat on a small bench, thinking he was unworthy of being received into the lap of a family armchair, and he felt as uncomfortable as if [a child had been tossed on him]. He hardly recognized the stranger in himself [*él también era desconocido de sí mismo*], disillusioned at being made of such base metal [*materia*]. But, to his surprise, a bit later, [...] he went straight to sleep. (199–200; 201–2)

After a metaphor so common in Felisberto that the author no longer seems to recognize it as figurative language—"his eyes" for "his sight"—the entire rest of the passage refers a series of similes to Horacio's point of view, phenomena of consciousness (in this case, a guilty conscience) before they are permitted to enter writing. What follows is a simile of almost Homeric length, comparing Horacio's look upon María's face with a look upon a place of former happiness, which expands (although without an explicit *como*) into a comparison with a landscape. Indeed, the simile is only completed on the next page/the next day, after María's oblivious considerateness has made Horacio feel even guiltier, and "his lips grazed her cheek. The kiss seemed to have dropped by parachute, onto a plain not yet touched by grief" (203). Typically for Felisberto, the simile moves the reader between the animate and the inanimate; here María becomes inanimate, while notoriously the Hortensia dolls frequently become animate in Horacio's mind. (Felisberto is sufficiently loyal to the clichés of Romanticism that María, the good object, is inanimate but natural, a landscape, while the dolls are un-natural or supernatural in their animation; and his kiss is a male invader to this territory, a parachutist.) The landscape simile involves shifting proportions (María's nose is a mountain); he moves away from her as he thinks this, and we may recall Horacio's earlier play with María's face and opera glasses: the play between nearness and distance is imbricated with a play between wholeness and fragments. He does not even see her cheeks as wholes but notices shadows on pieces of the cheeks; and he is already anticipating how the wholeness with which he can now see María's face will be broken by his treachery: "her face and all its features would be devastated." The passage is atypical for *Las Hortensias* for the prominence of idealized, sentimentalized vocabulary: *felicidad, inocencia, ternura, digno*. They correlate with Horacio's sense of domesticity, so that *ternura* (tenderness), for instance, stands opposed to *aventuras* with the dolls and, comically, is made equivalent with the *blandura* (softness) of the domestic chairs and perhaps even with the *criatura* he feels has been thrown upon him, an extra domesticity thrust upon him by a final simile just when he is unable to handle the domesticity he already has.

If the object (María) is draped in similes, the portrait of the subject is less adorned, indeed stripped bare. The *mancha* (spot or stain) of light that moves from Horacio's suit to María's dress is a concealed metaphor for his attention to her, but it is quickly unconcealed in the simile in which his (moral) stain is as if contaminating María. As the passage descends to self-chastisement, the *parece*'s and the *sentirse*'s fall off: "He hardly recognized the stranger in himself [*él también era desconocido de sí mismo*], disillusioned at being made of such base metal (*materia*)." Like the Freudian (especially the Lacanian) subject, both Horacio and María are *desconocidos de sí mismos*, unknowns or strangers to themselves. But the shifts in the *object* are described by similes to which the object has no access, while the *subject* is described through less and less figurative language. And yet the author is aware that these reflections are not as devastating to Horacio's peace of mind as Horacio himself would (melancholically) like to think: Horacio goes to bed and falls asleep instantly.

Did Felisberto *intend* this echoing of-*ura* to subvert an abstract language which expresses a guilty conscience that has no intention of reforming itself? Certainly mine is not the first analysis of Felisberto's style.[21] A common conclusion is that Felisberto prefers conceptual play and puns, mixing the figurative (a woman like a cow in the short story "Úrsula") with the literal (a cow is brought into the bedroom), and that sometimes he includes verbal and symbolic echoes which direct the reader toward a certain interpretation. An example of the latter in this passage would be the way *materia*, a word that seems to have an abstract meaning in this context—the (treacherously unethical) stuff of which Horacio's libido is made—, signals the increasingly wooden, mechanical, and doll-like madness that takes over Horacio over the course of the novella. Often the process involves a mix of accident and willful decontextualization. The couple takes Hortensia as the doll's name from María's middle name, which María never used; so too a remark by the butler Alex that the second Hortensia doll reminds him of a spy he once knew in Russia means that she will be called "la espía" by all of the servants, especially by the twin sister servants who were spying on María earlier in the novella, and María at this point in the novella tries to get the chauffeur to do a little bit of spying for her.[22] It is important to emphasize, however, that the similes, figurative words and nicknames of this type float somewhat unmoored in this text; they are not systematic enough to direct the reader to a specifically allegorical interpretation, yet they are there to be picked up and interpreted in a general way. They are, literally, the equivalent of the *presagios* Horacio feels when contemplating the dolls in his windows (and indeed the metaphor of the woman as landscape began in that first passage: the envious gazes of passersby "settled on the dolls' faces like clouds over a landscape, shadowing and blurring their expression" (187)). And just as Horacio often guesses wrong about what the *muchachos* have prepared for him, but the act of guessing reveals to him something about how his own mind and mood are working, so too here Horacio is wrong in the long run (María adapts, although with much pain and very slowly, to Horacio's perversions), but the habit of thinking long and privately about his wife, refusing to let her share in his own musings about her, abstracting her into an ideal version on which he can pile similes, takes its toll on the other *desconocido de sí mismo*, Horacio himself. By the end of the chapter Horacio has been "contaminated" by the simile he has been using for María: "He got up, feeling better. But he knew that the dark clouds of guilt were just over the horizon, and that they would be back with night" (202; II, 204).

It has certainly been remarked before that Horacio's dolls are an allegory for art and the Pygmalion-like difficulties that ensue when the artist falls in love with his art. This analogy is not perfect, although its imperfections are themselves interesting. Horacio does not make the art; indeed, he is explicit that he wants to guess the doll scenes, not create them, and will give the *muchachos* no hints as to the sort of scene he wants to see. If Horacio is an artist, he is an artist of thoughts and impressions, of absorbing the *presagios* which he claims the dolls channel to him. The Pygmalion theme, then, brought up by Horacio in a secret conversation with the dollmaker Facundo (" 'It may be crazy, but I've heard of sculptors falling in love with their statues' " (199; II, 201)), is a red herring. Horacio has fallen in love with what the dolls can mean to him, and thinks that these meanings will intensify if he can make the dolls anatomically correct. Yet the dolls retain for Horacio a sort of independence, alluring at first, but a rather hostile independence as the story progresses: without María in the house he can give himself over to his manias, yet "Every day it was harder to be alone. The dolls were no company but seemed to say, 'Don't count on us—we're just dolls'" (218; II, 220). The feature of Felisberto's art that resembles the dolls the most is his recourse to the simile.

There are some indications in *Las Hortensias* that Felisberto regrets his dependence on the simile in the same way that the narrative of the novella involves the downfall of Horacio. Horacio encourages the *muchachos* to experiment with scenes that use loose body parts he has found at Facundo's workshop, but is irritated and appalled with their experiments. They use too many of the limbs all at once, as if to say that, once permission is given to fragment the human body, the body parts immediately proliferate and the sentimental tableaux of the fates of beautiful women almost immediately become unintelligible. The similes' proliferation threaten in still another way. As it turns out, Felisberto's similes (or, if you insist, the similes that occur to Horacio) are very often, as here, narrative, like the *criatura* tossed upon Horacio. Even if the simile expands through further description, like the landscape of María's face, eventually it will spin out a story, such as the parachuting kiss and the foreboding clouds. Felisberto in this novella is committed to managing a story with many episodes nested within it, but the proliferation of narrative similes are a sort of overstimulation that finally causes Horacio to snap, and many readers have found the novella to accelerate inelegantly, and have reacted with the same sort of irritation that Horacio himself feels when the *muchachos* show him a busy woman with dozens of legs under her skirt: "what an undecipherable mess they've made of it (*esto es un jeroglífico estúpido*)" (219; II, 221).

These constant and constantly surprising comparisons which come to Horacio's mind as he contemplates the people in his life or the objects with which he surrounds himself bear a close relationship to the theorization we have seen around the relationship between fetishism and disavowal. Freud elaborated his theorizing on disavowal—different from either repression or denial—as a dissociation and preservation of affect from intellectual acknowledgment. The mother remains attractive and powerful even though she is castrated, and even though consciously the fetishist will agree that she is castrated: "I know, and yet nevertheless" I will be aroused by objects that are not a woman's genitals *as if* they were the genitals that she ought to have. The simile gives its due to the reality principle, as mandated by Freud—or by the independent woman, or by knowing how little money you will make through your concerts—. You do not have the poetic power to turn your love *into* a red, red rose, but you nevertheless state that your love *is like* a red, red rose. The object of your simile has been over-estimated in your fantasy of it, even as you settle for less by only claiming that it looks like or seems like what you are comparing it to. The proliferation of similes in Felisberto, many of which constitute small micro-narratives of their own, at times threatens the legibility of his text, even as their proliferation in *Las Hortensias* tempts us into comparing them with the proliferation of female bodies, animate and inanimate, postulated, "deduced," remembered, and mass-produced. The simile, like the female body around which one's penetrative imagination plays, reveals one's mood to oneself, eventually bringing about changes in the subject without having to change the object.

CONSUMER CAPITALISM HITS A MOVING TARGET (CHANGING THE OBJECT WITHOUT CHANGING THE RULES)

He did not feel like guessing [the doll's] fate, so he opened the door with the captions and read: "This woman is sick in the head. No one has been able to find out why she loves sponges." "That's what I pay them for, to find out," he said to himself.

(*Las Hortensias* 201; II, 203–4)

And yet of course objects do change in *Las Hortensias*. And because the object changes, because not all of its surprises are pleasant surprises, you ought to be prepared to *exchange* the object for some other desirable object. And if desirable objects are unpredictable, perhaps at least we can make the system of using them up and trading them in to be relatively predictable. It spoils the fun to know too much about how this system works. The drawbacks to this system are clearest when it goes into the overproduction of desirable objects.

The power of the Freudian narrative lies in its declaring that the fetishist's pursuits are a scattershot attempt to repeat a scenario from early childhood; when he finally hits upon the closest replica of that object from the scenario of that traumatic moment, he will have perfected the reassuring repetition that wards off castration anxiety. There is a metonymic shift of desire in the traumatic moment, but only one, a long time ago. What we see in *Las Hortensias* instead, however, is a continuous metonymic shift in the desired object. First María; then Hortensia who looks like María; then an anatomically corrected Hortensia; then an anatomically correct doll that does *not* look like Hortensia; and so on. To call such a pursuit a *fixation* is a complete misnomer. Horacio cannot be marginalized by that particular term of opprobrium. Indeed, part of Felisberto's point is that the objects which Horacio's eccentric psyche desires, and his strategies for acquiring the objects he desires, may be different in principle but not different in practice from business as usual in industrial-capitalist consumer societies.

It is of great importance to *Las Hortensias* that this sort of circulatable desire seem to begin at home, yet really precede and supercede the domestic. Chronologically, Horacio's obsession with the dolls begins when he owns a department store, but we do not see them in action there first, but rather in his private home. The dollmaker Facundo is introduced as "his friend, Facundo, the doll manufacturer" (187; II, 189) and indeed he is one of the guests at Hortensia's birthday party and we meet briefly his girlfriend Luisa. Even though the word *fabricante*, manufacturer,is a more industrial word than *hacedor* (or than referring to him as a *muñequero* would), Facundo, who repeatedly calls Horacio "brother" (in a text with virtually no colloquial speech), is on the topmost point in the hierarchy of laborers which we see in a novella that assiduously avoids the field of wage labor. We learn the names and idiosyncrasies of many of Horacio's house servants and employees, the "white Russian Alex" who would only take the job if he was allowed to keep his beard, the pianist Walter, the twin maids, one of whom is named María. Two groups remain corporate and anonymous, but the model for their work is the arts and crafts, not salaried labor: the *autores/artistas/muchachos* (II, 178) who compose Horacio's doll tableaux, and Facundo's *muchachas del taller* who work early on in the novella to help give Hortensia human temperature (Horacio "felt secretly pleased at the thought of girls working on Hortensia, putting something of themselves into her" (192; II, 194)). Insofar as these maids and *muchachos* are insubordinate, Horacio is not a successfully tyrannical father figure. Nevertheless, despite the *fábrica* next door, work and money—like desire—are talked about as if it stays all in the family.

The text emphasizes Facundo's status as a "brother," not just to demonstrate that he is an equal to Horacio, not below him with the other *muchachos* (Horacio and Facundo speak slowly, in turn, when conspiring to make Hortensia anatomically correct), but also to demonstrate that he is not Horacio's father. There is something Mephistophelian about Facundo, to be sure, insofar as a religious discourse of blasphemy is never permanently absent from the text (the note María leaves for Horacio accuses him of sending the doll to the workshop "to have those sinful things done to her (*a que le hagan herejías*)" (208; II, 210)); but, at least according to Girardian theory, in the relationship between brothers the older brother does not just furnish the object of desire but really teaches the younger how to desire in a sort of rivalry. And yet if Facundo is to be some sort of a modern devil, he is to be associated not with the savagery of the Argentine gaucho Facundo, only with his barbaric populism, a leader for a milder, gentler era and nation; he is not the Big Brother of Orwell but the manager of pleasures of Huxley's administrative brave new world (an aspect of Uruguay's self-image for most of the twentieth century was its elaborate welfare state). When Felisberto moves the scenes of desire outside Horacio's private home, his public spaces are only the semipublic spaces of the hotel/ex-brothel, the red-light district of the Park of the Acacias, and especially the department store, spaces where bedrooms and women's bodies can be purchased, spaces for the incitement of illusions.

One of the most heavily underlined aspects of Horacio's fetishism, where disavowal and commodity fetishism coincide, is his desire for "illusion," which involves an avoidance of the productive process, whether in love, art, or dollmaking. His first spoken sentence in the novella, to his wife about the doll tableaux, is a prohibition against speaking what they both know: "I know, but don't tell me anything" (175; II, 176). Felisberto seems almost delighted in finding variations on the theme of the pleasure of knowing-yet-not-knowing: Facundo should not tell him how the Hortensias are given human warmth ("Do what you want, just don't tell me" (187; II, 189)); he repeats this prohibition on the phone to Facundo later, although he is pleased to hear about the *muchachas*; and when María uses the phrase "human warmth" sarcastically during an argument, Horacio thinks irritatedly that the phrase "soured all the pleasures (*ilusión*) that he was looking forward to when Hortensia returned" (188; II, 190). The words *ilusión* and *desilusión*, illusion/hope and disappointment, are pressed into service often to describe the desirable and undesirable mental states involved in knowing-and-not-knowing, an inherently unstable state that must be finely calibrated if one is to achieve pleasure. Stealing the doll from "El Tímido" leaves him, as we have seen, "desilusionado," and the illusion has almost as much to do with the play between inanimate and animate as with a sexual disappointment: he fears to find in the doll's face her "lifeless scorn" (*la burla inconmovible de un objeto*) (221; II, 223). This vocabulary is not limited narrowly to the erotic sphere: after Hortensia has been attacked by María, and Horacio wonders whether he ought to repair her, thoughts of a repaired toy horse he had as child remind him of the "desilusión" he experienced then (207); when Horacio enters the doll tableau that shows a carnival scene, steps on a mask, picks it up and tosses it aside, "The gesture gave the objects around him physical reality (*un sentido material*) and he felt let down (*desilusionado*)" (190; II, 192). While it would seem that Horacio differs completely from the other Rioplatense radical idealists from Macedonio through Borges, always preferring the material to the ideal, such thoughts as these make one realize that the nego-tiations between the material and the immaterial in Felisberto are of a cer-tain complexity: both must be present to achieve the supreme pleasure. And indeed, as we have seen, Horacio also feels "disillusioned at being made of such base metal [*materia*]" (200; II, 202). After the muchachos fail to use properly the extra limbs he received from Facundo, "Horacio felt dis-appointed (*desilusionado*) with the boys, with dolls and even with [his cur-rent mistress doll] Eulalia" (219; II, 221). And when María returns and Horacio begs for her forgiveness, the word "desilusión" is used twice to describe Horacio's state (222; II, 224). So the wrong kind—really, any kind—of attention to the material will spoil the pleasure, the illusion caused by the erotic object.

Insofar as the dolls themselves are "producers" of the *presagios* and of shudders of Horacio's erotic pleasures, Horacio thinks they work best when they do not know what messages they carry: "at other times [...] the dolls were like creatures in a trance, on unknown missions, or lending themselves to evil designs" (185; II, 187). As the text shifts thematically from thrilling meanings to more overt eroticism, the dolls of the Primavera store windows "did not seem to care whether they were being dressed or undressed. They were like mad dreamers oblivious to everything but their poses" (227; II, 229). While Horacio is elaborating his theory of the source of the power of the dolls or the source of his various angsts, multiple interpretive solutions can be held in suspension, all held in the mind, none rejected. Once the dolls are made anatomically correct, however, ambiguity becomes dis-avowal. Horacio "knows [that the dolls are inanimate], and yet, all the same" will treat them as if they were human. Horacio, in an odd way like Lezama's protagonists, also retools the axis strong/weak to suit his own abnormal masculinity: he thinks that when he was younger he was strong enough to pursue his desires with less remorse, and certainly the story sug-gests that his constitution was too weak to withstand the illusions, or the constant cycle of illusion and disillusion, which the dolls fostered: even before María surprises him disguised as a Negress doll, he has begun taking on the fixity that objects are supposed to have while staring at the dolls in the department store display: "Carrying his small head stiffly, like another doll head, among the spectators, Horacio moved on to the forest" (227; II, 230). In his weakened state, there is no more play between *ilusión* and *desilusión*, only the part-self moving from object to object (*la cabeza siguió andando entre la gente*, untranslated in Harss: "the head kept going among the people" (II, 230)), chasing the moving objects of a fixated desire.

If the populace of this nameless city and country—all we know is that it can't be France, since that is where Horacio imports his wine from—does not appear as a citizenry or as a proletariat, they certainly appear as a market, a consumer society. Much as in neoliberal thought as it is praised and excoriated today, the novella sees the masses as individuals with desires, and their entry into the public space is (only) for the further incitement of these desires, which do not create a community but a mass.

We would hardly expect Horacio, who imposes silence on his wife, to find these crowds appealing, yet on the first of his two trips to La Primavera he decides to walk. Just as there is only one Hortensia in the store, hidden among the other dolls, "he walked, thinking about how he was going to tell his doll apart in the throng of other dolls. Now he was also part of a throng, pleasantly lost [...] in the holiday crowd" (224; II, 227). But indeed this noise does not resolve into a satisfying sort of silence, in the way that the noise of the machines is sometimes compared to silence: rather, "A child aimed a horn at him and let out an awful blast in his face" (224–5; II, 227),[23] In a public world without fathers, children can wield a phallic, gun-like cornet as a representative of the carnival masses. Following the novella's pattern of *ilusión-desilusión*, the preference for the imagined material over the real material, the crowds at the department store which Horacio sees are not the attractive masses he once imagined while wandering alone at night amidst his dolls:

> All sorts of faces enthralled by the scene went by outside the glass, looking the dolls up and down, and not only for their fashions. There were glinting eyes that jumped suspiciously from a skirt to a neckline, from one doll to the next, distrusting even the virtuous ones like the woman of the lake. Other wary eyes seemed to tiptoe over the dresses as if afraid of slipping and landing on the bare flesh. A young girl bowed her head in Cinderella-like awe [and thought that the splendor of some of the dresses had to do with the destiny of the Hortensias.] A man knit his brows and averted his eyes from his wife, hiding his urge to own an Hortensia. (227; translation modified; II, 229)

This is Felisberto's scene of Uruguay, of consumer society, reading the displays as commodity fetishists who, in a comic yet commonsensical spin on Freudian theory, understand that the invaginated object is the equivalent of the "phallic" powerful woman even though its/her anatomical modification is the very opposite of a penis. Felisberto also expresses the nineteenth century's common sense about the masses. The mass society is classless (*toda clase de caras*), and in its taxonomic enumeration of different types the passage recalls, a little, *modernista* vignettes of the nineteenth-century crowd by Gutiérrez Nájera or Casal which are themselves imitations of Baudelaire and other *chroniqueurs*. My point is that Felisberto is not breaking new ground in his conception of these crowds. Whereas the sophisticated fetishist searches for an ineffable nuance in the sublimely distracted poses of the dolls, the common gawker can only be (openly or secretly) for, or (censoriously or phobically) against, the realistic imitation of women's genitals.[24] The omniscient narrator participates ironically in the categories of the obsessives he describes, and we realize that we know what he means when he says that there are "virtuous" dolls as well as unvirtuous ones. If the crowds have changed from the idyllic first days of Horacio's mania when the gazes of envious women used to charge the dolls, it is in part because the dolls too have changed: even the young girls can deduce a relationship between glamour and prostitution; such thoughts about the "destiny" of the dolls is a far coarser tale than the melodramatically innocent stories that Horacio's *muchachos* told him, and Horacio told himself.

And Horacio is no more immune to these new dolls than he had been to the older ones; indeed, they are capable of fixating him in a way that the more demure ones could not. Perhaps because of his irritation with his wife's moral superiority, he chooses the single Hortensia in the Primavera store in his first foray because he "felt like humbling her" (225; II, 229) and is most passionate with her when he thinks that her eyes "took on the expression of humbled pride" (225; II, 230). The novella brings us through other variations on the theme of aristocracy and democracy, civilization and barbarism, first with the (supposedly national) legend of the "madwoman of the lake," and finally in a forest scene, where the dolls are half-naked "indígenas" and "caníbales" and "negras," dressed in ways that blend the natural animate with the human. Some are painted with eyes all over (we know that Horacio wouldn't care for them), but he does feel an immediate predilection for one of the black ones, whose breast are each painted as small heads where the nipples are lips (227; II, 230). The epicure used to use similes so as not to change the object, but, once his desires have been set into motion among a variety of objects and once they have been weakened and coarsened in the marketplace of niche-market desires, the glutton happily purchases an object which is itself changed. The process of moving these desires, as a department stores moves a line of goods, can so confidently depend on imperialist orientalism as fomented even by the avantgarde's taste for primitivism in artists such as Picasso and Gauguin that when Horacio asks which of the dolls in that display are Hortensias, Facundo can respond, "Why, dear boy, (*Mira hermano*), in that section they're all Hortensias" (230).

Disavowal is the space of any fiction; the granting of power to an object which you know-and-do-not-know does not "really" have that power is the equivalent of the willing suspension of disbelief in traditional fiction. In that sense, all fiction is disavowal just as all desire in consumer society is fetishistic desire. However, disavowal, represented along the axis of illusion/disillusion, coexists in this novella with the uncanny, the return of the repressed, represented by the noises of the factory and by what can only be called the machinery of consumer capitalism. The noises of the factory do not contribute to the scenes directly but, in Horacio's theories, use the dolls to communicate; they are the source of the *presagios* which take advantage of the tableaux to make themselves felt. In the first half of the novella, the silence Horacio hears in the brothel/hotel makes him wonder whether he ought to get away from the machines altogether (212); but by the last half of the novella he remembers the noise of the machines even while sitting alone by the lake: his soul "was like a gloomy silence over the dark water: a silence with a memory of its own in which he recognized the noise of the machines, as if it were another form of silence. Perhaps the noise had been a steamboat sailing by, and the silence was the memories of dolls left in the wreck as it sank in the night" (223–4; II, 226). Like the simile of the parachutist that profanes the landscape of María's cheek, the simile of the sunken steamship profanes the calm of the soul's silent black waters. The passage leads us from the good silence of the soul to the good noise of the machines to the bad noise of a shipwreck, which will lead to the bad silence of Horacio's madness (in the last pages we are almost never privy to Horacio's thoughts and perspectives). The impersonality of the noise of the machines has transformed itself into the anonymity of the crowd scenes. We could say that this clarifies the meaning of the sound of the noise of the machines, or we could say that it makes both impersonality and anonymity more sinister, even as the end of the novel makes clear that, for Horacio at least, the strategies of privacy and domesticity have lost all efficacy.

So in the end, the objects put on display by La Primavera, the *muchachos* and Facundo, energized by their absorption of the gaze of the mass public and participating in the mass narratives of national legend and imperial stereotyping, prove too strong for Horacio, who succumbs to their successful appeal to his fixated desire. Poor Horacio! Although his pursuit of the hidden meaning of desirable objects is too complex to be properly explained to his wife (and besides, to tamper with female innocence risks the loss of its *encanto*), consumer society can produce, with sufficient variety, enough desirable objects to harden and stiffen his subjectivity; and, being rich, he need not settle for window shopping, mere voyeurism, but can buy the objects that reduce the very mental complexity with which he began.[25] He does not even have the consolation of the moral high ground of Kafka's hunger artist, that most metaphysical refusenik of the European modernist canon: "If I could have found what I wanted to eat, I would have feasted happily; but I never did," he whispers on his deathbed, and with that he can become a symbol for the artist as an (ironic, involuntary) total negation of consumerist culture. I am sympathetic to attempts to show that, in his least narrative, most aleatory pieces, Felisberto pursues pleasures and meanings that are inimical to presence and form.[26] One would think that if others, or you yourself, cannot give a form to a pleasure, others would also be unable to market it and sell it to you as such. But in this novella, Horacio is simultaneously epicure and glutton, absorbing ever-increasing quantities of mass culture for what is only at first an idiosyncratic purpose. Lustful to contemplate the narratives and to generate the similes around the melodramatically imperiled woman, incapable of hunger-artist negation, Horacio is an antihero/victim of consumer capitalism, damned if his wife pulls him out of the field of centrifugal, ever-accelerating desires and damned if she doesn't.

RUNNING BACK TO THE MACHINE: FELISBERTO'S FAILURE: INTERPRETING/NARRATIVE/CLOSURE

> ... *the minute he felt her hand he straightened up, stiff as death, stretching his neck and gasping like a captive bird trying to flap its wings and caw. María took hold of his arm, but he pulled away in terror and began turning himself around in a little shuffle, as he had done the day she had painted her face black and laughed in his face. [...] [She and their servant Alex] were still looking for him when they heard his steps in the gravel of the garden. They saw him cut straight through the flower beds. And when they caught up with him, he was going toward the noise of the machines.*

> (*Las Hortensias* 230; II, 233)

In this essay, you will have noted a much more positive tone toward male fetishists than can be construed from feminist theorizings on the fetish, which have preferred to accept Freud's moralistic description of the fetishist's dislike of real women. For what it's worth, I distinguish in principle between the structural misogyny of Freud–Lacan, which argues that women are *a priori* castrated and for that reason incapable of an unproblematic subjectivity, and the less structural ambivalence of Felisberto's fetishist scenario, in which of course women can be subjects, whether their children/husbands like it or not. In the novella, the fetishist experiences his wife sometimes as a desirable objectivity, which inspires imaginative thoughts in the man, and sometimes as a discomfiting subjectivity, which faithfully but unpredictably puts her own imagination at the service of her husband, at first, but in the end demands a centripetal desire from her husband. With the guilty conscience of an adulterer Horacio's weak masculinity opts for the desirable objectivity of objects over the female subject of legitimate domesticity. Felisberto takes the next step from a post-Freudian critique of domestic desire when his thoughts about the desirability of objects blur the distinction between subject and object, or, if you prefer, between animate and inanimate objects, or, if you prefer, between "feitichos," powerful man-made objects, and commodities. This last blurring is one of the ways that *Las Hortensias* is unique in Felisberto's oeuvre, also the only one of his stories in which the fetishist protagonist slowly descends into depression and madness. So often the Felisbertian protagonist attributes his failure to poverty or some other externality, and his fetishism/voyeurism is his consolation prize, the less that he settles for. But here the implication is that his fetishistic approach toward satisfying his desires is the direct cause of his downfall.

In this story, and this story alone, the fetishistic subject's willingness to attribute independent life to inanimate objects has as its counterpart the conviction that the desiring part of him is not only independent of him (a motif everywhere in Felisberto) but also in some sense inanimate, that is, automatic, a pure desire for repetition without any real object. This aspect of the story is very deliberate, from the description—significantly, by the dollmaker Facundo—of Horacio, lying on his back after a pratfall at his birthday party, as one of those windup toys that has been knocked over (195; II, 197), to the "fixity of a doll" staring at the department store Hortensias (II, 230); to the slow circles in which he mechanically moves after being discovered the first time by María, angrily counterfeiting her husband's new Negress-Hortensia mistress (228; II, 231), to the novella's end, in which María's (actually rather tender) participation in her husband's tableau is a last invasion of his sphere of control, and turns him most fully into that minimum desire for the same, from the lover of the autonomous object to a mere automaton.

Notoriously, Freud theorized the repetition compulsion beyond the pleasure principle as the death instinct Thanatos, the ultimate noise of the machines in our lives. While I think that that is a plausible way to relate Freud to the pessimistic narrative arc of *Las Hortensias* and can offer no argument against that reading of the text, I have never liked that particular metaphysical move in Freud. Instead I would like to suggest some different readings of the relationship between Horacio's failure and Felisberto's failure—for, make no mistake, on a formal narrative level *Las Hortensias* is a failure, a fecklessly paced collection of provocations, conveyed through piling high and deep simile upon simile, each a small narrative of its own. The novella tries to rescue its problematic shape by resorting to a form of poetic justice in which the lover of dolls himself becomes a doll. Yet the text has been pointing in different directions throughout, leaving the reader with a sense that this particular card is being forced upon him—or has been forced upon the author. The story's treatment of money and consumer capitalism better explains the pessimism involved in charting Horacio's failure. Like many poor men, Felisberto tells a story of how money cannot buy happiness, or even pleasure; he argues that his rich protagonist fends off the subjectivities of others only to find that alluring objects also offer resistance to him, partly because they are built, by other men, and are circulated in public, among other women, before they can have the capacity to fascinate him.

Yet the noises of the machine, generator of *presagios* in good times and "unknown missions and evil designs" as the novella progresses, seem to require further interpretation. By now we are accustomed to read texts from the Freudian era against the grain, defending perversions which the narrative machinery of the text ineluctably punishes. The proliferation of incidents in the second half of the novella is quite different from the elegance of the narrative of origins in Freud's detective fictions, and different from Freud's fetish-narrative that proffers a single origin, a single traumatic misencounter, for the young fetishist. We can interpret *Las Hortensias*'s formal awkwardness in more than one way, not all of them mutually exclusive. We can believe that the author is actually in control of his text: Felisberto needs to show us that fetishistic desire is centrifugal and cannot be limited to a domestic space. On some other level, we might believe that the author is not in control of his text: delighting in inventing, if only this one time, a rich protagonist, Felisberto unleashes his imagination into a reckless proliferation of scenarios of perverted desire.[27] We might put this negatively: the author, recognizing the existence of social narratives which control any text, rebels for as long as he can and, sure that the end of his story will mark the end of the fetishistic party, Felisberto invents and invents in order to postpone the final curtain, thus spoiling still further the traditional form of the well-made novella.

After all, we too are implicated in Felisberto's fetishistic, voyeuristic fables of interpretation. We too take advantage of these and other narrative forms to "deduce many things," to fill in the blanks and provide beginnings and endings for the tableaux which we rob, like a woman's underthings, from the scenes we read in books of poems and in the glimpses we catch as we travel forlornly through worlds both fictional and real. If we have interpretive templates to help explain these worlds, and if we take pleasure in interpretation, we must accept that these interpretative templates may well impose a logic which permits us to "deduce" some outcomes but not others. Freud did not give his fetishists an unhappy ending—notoriously, he said that they enjoyed their games of disavowal and maternal lack and seldom came to him to have their fetishes removed. But when Horacio, mad, returns to the machines in the last sentence of the text, we should not just remark that another sexual pervert has been punished by master narratives of normality for lack of a supportive wife or community of like-minded individuals, or for lack of the proper mediations between an artistic avant-garde and the sexual avant-garde. We should also acknowledge that a man with a literary sensibility who saw a simile in everything, who also lacked a supportive community in his adult years, and who settled for less in his real life, forces us to examine the uncomfortable way that we too find meanings and pleasures in stories, as we move from textual object to textual object, until it is time for us too to return to the machines.

4. Fashionable and Unfashionable Perversions on the Latin American Rive Gauche: Cortázar and Pizarnik Read "The Bloody Countess" ∽

> *Masoch has been treated unjustly, not because his name was unfairly given to the perversion of masochism, but quite the reverse, because his work fell into neglect whereas his name passed into common usage. Although we occasionally find books written on Sade that show no knowledge of his work, this is increasingly rare. Sade is becoming more thoroughly known.*
>
> (Deleuze, "Coldness and Cruelty" (1967) 13)

> *[Nicole:]* "... *but it's not you who keeps me locked up in this inertia. There's only one thing I can't understand and that's why you're still with me, Mar[rast]."*
> *[Marrast:]* "Sacher-Masoch," *I say, stroking her hair.*
> "But you're not like that, Mar."
> "Existence precedes essence, love."
> "No, you're not like that. You weren't born to be like that."
>
> (Cortázar 62: *modelo para armar* 81; 75)

In Julio Cortázar's *62: modelo para armar* (*62: A Model Kit*, 1968), one of the secondary characters, the Parisian sculptor Marrast, accuses himself, using a name that has "passed into common usage," of masochism. His sex partner Nicole, who is no longer in love with him, hastily reassures him that he wasn't born to be that way. Neither of them may get what they want in life (she, too, is unrequitedly in love, in her case with the novel's protagonist, Juan), but whatever they were born for—especially, whatever Marrast was born for—it has nothing to do with *that name*.

At any given time among the members of a given group, some perversions are more fashionable than others. Perhaps it is true that there really is no such thing as a perversion that transcends all cultural difference; perhaps it is true that it is only the will of the lawmakers and their police forces that determine the sexual norm, encourage some behaviors, regulate or criminalize others, and reserve the right to define them all. It may also be the case that even as adults we retain a certain amount of polymorphous perversity that can actually be molded by our peer groups, tempting us into following the sexual fashions of our culture or our subcultures. And again, whether or not what we do, or want to do, or want to want to do, can be swayed by fashion, how we think about these actions and desires is almost certainly swayed by prevailing cultural and intellectual models. In the postwar West, the models of sexual discourse, with their general norms of acceptable and unacceptable behaviors and desires, were given a definitive shape in the twentieth century from the writings of Freud. But variations on the basic Freudian themes have abounded, and nowhere so with more vigor and tenacity than among French intellectuals. While not fully constituting an orthodoxy, and certainly with no police power to back up their opinions, Parisian writers of the late 1950s and the 1960s nevertheless devoted more energy to examining some perversions than others. And the voracious young intellectuals whom we associate with the term "el Boom" learned that landscape at the same time they were learning the streets which their characters sometimes traversed. An ambitious author such as Julio Cortázar might have a reaction to this intellectual landscape, but he would have had to learn it first.

Different perversions play different roles in sexual discourses, as we have seen in previous chapters. Sometimes a perversion is built deeply into the metapsychological edifice, as mother–son incest is an essential component of Freud's Oedipal theories of child development; from there the incest taboo as structure worked its way into meditations on comparative and structural anthropology in the late 1940s and 1950s by Levi-Strauss. (The attack by Deleuze and Guattari, *Anti-Oedipus: Capitalism and Schizophrenia*, would not come until 1972.) The effects of a Levi-Straussian, Freudian emphasis on Oedipus and culture can be seen in the notorious reflections on Cortés and la Malinche in Octavio Paz's *The Labyrinth of Solitude* (1949), and the sexually most conservative of the Boom novelists, Mario Vargas Llosa and Gabriel García Márquez, treat incest as the key explanation for family and history, the movement between past, present, and future. Sometimes a perversion is debated; the face of the homosexual in this period was shaken up by the coarse face of petty criminal and playwright Jean Genet, as championed by Sartre: a young Juan Goytisolo could find an erotic mentor that would allow him a position from which to polemicize, including if need be against other homosexuals.

Sometimes a perversion is "decriminalized," so to speak, no longer pursued by the police or the doctors, only to continue to lead a surreptitious life in folk thinking: Eve Sedgwick, following Foucault, has described the way that masturbation went from the scourge of the adolescent to an unproblematic private behavior over the course of the twentieth century, but (to judge from various conversations in Cortázar's 1973 *Libro de Manuel*) she perhaps should not underestimate the stubborn way in which mothers who need to train their young children continue to resort to similar threats and folk-medicine thinking before they pack their children off to bohemian Paris.[1] Onanism gained a theoretical cachet in 1967 when Derrida built an important part of his *On Grammatology* around an analysis of Rousseau's diatribe against masturbation, "that dangerous supplement," although, like *Anti-Oedipus*, deconstruction in many ways is beyond the horizon of the cultural moment which the writers of the Boom encountered in the Paris of the 1950s and 1960s.[2]

But one is tempted to say that masturbation is one of a whole raft of perversions which will always implicate writers, or at any rate the bourgeois individualist novelist and poet, by virtue of his or her pursuit of a silent, solitary pleasure. Fetishism, voyeurism, exhibitionism, are all metaphors for the act of reading and writing. These solitary perversions may correspond to real erotic drives; like masturbation, however, they can all be labeled "immature," and the dichotomy maturity/immaturity has produced *literary* normativity modeled upon models of *sexual* normativity, so that the Tolstoys, Balzacs, Goethes, and other "mature" geniuses stand higher on the scale of literary merit than writers who touch and retouch themselves. The avant-garde artist tends to mistrust the "maturity" of these Tolstoys and Goethes, especially insofar as these authors do not trouble the bourgeois sense of the individual self; Cortázar's texts in particular are full of attacks on "la seriedad (seriousness)," a false or unearned maturity that often appears as a fat woman, "la gran gorda, La Seriedad (that big fat woman, La Seriedad)," in his 1967 essay collection *Around the Day in Eighty Worlds*, and whose petty-bourgeois voice Cortázar imitates perfectly either in its French or its *porteño* inflections. In the novel *62* petit-bourgeois maturity is attacked most directly by the cast of minor characters in the novels called the "tártaros," friends who meet regularly around a table at the Cluny restaurant in Paris, various members of whom in this novel: convince a British group of "Neurotics Anonymous" to fixate upon a bad botanical painting in the Courtauld Institute; wreck a hotel room with experiments involving an electric shaver and bowls of porridge; get stranded on a small island in a lagoon in the gardens of a Parisian plant nursery; build a statue in Arceuil commemorating Vercingetorix with the pedestal on the top instead of the bottom; and get thrown out of the train on the way back to Paris from Arceuil for racing their snail Osvaldo on the backs of one of the train seats.[3] Yet many of the "immature" perversions, such as fetishism and voyeurism, never seem to fully throw off their middle-class connotations—isn't the fetishist collector always the museum curator? Isn't the voyeur in the strip club always the white-collar worker?—and are therefore still suspect for the avant-garde. What, then, was French bohemia's fashionable way to break the stranglehold of the bourgeois act of thinking and writing?

Perhaps there should have been other possibilities. But as it turns out, the fashionable way to attack bourgeois ways of thinking about sex and writing in the late 1950s and the 1960s before *mai '68* was a sustained reflection upon sadism. Although I will trace more than one influential line of thinking around the figure of the Marquis de Sade, I do so with the reservation that some Latin American authors' enthusiasm to repeat the bohemian party line upon Sade may not actually correspond to their fictional practice. Rather than a really helpful presence, the discourse on Sade might actually conceal other, less fashionable, libidinal and literary investments. My primary example for all this is Julio Cortázar, whose strategies for self-disclosure and self-concealment in the wake of his best-seller *Hopscotch* are particularly complex.

BEATING, AND BEING BEATEN, AND BEATING

"[My dearest fantasy is] To be the slave of a woman, a beautiful woman whom I love and worship."

"And who in return ill-treats you!" laughed Wanda.

"Yes, who fetters me, whips me and kicks me and who all the while belongs to another."

(Masoch, *Venus In Furs*, Deleuze 180)

There are probably multiple reasons why the writers of the Rive Gauche in the 1960s are turning away from Freud on the question of sadism and masochism when they remain loyal to him on homosexuality and fetishism. The power of a competing discourse, the Marquis de Sade's, is no doubt one of them. But my premise has been that Freud's success is due as much to his narrative skills as to any accuracy in describing psychical processes. Let us examine briefly the limits to his narrative of the pleasures of giving and receiving pain.

Unlike the Oedipal complex, which is both a structure and a narrative, the explanation for sadism and masochism is all structure, no narrative. After some suggestive comments in his 1905 *Three Essays*, Freud elaborates this structure most fully in his 1915 essay, "Instincts and Their Vicissitudes." For Freud, certain libidinal pairs are instinctual opposites, though not opposites in identical ways: he mentions specifically scopophilia (voyeurism) and exhibitionism, and sadism and masochism. Being two aspects of the same instinct, they supposedly easily flip from one to the other.

Freud's conclusion that sadism and masochism are reversible forms of the same instinct is of course debatable: the Rive Gauche countered this abstract positing of forces with the lush and frenetic literary outputs of the Marquis de Sade and Count Sacher-Masoch, claiming the independent status for each narrator of the perverse. But we might also take issue with Freud for the latitude which the notion of "vicissitude" introduces into the rules of interpretation. When a feeling is posited as being able to transform into its opposite, the interpretation of a dream or a sexual fantasy is very vulnerable to the analyst's own projection. The reconstruction of a patient's fantasy narratives will seem arbitrary, as we shall see.

Many on that same Rive Gauche also seemed offended by Freud's positing of "sadomasochism" in that it suggested that sadism and masochism were of equal importance in one's psychic make-up, but Freud not only does not think this, he changes his opinion on this topic in various ways. He posits at first only aggressive impulses, which themselves are almost equivalent to his use of the concept of libidinal impulses. But aggression is not in itself enough to form a sadistic character: to know that you are hurting someone by your behavior, you must yourself have experienced pain and empathetically, cruelly, imagine the pain of the other in the sadistic behavior you then turn upon him or her. This prior pain was probably inflicted by a parent, and partakes in the child's ambivalence towards his parents, so it has a masochistic component. In an oddly formal or abstract sense, masochism is psychologically prior to sadism. This mini-narrative of the perverse, aligning sadism with a prior empathetic imagination of the victim's pain and, thus, treating all empathy, all imagining of the other, as inherently masochistic, is an essential part of the process of the "vicissitude" in Freud and provokes disgust and irritation in those who will wish, as we shall see, to posit sadism as the absolute absence of empathy.

Yet masochism kept nagging at Freud, in part because of its deeply counter-intuitive aspect to anyone, but especially to a thinker who wishes to posit only need and aggressive instincts in the psyche. His final attempt to think through masochism, the 1924 essay "On the Economic Problem in Masochism," brings masochism into line with the later Freud's grand narrative of Eros and Thanatos, which does indeed bring something like a passive instinct (Thanatos) back on a par with an aggressive instinct (Eros), but which is alas both structural and now metaphysical, in ways that choke narrative. He also engages in taxonomy: masochism is either erotogenic, feminine, or moral. This trio maps suspiciously onto the id-ego-superego model of the self Freud had recently completed. The sensorium is aware that extreme pain and pleasure do meet, hence pain on the one hand is erotogenic, but too much of it, like other indulgences of the id, is pathological. If you *are* a woman, masochism is an expression of your feminine nature, but to behave like a woman if you are a man is a psychotic refusal of the ego as reality principle. Finally, if you provoke people into punishing you ("in the manner of characters in Russian novels," says Freud), you enact a moral masochism no less strong than the more visible case of the self-punishing ascetic.

This taxonomy only produces abstract narratives, but it is elaborated from a somewhat more recent and much more interesting essay, "A Child Is Being Beaten" (1919). As we would expect from the author of "Instincts and Their Vicissitudes," Freud tries to deal with both sadism and masochism at the same time, in a group of six patients, four women and two men, who all have variations on fantasies of watching a child being beaten (watching real children being beaten produces great anxiety in them). His interpretive moves as he tries to make "a contribution to the study of the origins of sexual perversions" (the essay's subtitle) seem at first to encounter frustrations: the patient's fantasies are brought forth reluctantly and with shame; the fantasies themselves evolved over the childhood and adulthood of the patients; genders of the children being beaten neither remained constant nor correlated with the genders of the patients; the gender of the beater remains (says Freud, at first) shadowy; it is only Freud's conviction that sadism and masochism are invertible sides of one instinct that makes it tolerable for him to have to confess, at the end of the summary, "In these circumstances it was impossible at first to decide whether the pleasure attaching to the beating-fantasy was to be described as sadistic or masochistic" (109).

The decision to summarize his findings from a group of six patients, instead of the in-depth analysis of just one patient (characteristic of the 1905–09 era of Dora, the Wolf Man, the Schreber essay, etc.) finds an odd echo in the way the beating fantasies themselves multiply for (one? some? all? of) the patients: attending school "noticeably modified the content [of the fantasies]. From that time forward it was an 'indefinite number' of children that were being beaten" (108), although Freud refuses to believe his patients who say that their fantasies began at school. Just as typically, but more sinisterly, he refuses to believe his patients who volunteer the information that it is their mother, or a woman, who is beating the child. In the 1924 essay he adopts the more knowing tone on this topic: although "the obvious interpretation, which is easily arrived at, is that the masochist wants to be treated like a little, helpless, dependent child, but especially like a naughty child," really "one easily discovers that in them the subject is placed in a situation characteristic of womanhood" (193). The man being beaten must be a woman.

Likewise, the person beating must be a man. In the 1919 essay, Freud eventually creates a narrative synthesis of the fantasies of the women patients (he postpones those of the men until the end of the essay). In the first stage of the fantasy, Freud reconstructs, "my father is beating the child whom I hate" (113), and gives nursery jealousy as the excuse for it (almost, but not quite sexual, says Freud), and posits the father as the one beating, for purely Oedipal reasons ("The affections of the little girl are fixed upon the father, who has probably [*sic*] done all he can to win her love" (114–15)). Freud then posits a second stage, in which guilt and disappointment lead to the masochistic fantasy that "the father is beating me, because he loves me." Freud blandly admits that none of his patients would actually admit to recalling this stage (only one of the men, he says, recalls fantasizing beatings, but these were by his mother, not his father). Conversely, he gives here a heavy weight to one of his patients' "artistic superstructure of day-dreams" (118), in which the boy-hero is regularly beaten by father figures. Freud was always receptive to narrators of the perverse, and always happy to avoid working out the ambivalences of mother–daughter relationships. In the final stage, it is boys whom the shadowy father is beating, not oneself, but the pleasure remains masochistic, with the women's masculinity complex allowing her to identify with the boys while also resenting their privileges in the world.

For the purposes of examining *62*, it is interesting to see the shift of tone in the 1919 essay when examining his two male patients. We have already noted Freud's impatience in his 1924 essay on the commonness of masochistic fantasies among his Viennese patients; there, as here, he refuses to believe that it is a mother–child scene which the masochist wishes to repeat, but rather a scene in which a father beats a feminized boy. While some of the patients admit that they take on a feminine role in their masochistic fantasies, "the persons who administer chastisement are always women, both in the phantasies and in the contrivances" (126). Freud overrides this and states flatly, based on "analysis of the earliest years of childhood" that the conscious fantasy of being beaten by one's mother is preceded by the ("invariably unconscious" (126)) fantasy of being beaten by one's father, a masochistic faith in his love for you.

Our late-1960s Rive Gauche defender of masochism, Gilles Deleuze, is not only irritated, as are the Rive Gauche Sadeians, that sadism and masochism are theorized as a single instinct reversible into two positions, he is also angered that Freud casts aside all the indications that the mother–son relationship can support the elaborations of heterosexual male masochism. Chapter V of his "Coldness and Cruelty," attacking both Freud and Reik, argues that "the belief in the determinant role of the father in masochism is . . . the result of the preconceived notion of a sadomasochistic entity" (59). As we shall see, Deleuze not only preserves the mother figure, but multiplies her function, a very satisfactory procedure for a novel such as *62*.

It is hard not to conclude that the typical Freudian maneuver of positing unconscious phases and fantasies which are the opposite of the patients' conscious thoughts and memories, producing narratives satisfactory to him and to his era but not always to us, are not interpretations but impositions, and that further interpretations (Deleuze's, my own, yours) merely add on further impositions. If the original patient accepts these elaborations, it may be because he understands it as a melancholy game, a practice in which we engage so as to keep our original fantasies, however distorted, in circulation. Cortázar's *62* is full of melancholy game-players (the novel's minor characters the *tártaros*, as well as its principal protagonists), and the novel in many ways is about the risks one takes in opening one's personal spaces out to further interpretation:

> And since it's a matter of dreams, where the Tartars consider as collective dreams material that parallels that of the city but is carefully kept apart, because no one would think of mixing up the city with dreams, which would be the same as mixing life and games and so they fall into a childishness that would be repugnant to serious people.

> > Polanco nearly always begins: Look here, I dreamed that I was on a square and I found a heart on the ground. I picked it up and it was beating, it was a human heart and it was beating, then I took it to a fountain and washed it the best I could because it was covered with leaves and dust, and I went to turn it in to the police station on the Rue de l'Abbaye. That's completely false, Marrast says. You washed it but then you wrapped it disrespectfully in an old newspaper and put it in your jacket pocket. How can he put it in his jacket pocket if he was in his shirtsleeves, Juan says. I was dressed properly, Polanco says, and I took the heart to the police station and they gave me a receipt, which was the most extraordinary part of the dream. You didn't turn it in, Tell says, we saw you when you went into your place and you were hiding the heart in a closet, the one that has a gold lock. Imagine Polanco with a gold lock, Calac laughs rudely. I took the heart to the station house, Polanco says. Well, Nicole

allows, that was most likely the second one, because we all know that you found at least two. Bisbis bisbis, says Feuille Morte. Now that I think about it, Polanco says, I found about twenty. Great God of Israel, I forgot about the second part of the dream. You found them on the Place Maubert, under a heap of garbage, my paredros says, I saw you from the café Les Matelots. And they were all beating, Polanco says with enthusiasm. I found twenty hearts, twenty-one counting the one I'd already taken to the police, and they were all beating like mad. You didn't take it to the police, I saw you when you hid it in the closet. In any case, it was beating, my paredros concedes. Could be, Tell says, the beating doesn't worry me at all. There's nothing like a woman, Marrast says, a heart's beating and all she sees is a gold lock. Don't be a misogynist, my paredros says. The whole city was covered with hearts, Polanco says, I remember quite well, it was terribly strange. And to think that at first I remembered only one heart. You've got to start somewhere, Juan says. And they were all beating, Polanco says. What good did it do them? Tell says. (46–7; 41–2)

The transpositions that Cortázar's Tartars impose on Polanco's dream are not, I think, different in kind than those that Freud, and we ourselves, impose on the erotic daydreams of Freud's Viennese women. From beating to beating, *golpear* to *latir*. Freud hopes to reduce the many beaten children to one child; Polanco, facing a chorus of voices, hopes to protect his first heart by multiplying the one beating heart to many hearts. If feminists and women join in the game, some of the moves the men make will be recognized as misogynist. The paternal function of the police is not punitive to begin with (Polanco gets a receipt for his heart), but the chorus of voices is hardly interested in that. Polanco sentimentally reassures us that all the hearts were beating, and the cold (Tell is Danish, and unsentimental) woman responds that that won't do them much good.

But the transaction between the sentimental man and the cold woman is a dream, not "life": there is an ambiguous distinction between this group's creative behavior and that of the life of the "City," the impersonal collective dreamscape of the novel, which will turn out to be nightmarish, true, and unable to be shaped at will by the characters. A different sort of language that eroticized the cruelty of the laws of life was far more privileged in the public discourse of the '60s Rive Gauche.

PHILOSOPHY IN THE BOHEMIAN BOUDOIR

Before writing about Sade was tantamount to writing about philosophy by other means, Sade was treated as a libertine. His works circulated underground throughout the nineteenth century, like the pornography they also are, and only achieved a certain kind of visibility in the fin de siècle: a writer in the Revue Independante of 1885 suggested that here was a writer for an age "whose nervous systems are worn out and overwrought" (quoted in Rosario, 149). Joining his colorful biography to his lurid yet chilly tales, French readers have been able to assimilate him rather easily to the category of *poètes maudits*; indeed, Sade could be said to inaugurate this tradition, with the result that the category of accursed poet is no longer so clearly understood to be a phenomenon of (what Mario Praz called) "the Romantic agony," but in some ways aspires to transcend the fin-de-siècle milieu.

The first literary students of Sade were the Surrealists, and it is amusing to consult their thoughts on Sade, available in the 1992 collection of "Surrealist Investigations" (i.e., transcribed conversations among themselves) from 1928 to 1932, *Investigating Sex*. Having already written, in the first Surrealist Manifesto, that "Sade is Surrealist in his Sadism," Breton gives the figure of Sade an even greater privilege in the first of these conversations, as the subject of homosexuality arises: "I accuse homosexuals of confronting human tolerance with a mental and moral deficiency [...] I make exceptions though—among them one for the unparalleled case of Sade [...] By definition, everything is permitted to a man like the Marquis de Sade, for whom freedom of morals was a matter of life and death" (5–6). Yet in practice in these conversations, in part because of Breton's own prudery about the perversions, the Surrealists refuse to "investigate" the more radical negotiations between sex and power.

Breton's enthusiasm for Sade, even as he declared himself more and more a philosopher of love, was a great frustration for one later Surrealist of the Latin American Rive Gauche, Octavio Paz. Paz wrote a poem in 1947 about Sade entitled "The Prisoner," after his first encounter with Sade's writings. His 1986 answers to a questionnaire list the various writers on Sade whom he read or knew, giving pride of place to Jean Paulhan and of course (as we'll see) Georges Bataille; more relevant for our purposes is Paz's 1960 essay "An Erotic Beyond."[4] Paz's hostility toward Sade is kept in check for much of the essay in his exposition of Sade's eroticism and in his comparison with "Freud as a philosopher" (i.e., the later, more conservative Freud, of *Civilization and Its Discontents*), especially as Sade is seen as a materialist philosopher who refuses to personify nature or to allow human value judgments to distinguish creation from destruction. Paz's disagreement with Sade is ostensibly over the logical contradictions of his anarchist politics, but on a deeper level it springs from Paz's blunt refusal to abandon his own dialectical approach to love, which for him must be a mutual opening of the self to the other. The sadist makes no effort to understand the victim, and Paz's analysis comes to a halt at the concept of the "erotic object": "(if it is an object, it is not erotic; if it is erotic, it is not an object)" (55), he harrumphs parenthetically, and that is that.

What ends Paz's reflections is unique, perhaps, to Paz, but it is not atypical to send Sade through some comparison to—or more likely, contrast with—Freud: by this point Sade as a name, a label, had already become attached to psychoanalytic discourse. Krafft-Ebing and later Freud disseminate the word and concept sadism, sexual pleasure in the pain of others. For Freud, the ability to imagine the pain one is inflicting comes from having experienced such pain at one time first, and this permutability from receiving pain to giving it allowed Freud to coin the concept "sadomasochism."[5] Literary and philosophical readers of Sade saw very little of such reversibility in Sade's own works—as we have seen in Paz, the sadists in Sade waste no energy imagining what it feels like to be their victims—; a different sort of reversibility obtains in Sade, in which the intensity of an experience turns a pleasure into a pain, and vice versa, but this is supposedly a fact of the human sensorium and not a tale of a disidentification and reidentification with a punishing father as it can be in Freud. Indeed, some readers of Freud seemed insulted that Sade's psychodramas should have led Freud to a psychological conceptualization. The historical–philosophical reading of Sade reaches a culmination at the end of the period we are examining, in Horkheimer and Adorno's *Dialectic of Enlightenment*, of 1969. Rather than associate the sadist with the psychology—or political economy—of a masochist, Horkheimer and Adorno take seriously the notion that Sade belongs to the Enlightenment, indeed that his almost impersonal *amorality* stands in perfect dialectical relationship to Kant's impersonal *morality* at the threshold of a shift into an industrial capitalism that rewards conforming to the impersonality of market forces.[6] By placing himself beyond good and evil, Sade becomes a precursor to Nietzsche, with the result that Horkheimer and Adorno denounce Sade together with Nietzsche (and capitalism) as precursors to the radical amorality of Hitler.

It was possible to have Surrealist roots, reread Freud carefully and think dialectically without concluding that Sade's Kantian impersonality was inherently the amorality of the Übermensch. Such was the situation of Jacques Lacan's 1963 essay "Kant with Sade," written in a prose of unusual difficulty, even for Lacan. Lacan translates Sade's philosophy of the boudoir into an impersonal categorical imperative: the absolute right of *jouissance* by anyone over anyone else's body. *Jouissance*, not mastery or the mere pleasure principle: the sadist's subjectivity is split even as the victim's body (and often his or her subjectivity), is split. For Lacan, Sade's assertion of (a split) subjectivity over the victim as object paradoxically frees both sadist and victim from the burden of a false subjectivity: the victim, treated as an object, need not pretend to be a unified subject; the sadist, identifying his actions with the Real and the Law (what Sade called Nature), is no longer quite the Nietzschean Will either.

But if Lacan's reading of Sade separated Sade somewhat from Nietzsche, it was far more fashionable to defend both Nietzsche and Sade together, often under the sign of the aristocratic rejection of egalitarian thought and the affirmation of ecstatic limit-experiences, no matter what the social cost. This reading begins with the renegade Surrealist Pierre Klossowski in the 1930s and 1940s, but the most persuasive champion of this reading of Sade as philosopher was Georges Bataille, who published in quick succession toward the end of his life *Literature and Evil* (1957), *Erotism* (1957), and *The Tears of Eros* (1961), in each of which he devotes substantial time to elaborating his reading of the Marquis de Sade.

Bataille is a particularly useful figure for this sort of intellectual history. Born in 1897, he was a medieval historian and librarian by profession; but he became involved with the Surrealists in the 1920s, until the rather prudish, always cliquish André Breton drummed him out of the club for his excremental visions.[7] Besides writing fascinating pornographic works in the 1920s and 1930s that curiously relate degradation to anti-fascistic struggles, Bataille was also a founding member of the Collége de Sociologie, whose theories of taboo, transgression, and sacrifice often used materials from Latin America, and one of whose members, Roger Caillois, became one of Victoria Ocampo's favorite refugees during World War II; after the war Caillois returned to France to be a publicist for Latin American literature. Bataille himself went underground during the War, legendarily with nothing but the complete works of Nietzsche, and there he extended his obsession with defending Nietzsche from charges of protofascism. Bataille's own intellectual and political theories, however, frequently come across as primitivist and/or antirationalist in their antiutilitarianism. His 1936 essay "The Notion of Expenditure" proposes a dualistic notion of the human self, on the one hand the rational, utilitarian self given over to the life of production (one's secondary self, according to Bataille), and on the other hand one's more primary desires to expend rather than absorb, to destroy what has been produced, to burn and smash and rape and draw the blood of others. It is completely unsurprising that Bataille was as disliked by the Popular Front Communists of the 1930s as he was by the Nazis; nevertheless, insofar as he identifies the bourgeoisie and its habits of rational accumulation as the enemy, it seems completely appropriate to award him the label "Gothic Marxist," as Margaret Cohen and other scholars of the mid-twentieth century have chosen to do. It is certainly pleasant to consider that label when examining the 1960s works of Julio Cortázar, who, along with Severo Sarduy and Alejandra Pizarnik, took very seriously the role of violence and transgression in eroticism, a theme they associated with Bataille's reading of the Marquis de Sade.

THE SATANIC DAUGHTER AND THE RELUCTANT SODOMIZER: PIZARNIK AND CORTÁZAR

Cortázar, over twenty years older than my other Latin American in this chapter and with a ten years' head start on her in Paris, certainly knew Georges Bataille's work before Pizarnik did. Yet the writer to have the most passionate and the least "fashionable" relationship to an erotics of transgressive violence is the younger, Alejandra Pizarnik. And, before Cortázar himself gives in to an aesthetic of fashionable sadism, she engages him in a complex and interesting dialogue about violence and madness.

I make no pretence of analyzing Pizarnik's poetry of the 1960s, and would not care to say whether or not it engages in a dialogue with the poetics of the French avant-garde. But it is extremely clear that in her nonfiction *prose* Pizarnik is doing exactly that—and she finds a way to include Cortázar in that avant-garde. Her essay rereading André Breton's *Nadja* is a shrewd and impassioned quasi-feminist critique of the book in which Pizarnik accepts the intellectual landscape of Surrealism, the search for transcendence through bodies and enigmatic souls of women, the significant chance that occurs through dream and random walks through cities. She quotes liberally from Breton's hallucinatory prose and seems at first to have no complaint with the way in which Breton's women all seem to blur into each other. However, she wryly notes that the model for his eroticism is, literally, a model, a mannequin adjusting a garter in a window, her head and eyes averted—for her, one of the many proofs that Breton is not really up to the challenge that wild women such as Nadja represent. Just as Bataille's excremental erotics were too strong for Breton, so too are the forces Nadja represents, even though it is Breton himself who describes them: Pizarnik makes it clear that Breton's dream of a naked woman in the forest, whom he ought to have pursued but did not, is a sign for the gestures *towards* transgression that Breton would make without actually transgressing. This is the first instance in which Pizarnik will play a role that Klossowski since 1933 emphasized in Sade's novels as the Satanic daughter: in the climax of Sade's *Philosophy in the Boudoir* a father figure and daughter conspire to rape and humiliate the mother.[8] Pizarnik reads the literary tradition and finds Breton not to be sadistic enough, and would like to goad him into much more destructive behavior than in *Nadja* he was willing to go.

Bataille would be a sufficiently ruthless father figure[9]; however, to collude with him Pizarnik must find a mother to kill, and also find a sufficiently savage female figure with which to identify. Pizarnik wrote a classic essay/prose poem in 1965, "Acerca de la condesa sangrienta (The Bloody Countess)," a review of a book on the life of Erzsebeth Bathory, "The Bloody Countess," the seventeenth-century Transylvanian aristocrat whose crimes were first mentioned in passing by Bataille (in *The Tears of Eros*, 1959). Pizarnik's text is a book review of the Surrealist collagist and poet Valentine Penrose's *The Bloody Countess* (1962). Through the figure of the Bloody Countess, Cortázar and Pizarnik will implicitly engage in a debate over the worth of sadism—and its far less fashionable half-sister perversion, masochism.

Most readers would agree that Pizarnik outdoes her source, Penrose's 1962 biography, which is a diffuse narrative that seems just as interested in heraldry, dynastic politics, and astrology as it is in the Countess Bathory's mind. Not so Pizarnik, who understands that our interest in the Countess is double. On the one hand, she must be seen as a test case in the Surrealist theory of convulsive beauty, the power of the limit experience to redefine what beauty is: the Countess and her behavior seen from the outside, so to speak. And on the other, reflections on the Countess must also pursue what it felt like to be her, to choose to torture young peasant virgins and bathe in their blood ostensibly out of a conviction that this would preserve one's beauty and youth: the Countess seen from within, seeing with the Countess. Here Pizarnik refuses to follow Penrose's lead, for Penrose's mass of circumstantial and historical detail detracts from the psychological issue.[10] Showing herself to be more philosophically inclined than Penrose, Pizarnik prefaces the entire essay and each of its eleven very brief chapters with an epigraph from the canon of Surrealism or Existentialism: Sartre, Artaud, Baudelaire, Paz on Sade, and finally Sade himself. Pizarnik runs through some traditional aesthetic categories as she sets up scenes to horrify her readers:

> Except for some baroque interferences, [...] the Countess adhered to a monotonously classic style of torture [...]
>
> Several tall, beautiful, strong girls were selected—their ages had to be between 12 and 18—and dragged into the torture chamber where, dressed in white upon her throne, the countess [Erszebet Bathori] awaited them. After binding their hands, the servants would whip the girls until the skin of

their bodies ripped and they became a mass of *swollen wounds*; then the servants would burn them with red-hot pokers; cut their fingers with scissors or shears; pierce their wounds; stab them with daggers [. . . .] The blood spurted like fountains and the white dress of the nocturnal lady would turn red. So red, that she would have to go up to her room and change (what would she think about during this brief intermission?). The walls and the ceiling of the chamber would also turn red [. . . .]

During her erotic seizures she would hurl blasphemous insults at her victims. Blasphemous insults and cries like the baying of a she-wolf were her means of expression as she stalked, in a passion, the gloomy rooms [. . .]

Her last words, before letting herself fall into a final faint, would be: "More, ever more, harder, harder!" (101–3, 378–9; italics in the original Spanish are direct translations from Penrose)

The accoutrements of the Gothic, with some Baroque interferences, all based on a "monotonously classic" style: Pizarnik summarizes concisely the aesthetic syntax of Sadeian fiction, outdoing Penrose in what she claims Penrose has already done successfully, that is, treating the Countess's behavior aesthetically. Pizarnik hardly ever quotes Penrose directly: this passage is typical in that Pizarnik is more likely to quote the Countess's direct quotations in the text than any turns of Penrose's phrases. In short, Pizarnik disaffiliates from Penrose in the way the Satanic daughter collaborates with the father against the mother.

Pizarnik does not merely repeat the Sadeian (Bataillean) project. True, the last paragraph of the essay's two last paragraphs ends on the theme of the Bataillean, the philosophical Sade:

She was never afraid, never trembled. And no compassion, no sympathy may be felt for her. Only a certain astonishment at the enormity of the horror, a fascination with the white dress that turns red, with the idea of total laceration, with the imagination of a silence starred with cries in which everything reflects an unacceptable beauty.

Like Sade in his writings, and Gilles de Rais in his crimes, the Countess Bathory reached beyond all limits the uttermost pit of unfettered passions. She is yet another proof that the absolute freedom of the human creature is horrible. (112–13; 391)

Pizarnik seems to be arguing that the reason to study the Bloody Countess is to judge the relationship between passion and absolute liberty. However, by positing in her introduction a second goal unfulfilled by Penrose, the examination of the Countess from within, Pizarnik encourages us to defer judgment as we learn empathy for the devil. Indeed, perhaps the real purpose of the essay is not in the ultimate but in the penultimate paragraph, namely, to feel, to feel "astonishment" and "fascination" in the presence of "unacceptable beauty." To convey this feeling is difficult insofar as "no compassion, no sympathy or admiration must be felt for her." This turns out, however, to be perfectly appropriate to the task: the Sadist is himself (or herself) a creature who does not believe in compassion or sympathy.

The Countess is most expressing herself when she is inexpressive. This inexpressiveness is multiple. The essay begins by arguing that howls and shrieks should be considered under the category of a variation on silence. In any case, in the earlier, long quotation with which I began, the howling and baying of a she-wolf in which the Countess engages during her erotic seizures is not her most complete or typical position. Rather, Pizarnik emphasizes the Bloody Countess's silence, either the trancelike state which she achieves while the blood of her victims drains onto her and onto her white dress from the lethal cage above her, or her melancholy in the face of the mirror. In my first quotation, the sentence in parentheses, "(what would she think about during this brief intermission?(*¿en qué pensaría durante esta breve interrupción?*))," is typical: it keeps our attention focused on the Countess, even as she "goes offstage," so to speak, not just on what she looks like but what she is thinking. Such asides, along with the strategic use of the first person elsewhere in the essay, positions Pizarnik as the mirror of the Countess, imitating the movements of her thought without volition but also without criticism.[11] Pizarnik, then, perfects a prose style that performs an ambivalent identification with the Countess. Withdrawing overt empathy with the Countess's victims, Pizarnik never descends into ghoulish enthusiasm for the Countess's crimes, but rather replicates the Countess's own trancelike distance from the events she brings about, which may or may not produce the supreme pleasure for Pizarnik the narrator as it did for the enigmatic Countess herself.

Of course, the ethical problem never goes away, but now it is refocused in an almost Foucaultian direction towards the negotiation between the self and itself, not the ethics of the other. Much like the Surrealists themselves facing earlier moments of "compulsive beauty,"[12] Pizarnik leaves ambiguous the status of the Countess's behavior: does it constitute the limit case of a doctrine of absolute liberty on an ethical level, as Sade is supposed to do for the Klossowski-Bataille-Lacan reading of his work, or is the Countess herself compelled by these actions, with little true interior/psychological liberty?

"The Bloody Countess," like the essay on *Nadja*, is a work of affiliation to the Surrealists: as a review of a book by one of the women associated with the Surrealist movement, Valentine Penrose, the essay should be read as an attempt to find and elevate a female equivalent of Sadeian, Bataillesque elements. Pizarnik manages simultaneously to remain the conspiratorial daughter of the sadistic literary father Bataille while complicating her position vis-a-vis the mother. And both the diffuse Penrose and the timid Breton must be rejected in order to maintain herself and Bataille in the Satanic, incestuous pose together.

Pizarnik takes on a different Surrealist father in an essay in 1966: Cortázar himself. She wrote a review of his short story collection *All Fires the Fire*, really only a commentary on the story "The Other Heaven." As is well known, Cortázar himself affiliates to the Surrealist tradition in this story: an adolescent in Buenos Aires in the 1920s finds that he can wander through the Pasajes Güemes and end up in the Passage des Panoramas of 1868 Paris, the Paris of available whores and a terrifying strangler and "the South American," the reclusive eccentric poet Lautréamont; these same covered arcades or passages were eulogized by Breton in *Nadja* and especially Aragon in *Le Paysan de Paris*.[13] In "The Other Heaven," the Franco-Prussian War happens to the Passage des Panoramas, World War II happens to the Pasaje Güemes, and business and family eventually drag the narrator away from his "secret homeland." The moment of the narrator's cowardice, as he himself underscores heavily ("I think that I messed up, that I was on the brink of an act that could have saved me" (146; my translation)), comes when he should strike up a conversation with "el sudamericano," helping him to join the group, but is afraid to and declines. Pizarnik reads this moment as the narrator's chance to accept the poet, however dangerous, within himself, and his failure to do so as a mark of the victory of the bourgeoisie: "But perhaps it is useful to pose again the never resolved conflict: the stock market trader manages to exempt himself from the most fearsome confrontations with madness and death; nevertheless, he understands that with this he let pass the occasion of saving himself from he knows not what" (409, my translation). So in her Cortázar essay, as she did with Breton, Pizarnik fixes upon a moment when a father figure tells the story of how he was not up to the task of living to the extremity of madness, ecstasy, and death.

There's no reason to believe that Pizarnik's voice was any more important than any other in the chorus of fashionable sadists of the era, and it is certain that Cortázar refers to the works of Bataille with more and more respect over the 1960s. Notoriously, Severo Sarduy in *Written on a Body* in 1969 points out that a series of photographs of tortured Chinamen in Cortázar's *Hopscotch* is taken from Bataille's *The Tears of Eros*.[14] In his second non-fiction collection, *Ultimo round* (1969), Bataille's fiction is also used as one of the touchstones for erotic writing in "/que sepa abrir la puerta a jugar," an important essay from *Ultimo round* worrying the issue of how to write erotically in Spanish, a problem that Cortázar says has been solved in English and in French by Henry Miller, Genet, and Bataille, all quite fashionable writers. As to specifically sadistic eroticism, Cortázar is virtually bragging about it in the book-long interview he granted to Evelyn Picón Garfield in 1973 after the publication of *Libro de Manuel* (A Manual for Manuel): "my personal eroticism is by no means inoffensive. It evidently contains elements of aggression which, at least on the literary plain, are fulfilled in a very explicit and frank way. It would seem to me to be hypocritical to disguise them in literature if they respond to deep drives of my own person" (102; my translation). Although there are other rough sex scenes in *A Manual for Manuel* and they all have different functions, the most controversial of them, and the one most necessary for the book's symbolism, is the final scene between the protagonist Andrés and his bourgeois girlfriend Francine.

Francine, like her counterpart Pola París in the dispensable chapters of *Hopscotch*, stands for sophistication and France, and she and Andrés have developed many lovemaking rituals around their rough sex; in an earlier scene she calls him "the smiling torturer" in one of their "ritual dialogues," and Andrés responds, "Oh yes: Francine Sacher-Masoch. Andrés de Sade" (139; 140). Their sex that night establishes that she is in control during their lovemaking, and that she refuses to have anal sex with Andrés. Hence, in the critical moments of the novel's plot when Andrés must decide whether or not he is to join the rest of the radicals in their kidnapping of a Latin American military man, Andrés decides to take Francine against her will and from behind. The language is cold and clinical, as befits the sadistic tradition; both of them lose their subjectivity, as Bataille's Sade would have wanted; the hotel room he has rented has windows that open on to a cemetery, so the symbolism of a dying bourgeoisie and of an ecstasy that both approximates and defies death is reinforced; and the breaking of Francine's taboos against sodomy ("that metal voice through which century-old interdictions return [...], the pouts from the no from mama and catechism and Holy Mother Church piled up into one single no" (152; 151)) is equated with revolutionary liberation when, after the act is over and they have talked about it, Andrés leaves the hotel to join his radical kidnapper friends.

Since it was published in 1973 after Alejandra Pizarnik committed suicide, we will never know what she would have thought about such a scene. We might be tempted to say, however, that Andrés's act includes some of the compromises that might have disappointed Alejandra yet again. Real sadists intend to demonstrate that sex is not about communication and that nature is cruel, whereas Andrés claims to be showing Francine that there are pleasures she has not yet experienced: "something new was being born in her weeping, the discovery that it was not unbearable, that I was not raping her even though she refused and begged, that my pleasure had a limit there where hers began" (314; 313). Hints of such ways to read the sadist's sexual act can be found in, say, Lacan's approach to Sade, but not Bataille's. In the end a Cortázar hero is a quester and a humanist; and while Anglo-American feminism makes such nonconsensual scenes currently extremely unfashionable, it is worth emphasizing that a more uncompromising Satanic daughter such as Alejandra might well find such a scene wanting from a completely different angle.

MASOCHISTIC POETICS

The only problem with Cortázar's self-definition as a writer in the Sadeian tradition, then, is that he isn't one. Or at any rate, I will argue that an aesthetics which derives its psychodynamics from that far more embarrassing perversion of masochism does a much better job of accounting for the features of Cortázar's oeuvre. Gilles Deleuze's "Coldness and Cruelty," a 1967 essay on the writings of Count Sacher-Masoch, tries to elevate Masoch's writings, if not into that of a philosophical equal to the writings of Sade, then at least a thoroughly distinct one which relates literary form to erotic attraction.

Deleuze emphasizes repeatedly the fundamental dissymmetry between a Sadeian erotics and a Masochian erotics. Sade takes pleasure in illustrating or demonstrating the abstract law of nature. Conversely, the heroes of Masoch's many novels may believe in a cold Nature, but it is a maternal coldness and has none of the bleakness of the father; they seek a woman who can embody this coldness, but these women must always be reluctant to take up this role; the women need to be persuaded to do so, and frequently claim to take no pleasure in it. Once they have been persuaded to do so, they sign a contract, giving them utter power over the masochist: Deleuze makes much of the difference between the implicit politics of the Sadeian aristocrat—anarchistic, arbitrary—and that of the Masochistic couple—contractual, feminist—. In even the most liberal realms of nineteenth century Europe, this privileging of the woman as mother or queen is understood as an exception and unstable: the father is banished from the masochistic scenario through these private contracts, and, Deleuze argues, the purpose of the whipping scenes is to beat the bad Father out of the son in order that the New Man may be born in him.[15] Nevertheless, hovering around the edges of the Masochian narratives is a male figure (in *Venus in Furs* he is called "the

Greek") who often goads the reluctant dominatrix into becoming a full-out sadist; this "hallucinatory return of the banished symbolic father" (Deleuze 65) puts an end to the masochistic scenario. Unlike the Sadeian's conviction that he is revealing the world the way it is, then, the Masochian is a sentimental idealist who persuades a reluctant woman to enter into a fictional game-playing, almost certainly temporary space. Sex as a short-term game (hoping for a long-term self-transformation) with agreed-on rules: masochism is an erotic which is also simultaneously a poetics.

The banishing of the father from the masochistic narrative permits Deleuze a greater attention on the cold maternal figure, which, he says, appears in Masoch in three different phases: the pagan, sensual woman who is a prime candidate for the masochistic contract; the cold dominatrix herself, reluctantly persuaded to enforce her contract ever more strictly; and the woman gone too far and become a sadist. (Deleuze correlates them with the uterine mother; the oral mother; and the Oedipal mother, who disappoints her son by returning to her husband and putting an end to the idyllic mother–son dyad.) The contract tries to structure the time and space between the undifferentiated womb/mother for which all interactions are acceptable, and the Oedipal mother to whom access is closed.

It is tempting to try to apply these characterizations to the women of *62*. The Masochian woman is the one, however reluctantly, to play the game; before her is the pagan woman who offers access without game-playing, and after her is the sadistic woman who brings game-playing to an end. In *62*, the pagan woman would be Juan's sex partner in the Viennese hotel, Tell, who is aware that Juan does not love her, but who on the whole does not mind; at the other end, of course, is the Countess Bathory, although her sadism is uncompromisingly non-Oedipal (her husband knows nothing of her activities and her castle is a world only of women). The sadistic woman is at the end, but also, notoriously, at the beginning of the story too: the novel begins with Juan's realization that the tale of Erzsebeth Bathory supposedly undergirds two other characters in the novel, Hélène and Frau Marta. Whereas Masoch saw the space of the contract as the civilizing of the pagan woman before she falls inevitably into the clutches of a man ("the Greek") more decadent than herself, here it is the urban and sophisticated Tell who watches, with Juan, the goings on in a Viennese hotel room, which themselves last only as long as we are unaware that they inevitably lead to the bloody Transylvanian castle.[16]

But what exactly is the game in Cortázar's novel? Like the supposedly sadistic scene in *A Manual for Manuel*, the masochistic scenario is supposed to thrill the one on the bottom, and already we can see that the Countess Bathory, as Penrose and Pizarnik present her, is an unlikely candidate as the dominatrix for a true masochist. It will be useful to take a look at her in action, then, in Cortázar's novel. One of the many threads of *62* involves the protagonist Juan and his sex partner Tell deciding, somewhat on a whim, that there is something fishy about one of the other guests in the hotel in Vienna where they are staying. This guest, Frau Marta, is showing too much interest in a young English girl. Frau Marta's hands in particular seem uncanny to Juan, who is sensitive to such things: he may be having regular sex with Tell, but he is unrequitedly in love with a cold super-rational anesthesiologist in Paris, Hélène. (The unhappiness of unrequited love is a repeated theme in the novel: Juan is in unrequited love with Hélène; in turn, a book illustrator Nicole is in unrequited love with him; and a sculptor Marrast is in unrequited love with Nicole.) Juan and Tell admit that their suspicions of Frau Marta are at first a game to allay their boredom; but one night they hear and see in the corridor appropriately spooky noises and go to investigate. As Juan and Tell watch, transfixed, in the hotel room they have entered without being noticed, Frau Marta hovers over the English girl:

> But they'd come too late, they knew it now [...] It was better to stay glued to the door in order to watch. ... Besides, the English girl seemed so placid and happy, watching the advance step of Frau Marta, who was outlined behind the dark lantern like a dry and angular old tree, one hand in the air near the one that held the light ... and Erszebet Bathori's light had also vaguely lighted up the black hair of the countess as she approached the bed where a servant girl tied hand and foot was struggling with a gag in her mouth, so different from the English girl, although perhaps after the first visit they all waited for the countess like that. All of them were probably sitting up in bed, no longer with bonds or gags, joined by another deeper bond to the visitor who put the dark lantern on the night table so that it would keep on lighting up the profile of the girl who hadn't moved, the throat which Frau Marta's hand slowly uncovered by pulling down the lace collar of the pink pajamas. (188; 174–5)

Juan and Tell see that the English girl has already succumbed to the vampiric love of Frau Marta, and Juan compares the scene to one he imagines between the bloody countess and her victims. In order to modify her to make her an interesting figure for the masochist, however, Cortázar has had to turn the Bloody Countess into a seductive, not sadistic, vampire. Unlike, say, Pizarnik, Cortázar imagines the victims to inhabit the same psychic space as the countess, to be in a reciprocal relationship with her—even to be in a bed; Pizarnik never imagines a bed—; in short, he updates histori-cally the cruel and somber seventeenth century of the Countess to the late nineteenth century of the Dracula novels and films, also the era of the novels of Masoch.[17]

Frau Marta, then, unlike Erzsebeth Báthory herself, is the sort of Bloody Countess a masochist could wait for in bed, writhing erotically.[18] According to Deleuze, the tense and excited wait for the dominatrix is a characteristic not just of the erotics of masochism but also its poetics. Indeed, for Deleuze masochism is an essentially theatrical mode, and its fetishes and its props (the furs, the whips) are part of an inherently literary strategy characterized by the heightening of anxiety ("It is no exaggeration to say that Masoch was the first novelist to make use of suspense in romantic fiction" (33)). Due to the constant crosscutting between so many plot threads and cities in this novel, the deflowering of the English girl takes almost a hundred pages to complete, and its almost infinite slowness wrings emotions out of Juan and Tell, who feel fascinated, forced to watch. A child is being vampirized, and I am probably looking on.

The role of the observer, not theorized as such by Deleuze, in this Cortázar novel takes on many of the characteristics of the masochistic contract. Of course it is the victims in the bloody countess's castle, and the English girl, who actually suffer under their cold cruel mistresses; nonetheless, Juan and Tell are just as transfixed as the girls are, just as held in suspense. Cortázar is familiar with the mechanics of Gothic and neo-Gothic reader-relations, the way the reader begs the author to manipulate him, dominate him, transfix him, and he has theorized this elsewhere in his oeuvre, always claiming that he, the author, was the first one to have felt that shudder of loss of control facing an inappealable, slowly dominating other. The author of the short stories refuses to take the position of the sadist facing the masochistic reader, but instead serves as a point of identification with other masochistic readers. If this is an indication of a sort of authorial bad faith, a disavowal that it is he who is taking over the house and he who is making the protagonist vomit bunny rabbits, to give examples from Cortázar's earliest published fiction, I repeat that some sort of bad faith or disavowal is characteristic of masochistic erotics, in which the masochist in the moment of painful ecstasy forgets that it is he who has written up the contract and handed her the pen. We will return to the theme of bad faith presently.

We are still seeking the woman who is worthy of a masochistic contract. Frau Marta, improbably oblivious of Juan and Tell's presence, will not fully do: she must be complemented by one of the novel's realistic characters. In a brief yet very suggestive article, Julie Jones remarked on the great similarities between the world of the characters of *62*, whose lives are free of material cares and are devoted to art and love, and the world of the lyric pastoral, despite the novel's urban settings; and the great thematic content of the lyric pastoral, Jones reminds us, is not just love but unrequited love.[19] As we have seen from this chapter's first quotation, between the painter Marrast and the illustrator Nicole (who does not love him; nor does she love the Argentine writer Calac, who also may love her; she loves Juan, who does not love her), unrequited lovers are pop-psychology's masochists, maneuvering themselves into a position in which the beloved disdains them. Cortázar is certainly interested in this position here; Cortázar's fullest attention is fixed on love's *desencuentros*, the failed encounters when bodies meet but not hearts, or minds or souls. Yet Nicole, in her absence and her passivity, is hardly the sort of woman to fuel a Masochian masochist's imagination and passion, and indeed Juan does not love her and sees her, at the end of the novel, in the dreamscape City's version of Paris's Canal St. Martin, as no more than the next victim of the vampiric Frau Marta, "the second figure on the barge, the tiny figure of Frau Marta coming up behind Nicole" (286; 267), Frau Marta rescuing her from suicide as she makes her the next woman in a sequence that began with the English girl.

No, clearly Nicole hasn't got the temperament to excite a masochist. But ah, Hélène: "Out of all that [idiot games, life] Hélène remained, as always, her cold shadow in the deepest part of the doorway [...] Her cold distant inevitable hostile shadow" (32; 31). Her coldness and her distance are symbolized in her profession as anesthesiologist. When we finally meet her in person, it is on a harrowing—yet for the unfashionable masochist, a secretly exciting—occasion: Hélène has accidentally killed a young patient who somehow reminded her of Juan. This is the mother–son dyad in *62*, and psychoanalytic critics of Cortázar's work, such as René Prieto, have shown how it recurs differently throughout Cortázar's writing. Hélène is certainly reluctant to enter into a relationship with Juan, and is resistant to game-playing with Juan, or with the other *tártaros* for that matter (she does not join in the collective dreams, or in racing *mi paredro*'s pet snail Osvaldo), so it is interesting to see the two games the novel does impose upon her: she will receive a doll from Juan via Tell; and Hélène, as often as or more often than Juan, will find herself traveling unhappily through the City, a heavy package in her arms. Hélène's burden, then, is not an interpretation of Juan's, but an objectively imposed aspect of her psyche and condition. It may need to be interpreted, by Hélène herself or by the impersonal mechanics of the City, but the burden itself is prior to interpretation.

We meet Hélène from the perspective of the (ostensibly) omniscient narrator first as she leaves the clinic after she has been informed of the young man's death. Distraught and with her other friends either in Vienna or in London, Hélène takes home a peripheral member of the group, the teenager Celia, who has just fought with her parents and needs a place to stay; somewhat drunk, Hélène molests Celia in bed. It is this repeated motif of an older woman deflowering a maiden in bed that makes Juan, in the novel's first scene, associate Hélène with the Bloody Countess. It is this scene which is most fully crosscut with the scene of Juan and Tell transfixed, staring at Frau Marta and the English girl in the hotel room in Vienna.

Foregrounding the presence of the voyeurs watching the vampire scene creates an interesting dissymmetry between Deleuze's and Cortázar's masochistic poetics. As we have seen, Deleuze has taken great pains to emphasize the mother-son dyad in which the father has been excluded, to return at the end to put an end to the masochistic game. The reader-voyeur, already doubled into both Juan and Tell, forms a triangle with Frau Marta and the English girl. Can we be as sure here as Deleuze was while reading the novels of Masoch that the frozen, suspended identification of the reader flows entirely into the victim's position? Might a Freudian language of sado-masochism more properly apply to this scenario after all, an identification unstably moving between vampire and victim?

Clearly this third voyeur's position is not Deleuze's return of the father. If Juan and Tell have any effect on what they watch, it would be not to stop the action but to shift the genre of the action. While Tell remains in the thrall of the neo-Gothic suspense, Juan begins to intuit that the scene has some relationship to Hélène and the Bloody Countess, but once again he cannot articulate it. Then, as they watch more closely, instead of biting her again Frau Marta undresses the girl, pauses, and then puts the pajamas back on her:

> Yes, love [Tell], we'll stay on guard, of course. The throat is still there, naked with its two small marks, but you'll see that she's not going to bite her, that everything's been overturned, that things have taken place in a diferent way, maybe because of us, because of something I was on the point of under-standing and didn't understand. (194–5; 181)

Juan's ironic, almost sarcastic commentary threatens to a certain extent the neo-Gothic reader-relations pact, not as a father figure but as a 1960s metafictionalist would. The events shift genre rapidly once again, and Frau Marta and the English girl lead the voyeurs through a secret passage and into the novel's nightmare landscape of the City, where Juan loses them all and finds himself pursuing Hélène once again.

Hélène is also in the City at this point in the novel, moving through its streets with a heavy package, after Celia has fought her advances, then given in but without pleasure, dressed recklessly, and left. The beginning of this lesbian rape scene, crosscut with our voyeurs watching Frau Marta and the English girl, eventually accrues its own voyeur. Juan had always accused Hélène of being too proud of her own order to share it with anyone, and now, she thinks, he would be interested to see that she is sharing the room with Celia: "Ironically, she thought about Juan […] Poor Juan, so far away and bitter, all that might have been for him in some way if he had been at the foot of the bed in the darkness" (183–4; 170). But this ghostly presence of Juan, doubled in the memory of the dead boy at the clinic, becomes part of Hélène's arousal at the sleeping Celia:

> Don't wake up, don't say anything. Let me go on listening to the coming and going of the little waves on your beach, let me think that if Juan were looking at me, something that would no longer be myself would emerge from a false endless absence to stretch out its arms to him. (191; 178)

Some Other Hélène stretches out her arms to the Juan fantasized to be at the foot of the bed, at the same time that the text's real Hélène stretches out her hands to brush against Celia's throat to begin the rape. This scene, in obvious parallel with the Frau Marta-English girl scene, escapes from Deleuze's mother–son dyad into a fascinating parody of the scene which Lacanians have toyed with positing as the source of all fantasy, the primal scene in which the child spies on (or fantasizes spying on) his parents having sex.[20] In this novel, however, the primal scene is not of a father figure seeming to be forcing a mother in bed but of an older woman molesting a younger one, with the infantilized or paralyzed man looking on, as if Freud had not analyzed the Wolf Man but Marcel the narrator of Proust's *Combray*. Having banished the father from the primal scene, the masochist-fantasist can split the scenario, making the victim desire the vampire in the neo-Gothic scene, and making the cold, cruel mistress sympathetic even in the act of raping the innocent girl in the realistic scene.

And yet, it could be argued, something like a father figure has not been banished from the (lesbian, masochist, primal) scene entirely. The night Hélène took Celia in she also received a doll, sent from Tell in Vienna. The doll was a gift from Juan; Tell, in one of her few moments of dissatisfaction with her (pagan, non-dominatrix) status, decides with annoyance that Juan really wished he could send it to Hélène instead, and so she passes it on to her. Tell is aware, but neglects to tell Hélène, that the maker of this doll, a M. Ochs whom Juan and Polanco have met, conceals disgusting surprises in the dolls' insides. As Celia is leaving Hélène's apartment in a reckless anger after the rape, she knocks the doll over, breaking it and revealing the (never named) horror within it. Celia's enthusiasm over the doll when she first sees it in Hélène's apartment makes the reader think that the author has given Celia to Hélène just as Juan via Tell has given a doll to Hélène, and in some sense this is true. But the doll watches Hélène and Celia in bed, and Hélène thinks, addressing Juan, " 'You should have come yourself instead of sending me the doll' "(184; 170), a sign that above all the doll is a representative of Juan. The voyeur's position, miniaturized into a doll, is backed up by an ambiguously potent male figure: M. Ochs has been briefly jailed because of these dolls and no longer makes them, but not only is this doll a successfully horrid one, it is a clear affiliation to the male Surrealist tradition, which Cortázar makes explicit in his *Ultimo round* essay "The Broken Doll."[21] However, rather than being the masochist's father who upsets the mother-son dyad and inaugurates an oedipal triangle, M. Ochs shames the mother by befouling the virgin whom she has just deflowered, and makes clear that the infantilized Juan's voyeurism was also an act of aggression. In a suitably minor key, M. Ochs and the doll are the Sadeian-Surrealist conspiracy of the father and daughter against the mother, an attack sanctified by the fashionable literary tradition against the rival primal scene of two women in bed and an infantilized male voyeur.

Cortázar's version of Deleuzian masochistic poetics splits the scene into two, and removes himself into the voyeur's position, supported by either a woman (Tell) or a weak father figure (M. Ochs). In each case the writer-masochist-voyeur acknowledges that he is affecting the scenes he claims his protagonist is just passively experiencing. In the first case, Juan and Tell invent the Vienna scene out of their boredom, and Juan's presence first makes it lesbian instead of vampiric, and then turns it into a scenario from the City. In the second case, Hélène decides that working through her ambivalence towards Juan is what has brought her to the vulnerable moment of pouncing on Celia, but Juan and the doll eventually ruin a scene that Juan eagerly, expectantly watched. Acknowledging his presence in these masochistic scenes is rather responsible of Cortázar. The novel will not continue to display such responsibility in dealing with Hélène, the object of its masochistic attention.

DISAVOWING MASOCHISM

So the novel *62* comes close to affirming the pleasure of yielding to and suffering at the hands of a cold, cruel mistress, despite the consensus of a fashionable avant-garde that sex is the apathetic demonstration of a law of Nature, and the proof of a transgressive aristocratic power over a woman's body, and a collusion between father and daughter against the mother. The novel comes close to affirming masochism, but in the end does not do so. It is not just a fear of seeming to be unfashionable that prevents Cortázar from affirming the self-transforming delight of playing the masochistic game.

It can't hurt to remind ourselves of the obvious: Hélène never signs the masochistic contract with our protagonist Juan. She never agrees to torture him on his own terms. Perhaps less obvious is that Hélène, who is supposed to be the real instantiation of the cold vampire between neo-gothic kitsch and historical archetype, is from the beginning almost as much a fictional construction, a subjective construction, as are the other two. The image of Hélène appears for Juan in the novel's first long section as part of the *coágulo en fuga*, the receding illumination which Juan experiences in the Polidor restaurant. He painstakingly inventories its various elements: the phrase "I want a bloody castle," a book alluding to Chateaubriand, the blood-red sunset on the streetcorner of the Rue de Vaugirard that put him in mind of the Countess a little while before entering, and so on. Yet Juan acknowledges that Hélène's position in this illumination is inappropriate: "cold distant inevitable hostile. What were you doing here? You had no right to be among the cards of that sequence, it wasn't you who was waiting for me on the corner of the Rue de Vaugirard" (33; 31). Hélène is part of the receding illumination only because he is always thinking of her (the phrase "and Hélène, of course" echoes frequently in his thoughts in this first section). It is not only that he cannot decide whether she sums up the other images ("he had felt the presence of the countess, remembered Frau Marta and the house of the basilisk, put all that together in the image of Hélene" (28; 27)), or whether it is the other way around ("There you were, Hélène, everything was still a small pin with the image of a basilisk, a square with streetcars, the countess, who in some way summed it all up" (27; 25); he concludes in the end that "in the last redoubt of my honesty she and the countess and Frau Marta were joined together in one same abominable image" (44; 41). More than that: Juan worries that Hélène might not exist at all, a thought that finds expression when reflecting upon the effect of telling his story to his friends at the Cluny restaurant:

> And you, Hélène, will you look at me that way, too? [...] I'll see Tell, Juan (because it might happen that I, too, will see Juan at that moment in the zone), I'll see Feuille Morte, Harold Haroldson, and I'll see the countess or Frau Marta if I'm in the zone or in the City, I'll see them leaving and look- ing at me. But you, Hélène, will you be leaving with them, too, or will you come slowly toward me, your nails stained with disdain? Were you in the zone or did I dream you? [...] But you, Hélène, can you have been once more a name that I carry against nothingness, the simulacrum that I invent

with words while Frau Marta and the countess approach and look at me? (22; 20–21)

Note the phrase "because it might happen that I, too, will see Juan at that moment in the zone": in the act of storytelling, Juan not only sees himself from the outside, but, possibly, Julio Cortázar acknowledges that he is outside his fictional universe, looking at them with eyes other than their own. Hélène is a name that Julio Cortázar carries against nothingness, at the same time that her image is a simulacrum that Juan invents to put into play with Frau Marta and, of course, the Bloody Countess. The real woman, the real Hélène cannot be reached. She may seem to be realer than her historical archetype or the rather kitschy version Juan and Tell will pursue in the Viennese hotel, but her realness is an effect of a secondary elaboration, a solidification over the course of the novel, less surprising perhaps than that of the other noncharacter *mi paredro*, but one that takes some of Hélène's behavior out of her own hands and into the hands of the desiring author or his stand-in who seeks a satisfactory illumination, however receding. But then, in this section we are warned: Julio/Juan tells us at the end of the first section that the conflict between the Masochian narrator and the woman who refuses to be the Masochian dominatrix will be a conflict between interpretations:

> I'll think to the very end that I might have been wrong, that the evidence they stain you with against me, which vomits me up every morning into a life I no longer want, is born perhaps from the fact that I didn't know how to find the real order and that you yourself never understood what was going on, Hélène, that you didn't understand the death of the boy in the hospital, Monsieur Ochs's doll, Celia's weeping, that you simply played your cards badly, you invented a great game that prophesied you into what you weren't, which I still persist in wanting you not to be. (41; 38)

Given this obstinacy of Juan's, we should hardly be surprised that some of Hélène's actions seem to be the inventions of an Unamunoesque author who makes the character do things that are outside her nature—and that *she*, not the author's stand-in, should be the one accused of inventing games.

Many of the novel's declarations of good faith (here, an acknowledgment that the Hélène that we are reading is his invention) trickle away into a practice that entails an act of bad faith (here, a claim that Hélène is the one inventing games contrary to her nature). All readers of *62* are aware of the way that the semi-character of *mi paredro* is introduced as a linguistic crutch, a way to shift the attribution of a phrase or opinion or event away from oneself, "not so much to avoid responsibilities but as if underneath it all my paredros was a kind of modesty" (29; 27). The argument that beneath ethics (*responsabilidades*) lies a sexual ethic (modesty, *pudor*) might reassure us at the beginning but by the end of the novel such linkages are more problematic. That this linguistic crutch solidifies into a character over the course of the novel suggests that avoiding responsibility and displaying a sexually tinged shame are not just a characteristic of these friends' conversation but part of the texture of the novel's strategies of characterization. Seen from this angle, the Marrast subplot feels designed to let Cortázar express the unfashionable emotions that spring from unrequited love which our more sophisticated and melancholy protagonist Juan is never seen to feel. This is clearest in the seven-page misogynist diatribe the drunken Marrast writes to Tell after Nicole has slept with the English musician Austin: "If I went back to the hotel now I'd kill her [...]/ Tell all of you women/whores all with birds whores and I am a man Tell" (213; 198).

But naturally we are most concerned with disavowal and authorial intrusion in charting the interaction between Juan and Hélène. M. Ochs's little surprise did not break off Hélène's relationship with Juan. They conclude, together, that the death of the young man at the clinic and the ugly surprise in the doll constituted a guilt without intention, a sort of objective *culpa*, a guilt, blame, or reproach cast by no one in particular:

"The blame, like a ..."

"Yes, I felt something like that, too. As if the blame had traveled in that doll on its own account. But then, Hélène ... "

"Then," Hélène said, looking straight at him, "it would seem that underneath it all neither you nor I had anything to do with it. But that's not how it is, and we know it. It happened to us, not to other people. The blame you talk about, that blame that goes along on its own ..."

Juan watched her cover her face with her hands and wondered, with a kind of panic and a horrible useless tenderness whether or not Hélène was going to cry, whether someone was about to witness that impossibility, Hélène's tears. But her face was the same as ever when she lowered her hands. (248; 232)

The phrase "the *culpa* that goes along on its own" allows the connection to be made with the other game that the novel has imposed upon Hélène, her participation with the other *tártaros* in the City, her fatigued wandering with a heavy package in her arms: "That was the package then," thinks Juan (248; 232), When Hélène finally explains to Juan about the boy in the clinic she returns to the language of generalized responsibility: "I killed you, Juan [...]. It wasn't you, of course, and I didn't kill him either, it was the same as this doll [...], a kind of total responsibility" (251; 235).

This confession of Hélène's, again leaving Celia specifically out of the story, comes from Hélène, but as if it were an Other Hélène Juan had never heard before: "Where did that voice come from that was so inconceivably the voice of Hélène?" (252; 235). Her weakness, her tears, shock Juan, and remind him that they will never truly encounter each other in a shared script. He reminds himself of his "interminable servitude" (254; 237) and he wants her to remain strong ("I should have tried to avoid it, bringing her back to her courteous distance") and yet at the same time there begins in Juan a different, not at all masochistic pleasure in seeing her downfall ("and at the same time I was giving in to a pleasure for which there were no words" (253; 236)). Hélène specifically offers not her stronger self to Juan, but this possible weaker self, which may or may not exist: " 'Take me if you want. You can see that I'm not promising anything, that I'm still the same. If you think you're stronger, if you imagine you can change me, take me right now.' [...] I offered him my mouth, which was dirty with words, thanking him for making me be still, for turning me back into an obedient object in his arms" (255; 238). Both Hélène and Juan seem to abandon a possible masochistic scenario (Juan has even mentioned the mythological fable of Diana and Actaeon, appropriately enough given the prominence of voyeurism in the novel's primal scene), and in an act of spectacular bad faith the strong woman asks to be turned into an obedient object. The Deleuzian tables are turned and we see that she is asking the Strong Man to beat the Bad Woman out of her so that the New Woman (really, an appallingly old-fashioned woman) can be born.[22]

Not having agreed to satisfy his masochistic desires, Hélène even in her surrender to him is a danger for Juan. Things are the same as they were before they had sex. Worse, Hélène's postcoital laughter shows that the destructive Bloody Countess has been released in her:

> "Please," Juan said, looking for her mouth. "Please, Hélène."
> But Hélène laughed again in the shadows, and Juan leaped back and looked for the light switch. [...] The jab of light speared the end of Hélène's laugh and in her wide-open eyes with dilated pupils Juan saw an expression of primordial evil. (276; 258)

Facing primordial evil or not, he resumes sex with Hélène, first with Hélène on the bottom and then on the top; while on top she tells him all the things he wants to hear ("she told him yes, she would stay with him, he could throw the doll in the garbage, he could free her from the last remains of the smell of death" (277; 259)), and only in the second postcoital moment does she tell him about Celia. She had wondered whether sex with Juan might have rescued her from her predatory lesbianism, equated with this smell of death:

> [. . .] who knows whether or not I was expecting to find you here, too, that this was what you wanted, that something in me wanted, too. Now I know that it wasn't, and then only this was left, telling you the end of it, finishing it clean. I love you in some way, but you also had to know that Celia meant the same as you or whatever tomorrow brings, because I'm not entirely here. Something is still somewhere else, and you know that, too. (280; 261–2)

Juan thinks a simple answer to this: the somewhere else is "In the Blutgasse."

Cortázar is not content to declare that Juan's passion for a lesbian is unrequited, even after he has made her let his stand-in sleep with her to see if he can turn her into a real woman. He is not content to let her say that the darkness in her is metaphysical, to be slaked by neither men nor women ("Celia meant the same as you"). In extraordinarily swift fashion—the sex and postcoital conversations are narrated the next day in flashback as if deliberately to shorten the narrative time between Hélène's crime of not loving Juan and the narrative's punishment of her—Hélène moves from the Parisian train to a train in the City to one of its hotel rooms, where she is murdered by Celia's new boyfriend Austin to avenge Hélène's rape of Celia. Austin, like Celia, is a peripheral member of this group, and it is improbable that he should have access to the City.

The relation between the three female figures of the Masochian woman, the Bloody Countess, Frau Marta, and Hélène, is then a complex disavowal: Cortázar works out frustration and anger in the unrequited love scenario in this novel by having someone—but not any of his favored characters, of course—kill the lesbian who refuses to sign the masochistic contract with his main male protagonist. Casting about to find a moral reason to punish her, Cortázar resorts to a sexually conservative script that is acted out only by an Other Hélène within the more fully drawn woman that we already know. Even though following this script might not have made Juan and Hélène happy either, Hélène renounces it and declares herself incapable of love, which makes her so much easier for the novelist to kill with a clear (if melancholy) conscience.

Alejandra Pizarnik did not delude herself about the moral potential in the Bloody Countess story, as she hews to a sadistic scenario with which she is not afraid to identify. As for any moral potential in the masochistic scenario, much of the political progressiveness that Deleuze saw in it derives from the reversed genders of the power play. In *A Manual for Manuel* and other fictions, Cortázar turned the genders back around to create male sadomasochists that a female masochist can love, hoping in a general way to be obedient to the moral and sentimental project that Masoch sketched out in the fin de siècle, without abandoning the prestige of calling himself a sadist. However, in *62* itself, Cortázar has interpreted a Bloody Countess who presides over a much less stable field of morality, leading to acts of novelistic bad faith in which violent impulses toward (perhaps predatory) lesbians are expressed but also disavowed, even if the male characters who survive the novelistic plotting gain no satisfaction from this outcome. Such is the punishment meted out to those fictional characters who threaten our status, and our self-understandings, as the fashionable perverts.

CODA: CORTÁZAR PROTECTS HIS TEXTS FROM FASHION (DIFFICULTY, HANDWRITING, POSTHUMY)

I hope I have traced, however sketchily, a story in which Freud's stories of sadism and masochism were found wanting in the Rive Gauche of the 1950s and 1960s, although we might wish to steal some of his ideas anyway, and how instead this literary and intellectual subculture came instead to privilege Bataille's reading of Sade as a *poète maudit* of apathetic, taboo-smashing ecstatic sex who displays the reality of Death in the very center of coitus and of bourgeois habitus. I also hope I've shown that Alejandra Pizarnik found this Sade to be strongly attractive, and that she and a long line of French Nietzscheans imposed these philosophical erotics as a sort of lingua franca on bohemian Paris in the day, such that Pizarnik, and the Rive Gauche generally, could goad Cortázar into experimenting with its erotics as a form of political liberation. In his most public works of this 1960s moment, *A Manual for Manuel* and interviews and *Ultimo round*, Cortázar seems almost comfortable abjuring his masochistic ways and glorying in what he thinks are a liberatory sadistic ethics and politics.

It is not just in his novel *62* that Cortázar expresses, through a repeated scene and a repeated tactic, his dissent with this fashionable sadism, without challenging it directly. The scene is lesbian, and the tactic is illegibility. As I hope I have shown, the descriptions of Frau Marta's seduction of the English girl in *62* are played more for masochistic thrills than for sadistic ones: it is supposed to stand in analogically for the novel's other lesbian scene, in which Celia is taken advantage of by Hélène, and the lesbian who would not sign the masochistic contract is punished by a minor character. However, to piece together this sequence, as we have done and as Steven Boldy and other critics have done, is relatively difficult: the novel is constructed out of fragments which violate ordinary space and especially time, hence causality also; and as a result *62* is one of those great unread or under-read novels. If the novel is politically incorrect in its anger at lesbians who won't play the dominatrix game with men, and—in the context of my analysis—if it puts forward a poetics that is more masochistic than sadistic, then relatively few readers will find it legible as such.[23]

A variation on the protective tactic of illegibility, quite common to Cortázar as we have found out since 1984, is to reserve publication until after he is dead, or nearly dead. This turns out to have been a strategy he used in dealing with his powerful yet also so helpless rival, Alejandra Pizarnik.[24] At the very end of his life Cortázar completed the poem collection *Salvo el crepúsculo* (Except for Twilight), which includes an entire suite of poems which he labeled "La noche de las amigas (The night of the girl-friends)." The prefatory section reads like something out of *62*: he had received a beautiful notebook from one of his women friends, "I kept it virgin for a long time," and, when he finally decided to write in it, it became a place for a suite of lesbian poems, "I saw the girlfriends, real and imaginary, dead and alive, meeting in a room with thick air [...] a little *belle époque*, lamps on the floor, hashish smoke, glasses and clothes, mixed up with open books and caressed and abandoned bibelots"; while he was "the voyeur of my own magic lantern" he was also absent, "all so lesbian without being it and being it" (261, translation mine). The whole last section is entitled, "Here Alejandra," and has been used as a poem-hommage in an anthology of Pizarnik's work. It's clearly Pizarnik (Olga Orozco and Silvina Ocampo are mentioned, for instance), and Cortázar generously shows her challenging him as she challenged him more formally in her essay on "The Other Heaven":

> quisieras insultarme sin que duela
> decir cómo estás vivo, cómo
> se puede *estar* cuando no hay nada
> más que la niebla de los cigarrillos
>
> cómo vivís, de qué manera
> abrís los ojos cada día
>
> no puede ser, decís, no puede ser (281)
>
> [you would like to insult me without it hurting
> say how can you live how
> can you *be there* when there is nothing
> but the mist of cigarettes
>
> how are you alive how
> do you open your eyes every day

it can't be, you say, it can't be]
(Translation mine)

Alejandra intransigently speaks for a nihilism associated with Sade and the French Nietzscheans, in a dreamscape that Cortázar tenderly wishes to bring back to the fin de siècle of Masoch's heyday, specifically the bibelots and magic lanterns of the *belle époque* lesbians of Marcel Proust, captured in a yellow silk notebook in handwritten free verse which he photocopies for us to see but which is therefore somewhat difficult to read.

In doing so he exacerbates the contrast between two eroticisms at cross purposes in a bohemia from which we are separated by an ocean, thirty years, suicide, death, and the loss of certain political clarities and a certain erotic ambiguity; but we love them both, each in its way, and each, no doubt, in our own way.

5. (Triple-) Cross-Dressing the Boom: Fuentes, Donoso, Sarduy, and the Queer Sixties ∽

LIP-SYNCHING "WOMAN"

Transvestism has often been trivialized and domesticated into mere "crossdressing," as if its practice had principally to do with something that can be put on and off as easily as a costume ... As such, it is sometimes treated as sinister—when men are seen as being empowered by a pretense of femininity they can doff at will, leaving their underlying gender identity and privilege untouched or indeed enhanced. Alternatively, a very similar understanding of transvestism can take on a utopian tinge: as a denaturalizing and defamiliarizing exposure of the constructed character of all gender; as ... a caricatural, exciting, chosen plane of arbitrariness and free play.

But ... some people can cross-dress convincingly and others can't.

Some people's bodies make more sense to themselves and others when they're cross-dressed than when they aren't.

Some people get turned on when they cross-dress and others just feel at home.

Cross-dressing crosses between public and private differently for different people.

For some people cross-dressing signifies their hetero-, and for other people their homo-, sexual identity.

The embeddedness of cross-dressing in routines, in work, in spectacle, in ritual, in celebration, in self-formation, in bodily habitus, in any sexuality, can vary infinitely from one person to another.

Some people's cross-dressing is consistently treated as a form of aggression and responded to with violence.

(Eve Sedgwick and Michael Moon, "Divinity" 219–20)

It is about time to restore complexity to a moment in Latin America's literary past that threatens to become all too simple, and I intend to do so by examining a figure that also, for all its gaudiness, has been treated all too simply. The moment is the Boom; the figure is the transvestite. The better to differentiate it from what comes after it, the Boom is characterized by recent literary histories in a monolithic way, and books that do not fit that characterization are shelved elsewhere in the mind, although their authors often shared the very same cultural and social space of that moment in the sixties. For this project I would like to direct your attention to the three authors whom Suzanne Jill Levine translated in an English edition aptly named *Triple Cross*: Carlos Fuentes, José Donoso, and Severo Sarduy, who shared cultural space on very interestingly unequal terms in the Paris and Mexico of the 1960s. All three of the novellas in *Triple Cross*, as you may already know, have protagonists who engage in transvestism: La Manuela is the full-time tragic-grotesque drag queen in Donoso's *El lugar sin límites* (Hell Has No Limits, 1966); Guillermito, or Mito, dresses up as his mother in the penultimate scene of Fuentes's *Zona sagrada* (Holy Place, 1967); and—well, it seems sometimes as if all or any of the characters in *De donde son los cantantes* (From Cuba With a Song, 1967) could be a transvestite. For convenience's sake instead I will begin by examining Sarduy's theories of transvestism, as exemplified in two essays from his 1969 collection *Escrito sobre un cuerpo* (translated, with other relevant essays, as *Written on a Body*), one on Fuentes's novel and one on Donoso's novel; from there I will examine Sarduy's practice in his 1972 novel *Cobra*. Fuentes and Donoso's protagonists, La Manuela and Mito, each have a story to tell; I admit that I am almost as interested in the story that each refuses to tell, the origin story of how the protagonist became a transvestite. This origin story is displaced onto other origin stories, and these stories reflect back onto the complex origins and stories that we tell about the Boom itself. In his tale of how a transvestite makes the decision to become a transsexual, Sarduy plays a complicated game with referentiality beyond origins which also reflects upon the Boom, upon literary–historical terms such as "Neo-Baroque," and ultimately upon our desire to create origins *ex nihilo*.

Package Deals

> *Moronic reader: if even with these clues, thick as posts, you have not understood that we're delaing with a metamorphosis [...] abandon this novel and devote yourself to screwing or to reading the novels of the Boom, which are much easier ...*

(Sarduy's footnote, *Cobra* 37; 66)

A principal way in which the Latin American literary past threatens to become too simple is in the segregation of the Boom authors from other literary currents of the day in Latin America and in Europe. Some of this segregation comes from others who disassociated themselves from the Boom, as Sarduy naughtily does in the passage above from *Cobra*. However, some of the segregation comes *ex post facto*, especially around the specific stigmatization of the Boom as too sexist to be worth imitating in contemporary times. A closer examination of this topic suggests it might be a bit to hasty to bundle all these texts together under the term "sexist," insofar as the sexism of these authors, which did indeed exist throughout this period, served so many different functions in their texts and expressed itself in so many different ways.

An increasingly common strategy in the writing of Latin American literary history in the last twenty years is to argue that the "post-Boom," to which Sarduy is assigned, as is Manuel Puig, is a complex phenomenon which attacked the Boom's literary elitism and heterosexism and Eurocentrism: after 1973 (or whatever date you prefer), Latin American literature turned to the oral history or the *testimonio*, to women and gay men's writing, to literature that was not so experimentally formal and that did not ground itself so showily in the classics of Western literature in order to compete with them in an Oedipal struggle.[1] If we define the Boom narrowly, as the usual four authors and their close friends (such as Donoso), this statement need not be disputed. García Márquez's friendly if uncomplicated sexism, Fuentes and Vargas Llosa's playboy-antics sexism, and the structural sexism that Cortázar inherited and then propagated from the Surrealists certainly at times seem to have come from a past to which nobody would wish to return, even if Isabel Allende, Laura Esquivel, Angeles Mastretta, as the newer wave of "bestsélers," cannot or will not embark upon the task of constructing fictions as complexly polyphonic as did the generation before them. However, such generalizations of literary history obscure other authors writing from between 1959 and 1975 who did not sign on to the Boom's machismo yet created formally experimental writing; and on the other hand it encourages us to read the writings of the Boom as if they were unrelated to what many have portrayed as the growing crisis of post–World War II Western masculinity, as if they were not living in an era shot through with anxieties that the novelists' public performances at writers' conferences and in the pages of magazines like *Mundo Nuevo* took great care to conceal.

It is easiest to demonstrate the first point with women writers. The literary establishment of the Boom years was certainly sexist; it is not as clear that the literary forms of many Boom novels are. For every Elena Poniatowska who genuinely breaks with the forms of the Boom novels as I have been describing them, there is a Clarice Lispector whose fiction contains many traits in common with them. The case of Elena Garro is exemplary: of course her 1963 novel *Los recuerdos del porvenir* is part of the late-modernist formal experimentation we see everywhere in the Boom years, with a prose style that owes as much to Woolf as Fuentes's and García Márquez's styles owe to Faulkner. Because her return in the early 1980s from a silent self-imposed exile in France coincided with the growth of feminism in Latin American literature departments in the United States, Garro's novels and stories belong perhaps to the post-Boom's habits of *reading*, but not to its varied modes of writing: Garro's 1963 work is in many ways a Boom novel. It seems equally unjust to restrict the label Boom to "sexist fictions by four men and their friends" when one reflects upon their friends: consider a startlingly original novel like Albalucía Angel's 1975 *Estaba la pájara pinta sentada en el verde limón*, as epic and wide-ranging in scope on Colombia's years of *La Violencia* (1948 through the 1960s) as Fuentes achieves for the betrayal of the Mexican Revolution in *La muerte de Artemio Cruz*; and Angel's novel is also a female *Bildungsroman*, which mixes the voices of many social classes, newspaper reportage, and the like. How ironic it is to read in her 1985 interview with Magdalena García Pinto that Angel was composing this novel in the same years when she was an occasional guest in the house of García Márquez in Barcelona, taking breaks from her gigs as a Paris cabaret singer.

But what anecdotes such as these prove, I hope, is that the Boom was sexist, and the contemporary journalists and literary historians who promoted and codified (only the male) Boom writers were sexist, but that the *nueva novela*, merely by virtue of being a late-modernist formal experimentation with reflections upon Latin American politics, culture, and myths written in the 1960s and 1970s by a Latin American, is not necessarily sexist. We could say that this is a characteristic the *nueva novela* shares with that larger Euro-American phenomenon, The Sixties: the new social, cultural, and at times artistic forms which came into being in that long decade were first, or most loudly, put to the service of masculinist liberty; yet this freedom was not only expanded into what we know now to be women's liberation, it also was exercised at times by women, such as Julia Kristeva, Susan Sontag and Angela Carter, who loved the forms and let the critique of sexism eventually catch up with their social, cultural, and artistic experimentation. Patricia Juliana Smith's label for the sexual experimentation and mixing of gender signs in this period, "the Queer Sixties," seems particularly apt for those women artists who experimented in life and art without yet applying the formulas of a 1970s critique of gender roles.

For the most part, however, I wish to question the other side of this equation, which is also part of what anyone would wish to call the Queer Sixties, namely the experiences and the texts of the hegemonic male avant-garde writers. Both on the Euro-American front and in the case of Latin America we must not assume that the texts that the sexist authors of the Boom wrote are actually as sexist, or as unproblematically sexist, as they themselves were. If we look at them, we may find anxieties, unconvincing bluster, dirty tricks, attempts at bargain and compromise, in these texts by authors who revered sexually ambiguous authors such as Proust, Mann, Gide, and Woolf, even as they befriended contemporary *machistas* such as William Styron and Norman Mailer. Indeed, the infighting and the trench warfare of the gender wars in the writings of Boom authors is a chapter of literary history still largely to be written. It could even be argued that there is little incentive to write it, that is, that the liberal pluralism of most literary historians finds it convenient to describe the Boom as all macho, the better to contrast it with the minority, nonelite literature that supposedly follows it and to produce those nice Hegelian-liberal and Marxist narratives by which through dialectical reversals the World-Spirit and historical agency gets expanded just a little more each and every day.

Further, it is always perhaps a bit too convenient for Euro-American writers and readers to exaggerate the machismo of any male Latin American cultural product (and, I might add in passing, either the stereoypical passive piety or spitfire rebelliousness of any female Latin American cultural product): if so, this has been the case for a long time. Perhaps it is not merely a retrospection that makes these little novels of transvestites disappear when we look back to Latin America's Sixties. It may be that the European and North American contemporaries of these novelists were also uninterested in the dissemination of unorthodox sexuality. The English translator Suzanne Jill Levine noted pragmatically in her book *The Subversive Scribe* that it was only Fuentes's charisma that got the translation project through,

> which also had its incestuous side since Donoso had dedicated *El lugar sin límites* [*Hell Has No Limits*] to Rita and Carlos Fuentes. Because these unholy three [novels] were neither family sagas nor historical novels about dictators but weird carnivalesque fantasies—and Sarduy was an unknown— this "package deal" seemed the only way to make these novellas even marginally palatable to commercial publishing. (141–2)

I return later to Levine's metaphor of incest; I will argue, albeit in the case of *Holy Place* a bit perversely, that both Fuentes and Donoso's novellas have a sort of dictator presiding over it. For now, however, I wish to note that, on the one hand, in 1970 the marketing arm of the Euro-American literary establishment was already demanding only a certain product from Latin

America; and that since, say, 1990, the academic arm of that Euro-American literary establishment has been deploring that this is the only product 1970 had to offer, but neither 1970 nor 1990 was or is willing to linger to examine what was, at times, actually offered: ecstatic, anxious, tragicomic male subjectivities in the margins.

Missing Origin Stories

Martín had now made a definite choice, to become Marta:

"There comes a moment when you have to decide for yourself. And I felt locked in men's clothes; there came a moment when I said 'away, away all men's clothes. I don't want it anymore.' And I put on women's clothes. I felt like Cinderella, I shed the old clothes and put on the new ones. What I now wanted to be."

(Annick Prieur, *Mema's House, Mexico City: On Transvestites, Queens, and Machos* 106–7)

Surely realistic novels with transvestites as protagonists are expected to represent at least one subjectivity and tell at least one story: the one subjectivity is that of the transvestite, what it feels like to be a man who dresses as a woman; and the one story is that of how a boy becomes a woman. A social anthropologist such as Annick Prieur, quoted above, asked her subjects, transvestite prostitutes living together in a slum of Mexico City, to tell their stories, and they did so with gusto and in detail. Each of my authors makes an attempt to achieve that subjectivity, in very different ways: but, surprisingly and fascinatingly, each one seems determined to avoid the narrative of the transvestite, how one becomes one.

Let me give brief summaries of my first two novellas. In Donoso's *Hell Has No Limits*, an aging transvestite, La Manuela, runs a brothel in the backlands of Chile with her daughter, La Japonesita. (At one point La Manuela imagines her given name—Manuel González Astica—on her tombstone, but otherwise she refers to herself as a woman throughout, and henceforth so shall I.) While the brothel awaits the arrival of a truckdriver, Pancho Vega, who is violently yet homophobically attracted to La Manuela, the novella flashes back to the night eighteen years ago when La Manuela was seduced into impregnating the brothel's main prostitute, La Japonesa. La Manuela was part of a visiting troupe of prostitutes who came to the little town to help celebrate the election victory of local cacique don Alejo Cruz, and after her star turn as a flamenco dancer she was dragged into a bet between La Japonesa and don Alejo. By performing sexually in bed with La Japonesa, La Manuela won for them co-ownership of the brothel (and inadvertently sired La Japonesita). In the novella's present, La Japonesa has been dead for some years and the brothel is decrepit. Pancho Vega arrives, La Manuela captivates him with a flamenco dance, but Pancho is shamed into a show of machismo by the presence of his brother-in-law Octavio and they beat La Manuela up. La Manuela desperately races to beg for don Alejo's help, but the cacique is ill and his savage dogs have been let loose to roam freely; they attack La Manuela, probably killing her.

In Fuentes's *Holy Place*, the protagonist is the twenty-nine-year-old son of the greatest Mexican actress of the day, Claudia Nervo, based very recognizably upon the actress María Félix. Obsessed with Claudia, Guillermito or Mito goes through a progressive series of degrading events— snubbed at a photo shoot of hers, nagged for having stolen a cashmere sweater of hers, sleeping with a member of her entourage who is dressed to look like her, having his monthly allowance cancelled when she is irritated with him, participating in an orgy with his mother's entire female entourage—all mixed with flashbacks to his childhood, and framed by the moment of narrating all this to an old Italian schoolmate of his, Giancarlo. When the narrative catches up to the present, the novel ends three times. First there is the staging of a grotesque art-film-cum-orgy, filmed in Giancarlo's Italian castle, in which it becomes clear to Mito that Giancarlo is now Claudia's current lover and has divulged Mito's secrets to Claudia and to the director. Second, back in Mexico, after he has been in a sanatorium, Mito enters his mother's bedroom and dresses himself entirely in her clothes before the mirror (this is the only actual scene of cross-gender masquerade in the novel).[2] Finally, back in his own apartment or "zona sagrada" as the novella's ruling mythical intertext shifts from Ulysses and Telemachus to Ulysses and Circe, Mito metamorphoses into a dog, who watches helplessly as his servants destroy his apartment in their noisy love-making.

With stories such as these to tell, and compared to an aggressively non-representational author such as Sarduy, it is hardly surprising that we as readers would group Donoso and Fuentes together, as roughly realistic narratives in the modernist mode of Henry James and Joyce.[3] One technique of realism which both Donoso and Fuentes employ extensively is the layering of times, which permits a depth of characterization at the same time that it increases narrative suspense—we stop to find out more about the main characters' past just when we impatiently want to know what happens to them next. Fuentes complicates the temporal schema still more by leaving unclear for most of the novel the temporal relationship between the first chapter, in which Mito begins to tell Giancarlo about his obsession with his mother, and the rest of the narration, an ambiguity to which I shall return.

With all these flashbacks, then, it is all the more surprising, then, that neither Fuentes's nor Donoso's characterological trajectories include what one might call the "transvestite's narrative," the flashback to the moment when the character was first attracted to or aroused by women's clothing. Donoso's La Manuela arrived in Estación El Olivo at the age of forty, and we learn virtually nothing about her interior life before her arrival. In this sense there is nothing "behind" the transvestite. Sarduy stresses this point in the second half of his essay "Writing/Transvestism":

> Transvestism, as practiced in Donoso's novel, may well be the best metaphor for writing: what Manuela makes us see is not a woman who might be hiding a man *beneath her appearance* [...], but *the very fact of transvestism itself.* (37; 1150–1, emphasis Sarduy's)

This argument would, of course, fit Sarduy's own fictions better than it does *Hell Has No Limits*, whose layers of reality are very closely hierarchized, and whose La Manuela clearly wants to be treated not like a transvestite, but like a lady. The first half of Sarduy's essay affirms what can be affirmed and concedes what must be conceded on this topic. The novel's characters in their sexuality undergo constant inversions without ever turning right side up, so to speak. At the same time, this constant inversion is limited to a single plane:

> This series of twists with turns, however, never provides an image analogous to that of "the world right-side-up" [...] because what is inverted in each instance is not the entire surface—economics, politics, class tensions are not included in the twists of the plot, and they always correspond to "reality"—, but only its continually changing erotic signifiers. (36; 1149)

I am prone to think this concession weakens Sarduy's hope that *Hell Has No Limits* must be seen as a post-modernist linguistic artifact; rather, Donoso gives us a plausible subjectivity of a transvestite in a realistic milieu. To maintain this plausibility, to herself if not also to the reader, La Manuela never tells herself the story of how she became a transvestite.

Of course, the perversion of transvestism can produce an equal and opposite perversion, and it is worth pointing out that Donoso does suggest an origin story for the latent homosexual of the *mayate* type, the man who goes for effeminate men, in Pancho Vega's flashbacks to his own childhood.[4] A child of one of the local peasant families, Panchito was drafted to play with the Cruzes' daughter Monica (97–9; 91–3); while they played house and he was rocking the doll who was their baby, older boys came by and called Panchito a "sissy" (*marica* 98; 97). He avoided the Cruzes but couldn't help spying on them; when he was grabbed by don Alejo, who only wanted Panchito to keep playing with Monica, Panchito found don Alejo's vicuña poncho to be warm and arousing: "I hang from his cape kicking, him so big and me so small looking up at him, like looking up a cliff [...] I hang onto his cape because it's so soft and so hot and he drags me along" (97). Such scenes are invoked by social-realist interpretations of the text to describe the neo-feudal dependence of Pancho on don Alejo, but this emotional dependence also brings with it a characteristic eroticism. Panchito's interest in tenderness, playacting, and the authority of a man beneath a sensuous exterior all mark him as a future lover of transvestites, though not a transvestite himself.

But as for the origins of La Manuela, nothing. Whereas for *Holy Place*, I think Fuentes thinks that his entire novel *is* an origin story for Mito's transvestism, yet it is a very specific woman that Mito's drag imitates. The two most important features of Mito's family situation are the strength of his movie-star mother, and her physical absence in the early part of his life. Mito's father is weak, but his conservative family tried to keep Mito away from his glamorous and powerful mother; in an early flashback in the novella, we see Claudia Nervo kidnapping her own nine-year-old son on the streets of Guanajuato: Mito cannot even be sure it is her. The result of Claudia's intermittent availability to her son, coupled with the country's saturation of her image, is that Mito careens wildly from adoration to hatred of his mother. In the novel's present, Mito has stolen one of his mother's cashmere sweaters, but he has not, as it turns out, worn it himself; it is soiled because Mito gave it to his maid's working-class boyfriend to be defiled. Mito only dresses up as Claudia after he has definitively lost her, symbolically to the apotheosis of the Felliniesque orgy, and erotically to his high school classmate Giancarlo. In other words, Mito is not a transvestite for seduction or for gender identity, as La Manuela is in *El lugar*; he dresses up neither to attract men nor to express his identification with a generalized femininity. It is a negotiation with the image in the mirror.

Sarduy's essay on *Holy Place*, "A Pearl Grey Cashmere Fetish," becomes especially interesting at this point for us. Quite intelligent in its own right, it is also revealing of the limits to a Freudian basis for the narratives of the perverse. As we have seen in previous chapters, Freud's strongest *narratives* of the perverse are the story of the Oedipus complex and the various ways in which the child does not successfully negotiate it; among the narratives of Oedipal failure which produce perverse sexualities, the strongest narrative is the narrative of the fetishist, who recoils in horror from the "fact" that women are inferior to men. The fetishist's narrative draws from the power of a reconstructed fable. Despite the title of the essay, Sarduy correctly "diagnoses" the problem of *Zona sagrada*'s Mito not as a case of fetishism but as a narcissistic wound. When he does so, Sarduy is faced with a rhetorical and conceptual problem: Freud's texts on narcissism do not have the same narrative energy that the fetish text does (Freud never quotes Ovid on Narcissus the way he quotes Sophocles on Oedipus, for example).[5] Sarduy turns instead to a range of his contemporaries in Paris who have been interpreting Freud along a very specific line.

After the first third of the essay, in which Sarduy invokes Roland Barthes's essay on the iconic character of the face of Garbo and claims that Mito's actress mother Claudia has a similar power (and is hence *not* the face of an individual but a sign of femininity itself), Sarduy goes on to invoke the prestigious psychoanalytic narrative of Jacques Lacan's brief but much-invoked essay on the pre-Oedipal mirror stage. When the infant looks into the mirror and (mis)recognizes himself, the mirror projects a wholeness that the infant has yet to achieve; it gives the child a false (or premature) sense of self-mastery. As Lacan elaborated the stage to be called the Imaginary, it was coded feminine. By rights, then, little Mito should have been able to have seen himself in the mirror of his mother; without that fundamental reassurance and protection, he is doomed to a life of recreating the womb in his childhood bedroom or his adult apartment (financed by Claudia); striving to get his mother to recognize him; and to be able to at last see her when he looks in the mirror. A failed Oedipal complex produces perversions; a failed pre-Oedipal stage produces perversions too.

(A final question before we leave the first third of Sarduy's essay: how true is it that the face of Garbo in Barthes's essay is the equivalent of the face of Claudia/María Félix in Fuentes's novel? To call both of them the face of *terror* is no betrayal of Fuentes's novel, certainly. But the seamlessness by which European cinema can override the specificity of Mexican cinema, even here on the level of theory, performs a collusion with Fuentes's own cosmopolitan desire to equate Mexico with Italy with Paris. Amidst all these missing origin stories, there is also at least one missing terminus, Mexico as a late comer, the end of the line of French influence.)

Lacan's mirror stage theory, then, contains a level of sexism which Sarduy does not investigate and which Fuentes's novel lays bare: the child is supposed to use the mother as the mirror, the reassurance of a future mastery of the world and of the self; he is expected to look at the mother and see himself.[6] To be unable to do so fractures the subject in a way different from that of the split subjectivity we are all supposed to have when we discover that we do not coincide (yet, ever) with the image we see of ourselves in the mirror. Claudia as a mother-function was both absent and too visible in her own right, and the novel explores both the dynamic of a son who compulsively makes (unmet) demands for his mother to be there only for him, and the dynamic of a son, and a culture, who is presented with the image of a powerful woman who makes her own demands upon all Mexicans. Claudia really did wrest power from a male-dominated industry (partly because it is an industry organized around the dissemination of the image of the woman); in that sense she is the real thing, the phallic woman (and mother) who exists only as a phantasm in Freud's theories. Insofar as *Holy Place* is (in Wendy Faris's acute phrase) a "case history," the transvestite is a figure blocked from access to a powerful mother, a phallic mother who has never been castrated. He looks at himself dressed as her in the mirror, not to reassure himself that his own penis is there, but to try to convince himself that her penis is there, there for him and for no one else.

A Digression: On the Realness of Drag Queens

To Be Real—

(Soundtrack of *Paris Is Burning,* dir. Jennie Livingston, 1990)

The most essential feature of his mission of redemption is that it must be preceded by his transformation into a woman. It is not to be supposed that he wishes to be transformed into a woman; it is rather a question of a "must" based on the order of things, which there is no possibility of evading...

(Freud, *Three Case Histories* 112; italics in the text)

The language into which Sarduy and I are translating *Holy Place* is Freudian. However, this language of anxiety and reassurance around the phallic mother is not taken from Freud's story of the origin of transvestism, because Freud never provides one—another missing origin story, if you like. It is tempting to say that mid-century novelists in the Queer Sixties do not provide "the" story of the male transvestite's discovery of his own desire because Freud did not. It is also tempting to say that the heft and exciting slipperiness of Marjorie Garber's monumental 1990 book, *Vested Interests: Cross-Dressing and Cultural Anxiety* is also due to Freud's silence, encouraging her and other critics to mix and match various Freudian texts to create an ensemble of transvestite theory, much as we, and Sarduy before us, are cannibalizing bits of Lacan and fetish theory to help schematize Mito's actions. In *Vested Interests,* Garber squeezes in a page praising the opinions of Sarduy on the topic of the relation between writing and transvestism, which is hardly surprising, since both he and she share an enthusiasm for the works of Lacan. When she is willing to be pinned down on the topic,

Garber argues that the transvestite should be seen as what at times Lacan called the third term, the one that interrupts binarisms: the transvestite neither *has* the phallus (the male) nor *is* the phallus (the female), but rather "seems" to be the phallus. In this reading, the transvestite marks the space of appearance, of fictionality itself.

In this reading, the drag queen occupies a space which, in its purest form, is disconnected from reality altogether, and inhabits a realm of pure seeming. Such language is fruitfully, but also dangerously, ambiguous: from whose (definition of) reality has the drag queen detached herself? The logic that led us to this statement was Lacanian, yet it may not correspond to the Lacanian theories of the Real.[7] Were we to be somewhat sloppier, and claim that the drag queen in her perfect seeming takes leave not of the Real, but of the Freudian reality principle (which corresponds mostly to Lacan's symbolic order), we would have a formula that would give us access to: popular stereotypes of the dizzy drag queen; the high-modernist realist conventions that inform the perspective shifts in *Hell Has No Limits*; and the common-sense description of psychosis. A famous psychotic who abandoned the reality principle is Freud's only famous transvestite case history, Doctor Schreber. Doctor Schreber, a prestigious judge and pedagogue of Wilhelmine Germany before his illness incapacitated him, told in his memoirs not just of supernatural aliens who were torturing him through a series of hospital doctors, but also of the heroic efforts he made to thwart the aliens by attracting their energy beams, or rays, up his anus, a task he could perform most efficiently, he assured the reader, by dressing as a woman in front of a full-length mirror.[8] Surely this is not what Sarduy meant when he spoke of the perfect performance of Woman; and yet, as we will see in our reading of *Cobra*, Sarduy never wants to completely eliminate the possibility of a popular uprising against the empire of signs.

But if the Garber-Lacan reading of the transvestite as the third term is unsatisfying, it is less so for the analysis of Sarduy's own fictions than for the analysis of realist fictions. One must be skeptical of the way that this metaphysics of being, having, and seeming-to-be the phallus eliminates once again on the theoretical level the occasional reality that sometimes women really do have power, on whatever limited terms. It might be, then, that some transvestites do not dress up in order to seem to *be* a phallus, to be the trophy wife and sign of status around some other man's waist, but rather in order to seem to *have* a phallus, to wield the power that a female movie star in the Golden Age of Mexican cinema actually wielded, and wielded differently than her male co-stars did. If we must use Lacanian language to describe our *vedettes*, we can say that, yes, Donoso's La Manuela dresses up in order to seem to *be* the phallus for Pancho Vega and don

Alejo, but that Mito Nervo dresses up in order to seem to *have* the phallus that his mother already has in a man's world.[9]

Seeming-to-have-the-phallus is a transvestite practice most suited for an audience of other gay men, and for oneself; it is not surprising that Mito does it in the mirror, and it is not too surprising that Lacan omits it as a theoretical possibility. Seeming-to-be-the phallus is supposed to inaugurate or maintain the space of desire as autonomous fiction, and vice versa; that it does not do so for La Manuela suggests how vulnerable, not just transvestite prostitutes are, but also how vulnerable fiction and the space of desire are, always least autonomous when making a claim to be no more than seeming, in part because a phallus is always wielded by *somebody*. While she is dancing, while she creates herself as phallus, La Manuela suspends and transfixes (indeed, we barely get a description of her dancing, in the bar eighteen years ago or in the novel's present); but once the dance is over, La Manuela gives the phallus she seems-to-be to the men to wield it. Conversely, even after the director cuts the camera, Claudia continues whipping the actor in her portrayal of *Doña Bárbara, la devoradora de hombres*, and Mito has the outtakes to prove it (119; 152–3). If Lacan and Garber limit themselves on a theoretical level to speaking of "seeming" as if all scenes of seeming are of seeming-to-be, then their approach to the varieties of desire incited by the drag performance will be limited.

Garber's approach has other virtues, of course. Her description of the epistemological allure of the seeming of the transvestite, the site which drives the drag queen's audience to want to know what lies beneath the seeming even as she warns us that there is nothing—as well as the wrong thing—there, corresponds nicely with the arc of the main narratives of Sarduy's *From Cuba With a Song*. Her chapters on the paradoxical way that the transvestite and the transsexual narratives can frequently be employed to reinforce conservative notions of gender, whenever men trapped in their male bodies yearn to seem to be, or to become, "real" women, are useful for examining the narrative progress of Sarduy's *Cobra*, in which Cobra undergoes a sex-change operation so that she will become a perfect woman. Finally, Garber's style, an extraordinary patchwork of anecdotes drawn from the highest and lowest levels of culture, shows a great respect for narrative *per se* as a mode of persuasion. Sarduy does not show such respect, either in his essays or his fictions.

This lack of interest in certain narrative categories combines with his scorn for realism to give a specific twist to his reading of certain psychoanalytic narratives. In the essay on *Holy Place*, for instance, Sarduy's main conceptual tool is the fetish. Freud's essay on fetishism is an origin story par excellence; as we have seen, this origin story has its own missing origin, the mother's missing penis. Because he has no love for realism, Sarduy does not expand on a crucial aspect of the fetishism origin story, that of disavowal, the double consciousness the fetishist has which is different in kind from the denial we see in repression and which is summarized in the phrase, "I know, but yet…"—I know that the object I revere is not the woman's phallus, yet I will be aroused by it just as if it were. Such a double consciousness is most appropriate for La Manuela in *Hell Has No Limits*, who is angry every time her daughter calls her "papá," since the name threatens her illusion and pleasure, and who knows that Pancho and Octavio are assaulting her because she is really a he. Sarduy may feel freer in sidestepping this aspect of the fetish story in the case of his essay on Fuentes because Fuentes himself does not practice the disavowal of and return to reality (after all, the third of the novel's three endings involves Mito's transformation into a dog). Besides, Mito before the mirror does not feel that he has become a woman, nor even that he "knows he is not a woman, and yet…": Mito is too ambivalent about this mother figure to take a fetishistic pleasure in the transvestite act, at least as disavowal is supposed to promise us.

Sarduy's idiosyncratic use of the fetishist origin story is nevertheless true to some aspects of both Freud and Fuentes. As did Freud, Sarduy felt that fetishists like Mito are filled with anxiety and use fetishes such as his mother's sweater to gain reassurance. But he expands on the Freudian paradigm to explore the ambivalence the fetishist feels about the object, and about the mother. Imitating similar schemata in Levi-Strauss's readings of myths and Barthes's semiological analyses, Sarduy maps out the movements of the cashmere sweater from various "safe zones" to "danger zones," and shows that Mito needs both to revere and to defile the fetish-object, because he needs to revere and defile his mother Claudia. Mito takes the final step of dressing up entirely as his mother alone in the privacy of her boudoir, because seeing himself dressed as her in the mirror returns the image of her to himself as an exclusive observer, but it is an image that humiliates both of them at the same time.

Sarduy's emphasis on ambivalence toward the phallic mother whom the transvestite embodies works itself out differently in his own fiction, and this ambivalence is worked out differently again in *Hell Has No Limits*. But at least the phallic woman or phallic mother is not *necessarily* a phantom for him or for Fuentes or for Donoso, as it is for Freud who systematically undermines the social and familial position of the mother, and for Lacan who cannot let the phallus on a theoretical level be wielded by a woman (or by a drag queen). In the real world real women sometimes wield the phallus.

And in *Hell Has No Limits*, the plot (or the plot of eighteen years ago) turns on whether a woman can wield La Manuela-as-phallus.

Triple-Crossing the Patriarchy

Donoso saves the best flashback for last in *El lugar sin límites*. We have already had two chapters of an objectively related flashback to that fateful night eighteen years ago when La Manuela performed flamenco for don Alejo's victory party, and we saw her in command, the powerful phallic woman who incites men's desire; in a pattern common for her, however, that moment faded, and the men who vied for her turned upon her, dumping her in a nearby water-filled ditch. Two chapters later, when Pancho Vega forces his way into the brothel, La Manuela takes refuge in the chicken coop. There she again thinks back on the night eighteen years ago: La Japonesa had bet don Alejo that she could seduce La Manuela into having sex with her, and Don Alejo would watch from a nearby window. The seduction, which is worth quoting at length, was successful, partly because of La Japonesa's warmth, but also because of her shrewd manipulation of La Manuela's *non*-phallic femininity:

> I don't have fists to protect you, I only know how to dance and to shiver here in the henhouse.
> ... But one time I didn't shiver. Big Japonesa's naked body, oh, if I had that warmth now, if Japonesita has it so she wouldn't need other heat, Big Japonesa's naked, repellent, but warm body surrounding me [...] by the lamp light that we didn't put out so they could see us from the window. They insisted on at least that much proof. And the house would be ours. Mine. And me smothered in that flesh, that drunken woman's mouth searching for mine the way a pig roots in a swamp though we agreed we wouldn't kiss because it nauseated me [...] I was terrified to see Japonesa violating our agreement, something was beginning to stir and I didn't ... I didn't want to be sickened by the flesh of this woman [...] and me realizing that all this is monstruous, unnecessary, they're betraying me, oh how clearly I saw it was a betrayal to capture me and lock me up in jail forever because Big Japonesa was utterly reckless with that odor [...] that boiling so different from mine, my foolish doll's body, depthless, everything on the surface, useless hanging, while she caresses me with her mouth and sweaty palms [...]. She's pleased that I can't; not with anybody, tell me, pretty Manuela, tell me not with any other woman before me; tell me I'm the first, the only, so I can have you all to myself my pretty little girl, my love, Manuelita I'm going to have you, I like your terrified body and all your fears and I want to destroy your fear [...] to reach a part of me that she, poor Big Japonesa, thought existed but doesn't exist [...] No honey (*mijita*), Manuela, as if we were two women,

look, see, our legs wound together, sex in sex, two identical sexes, Manuela, [. . .] like two women when the gentlemen in Wooden Heart's house pay the whores to let them watch . . . no, no, you're the woman, Manuela, I'm the man (*la macha*), look how I'm taking off your panties and loosening your brassiere so your breasts will be bare and I can play with them Manuela, don't cry, you do have breasts, tiny like a little girl's but you have them and that's why I love you. You talk and caress me and suddenly you tell me, now darling Manuela, now you can . . . I dreamed about my breasts being caressed and something happened while she was saying, yes little girl (*mijita*), I'm making you like it because I'm the man (*la macha*) and you're the woman, I love you because you're everything, and I feel her heat devouring me, me, a me that doesn't exist, [. . .] and what does it matter if they're watching us from the window, that makes it better, sweeter, until I shudder and am mutilated, bleeding inside of her, while she screams and clutches me and then falls, my precious little boy (*mijito*), what a sweet thing, it's been so long [. . .] and she says into my ear, as if in a dream: my sweet girl, my sweet boy (*mijita, mijito*), her words muffled in the pillow. (107–10; 106–9)

Why does La Japonesa's seduction succeed? When at first she calls La Manuela "mijito," it doesn't; but she shifts tactics and permits, even builds up, La Manuela's imagined femininity. This begins with La Japonesa's expressions of pride in being in bed with a "virgin," and then—and this is such a surprising move that some critics pass over it—La Japonesa declares that the two of them are performing a lesbian scene. La Japonesa is willing to declare herself a *macha* but not a *macho*. Perhaps if La Japonesa had portrayed herself as a man, La Manuela would have responded by eroticizing her ass and looking for La Japonesa's penis, but this La Japonesa chooses not to do: one of the overriding image patterns in the passage is the traditional association of woman and house, all associated with La Japonesa's mouth and vagina. After all, La Japonesa wants to own her own house, and her proximate goal is to get La Manuela to enter her "house."

In "Writing/Transvestism," Sarduy is indeed one of those critics who does not deal explicitly with the "lesbianization" of the sex scene between La Japonesa and La Manuela. Sarduy has much invested in the notion that La Manuela is the sort of drag queen whose signs of masculinity and femininity are both on the surface: he claims that La Japonesa is attracted to La Manuela for something masculine in La Manuela: "as a man he attracts La Japonesa" (34; 1148). (We —and La Japonesa—know from an earlier scene that La Manuela is well-endowed; Sarduy presumably is referring to this, since even offstage La Manuela is stereotypically feminine.) Recall that Sarduy argues that the plane of sexuality permits inversions that never "turn right-side up"; while all this is true, it is inconvenient for Sarduy's argument that La Manuela's fantasy of herself is not of a being who mixes male and female signs, but of being a real woman, and that it is La Japonesa's ability to manipulate La Manuela's fantasies that bring the transvestite to orgasm and the double cross to fruition.[10]

But this double cross, recall, is not a *menage à deux*, and it is the presence of a third person which brings it into a triple cross. La Japonesa tells la Manuela that they should imitate the prostitutes of the more sophisticated brothel in Talca of Wooden Heart: "like two women when the gentlemen in Wooden Heart's house pay the whores to let them watch." Rather than ignoring don Alejo's male gaze upon them, then, La Japonesa builds it into the love scene.[11] I call this scene a triple cross of the patriarchy for this reason. Nobody crosses don Alejo and gets away with it: in this flashback, he has just won an election. (The social-realist interpretations of *Hell Has No Limits* emphasize that, in the present time of the novella, eighteen years after the sex scene, don Alejo is defied directly by Pancho Vega's brother-in-law Octavio, who is neither economically nor erotically dependent on don Alejo as La Manuela and Pancho are, each in his own way. Octavio had been so irritated by don Alejo's patriarchal ways—and Pancho's submission to them—earlier in the day that he lent Pancho money to repay don Alejo for his truck that very day. But of course in the brothel and later, outside, Octavio is the enforcer of sexual orthodoxy by watching Pancho's behavior: he may represent the overturning of a feudal economy and psychology but he has inherited the patriarch's gaze.) La Japonesa proposed to La Manuela the double cross of only pretending to have sex with each other, swindling the house from don Alejo. Sarduy suggests a double cross in both directions, emphasizing that La Japonesa misled La Manuela into thinking that no sex would actually take place. True enough; but he overstates the case when he says that La Japonesa's ambition "is only a pretext, the pretext used by money to justify all transgressions" (34; 1148). It was not by an appeal to money that La Manuela achieved her male potency. But when La Japonesa aroused La Manuela by reinforcing their femininities as a display to be watched over by don Alejo, this reinstallation of the patriarchal gaze into La Manuela's sexuality is a *triple* cross which does indeed "turn the world right-side up" for the patriarchy, undoing any long-range subversive potential in La Manuela's transvestism and leaving the cacique's phallus as the only one in the scene (although La Manuela's penis is erect and actually impregnates La Japonesa)—or, if one prefers the Lacanian vocabulary, leaves La Manuela as the phallus wielded, not by La Japonesa, but by don Alejo. La Manuela's doublethink goes beyond the "I know, but yet" fetishistic construction of her own transvestism: faster than any of the other characters she sees through don Alejo's stratagems to deny the town electricity and buy it up to replant it as vineyards, but nevertheless in fantasy moments, and moments of stress, she continually returns to him as rescuer and savior. The powerful maternal La Japonesa called La Manuela "mijito, mijita" indiscriminately, but in either case the phallic woman La Japonesa turned out to be wielding La Manuela as the patriarch's phallus, not wielding her own.

Double Crossing Your Brother

I have one more origin story to bring to your attention in relation to Fuentes and Donoso, and in this story I fear that once again the patriarch will win, if not perhaps in the long term; and with this story I hope to explicate some of the energy that informs *Hell Has No Limits* as well as to cast some light on some of the odd formal decisions Fuentes makes in *Holy Place*. I refer to *Holy Place*'s first chapter's foregrounding—and temporal unmooring—of Mito's conversations with Giancarlo, and the multiplicity of the novel's endings.

These odd formal decisions are passed over in total silence by Sarduy in his essay on *Zona sagrada* in what is otherwise quite a responsible essay in its focus on the combination of frustrated narcissism and ambivalent fetishism at work in the psychology of Mito's relationship to his mother Claudia. Due to that focus, however, Sarduy virtually eliminates Giancarlo from his analysis. Instead, Sarduy follows his own understanding of how fetishism works in real life and Lacanian theory, and in doing so hits a discrepancy, which he explicates as the conclusion of his essay. In the novel, the "zona sagrada" is Mito's apartment, the protected space, heavily laden with European and *modernista* fin-de-siècle memorabilia—photos of Sarah Bernhardt, a Beardsley engraving of Salomé, novels by Wilde and Baron Corvo—which Mito rents and decorates with the allowance his mother gives him. This should not be the "zona sagrada," Sarduy reasons; rather, the sacred space should be Claudia's boudoir, and yet Mito invades that space rather easily, and more than once in the novel. This "profane space" is where he dresses up as the mother; immediately afterwards we see him back in his own apartment, the supposedly holy place, where he has metamorphosed into a dog.

This discrepancy permits Sarduy a very Barthesian, proto-poststructuralist rhetorical flourish for a conclusion: the *zona sagrada*, coded as the aesthetic, is the space in which Fuentes ascends from psychological realism (transvestism into the mother) to mythic fantasy (metamorphosis into a dog); therefore the *zona sagrada* is the space of literature itself:

> In this way Fuentes confirms the autonomy of the esthetic process and uses words to sketch the limits of that other zone (which is also sacred because it

assimilates and converts into its own substance everything that passes
through it), the zone of literature, of the inexhaustible symbolic production
of language. (32; 1146)

I am not really satisfied by this move of Sarduy's (although some readers of
Fuentes may have at times felt that "inexhaustible symbolic production" is
an all too accurate characterization of his longer books). Before crediting
Fuentes with the noble goal of rescuing Language from Psychoanalysis, Art
from Science, I would like to examine more ignoble motives that might lie
behind the discrepancies and quirks in the novel's form—such as envy, or
sibling rivalry. Were we all still structuralists, no doubt we would turn to
the writings of René Girard for enlightenment on this topic; but for an ana-
lyis of how sibling rivalry and envy affect a novelist, let us turn to my final
origin story: *Historia personal del Boom* (The Boom in Spanish American
Literature: A Personal History), by José Donoso.

I suspect that for many Latin Americanists the "plot" of this 1972 essay-
memoir is more familiar than the plot of *Holy Place*. Once upon a time José
Donoso was languishing in the backwater of Chile when Carlos Fuentes,
cosmopolitan, impassioned, radicalized by the Cuban Revolution, showed
up at a writer's conference in Chile in 1962 and inspired Donoso and all
and sundry to write with a transnational, universal audience in mind. The
success of these new novelists—Fuentes, Vargas Llosa, Cortázar, eventually
García Márquez—would inspire warm friendships, and also the envy of
their contemporaries, but surely not of Donoso himself. After all, Fuentes
recognizes Donoso as an old high school acquaintance. He introduces
Donoso to agents and to celebrities; he throws sybaritic parties (and the
conferences these writers attend also lose that nasty ideological strain and
become rather sybaritic too). Fuentes's wife and step-daughter are actresses
and his house is used to film a version of his short story "Las dos Elenas"
which features an actor who is the son of María Félix. Donoso knows all
this because he and his wife Pilar, down on their luck, have been given rent-
free a small house in the back of the Fuentes garden, where, humiliated by
a debt to a publisher back home and by writer's block on his great novel to
come *The Obscene Bird of Night*, Donoso will write in two short months the
novella *Hell Has No Limits*. When years later he is finished his great novel,
alas, politics—Cuba again, mostly—will have broken up the Boom, but
that puts Donoso in the best vantage point to tell his personal history, neither too close nor too far from the people and the success that inspires
envy … in others.

I suppose it is possible that Donoso would have rejected a reading of
Hell Has No Limits as a fantasy autobiography, the tale of an emasculated

man living in a shack due to the calculated generosity of a *cacique*; sometimes he can see right through the *cacique*, but he always falls back on an eroticized hero-worship; he has an artistic talent of creating illusion which emasculates him further and does not earn him a living; by some theatrical magic that feels utterly uncharacteristic of him and partly due to the intervention of a sexy actress wielding the boss's phallus, the little man gains a sort of literary potency while never feeling any less emasculated. Pancho Vega, although he is the sort of blue-collar man whose outward shows of virility many gay men have eroticized, is also a figure for the novelist in his eroticized dependence on don Alejo; Donoso is simultaneously La Manuela and Pancho, and it is more important for Donoso to tell the story of the closeted Pancho's sensitive childhood than to tell of La Manuela's. With names of sexist literary patriarchs like Alejo (Carpentier), (Fuentes's Artemio) Cruz, and Octavio (Paz) pulling the strings, the interior drama between the hopeless queen artist and the closeted married man must end in retributory violence, finished off by the boss's dogs. The hero-worship so warmly expressed toward Fuentes in *A Personal History* finds its counterpart in the eroticized *ressentiment* in *Hell Has No Limits*, and while I am hardly calling the novella a *roman à clef* I find this aspect of the work so obviously there that I presume that Donoso tailored his 1972 account of the summer of 1965 so that the analogy could leap to anyone's eye, and it is only various codes of literary decorum that have prevented previous academics from saying so explicitly.

Did the ebullient overproductive Carlos Fuentes of the summer of '65 see himself as the old, cruel, manipulative don Alejo in his friend's novel? I should think not; but I suspect he did read La Manuela as some sort of self-portrait of Donoso, and in October of that same year he amiably set out to steal his starveling friend's thunder, by writing his own novel of an emasculated man and the woman he tries to see when he looks in the mirror. Donoso was not the only reader who identified Claudia Nervo as María Félix in the main part of *Holy Place*, and naturally it was quite a scandal to seem to be calling Enrique Alvarez Félix an orgiast and transvestite; the author of the 1972 Twayne's World Author Series book on Fuentes sniffs in his main text that *Holy Place* "cannot by any means be called an important work," and reserves for the footnotes that it was "in singularly bad taste, to say nothing of betrayal of friendship."[12] Yet I would argue that Fuentes is betraying more than one friendship in this fictional portrait.

The meat of the book ends after Claudia has flown off to Italy, with Mito screening outtakes he has of her on various movie sets engaging in spiteful acts of cruelty—such outtakes, excesses or violations of the public-private division, point towards the *roman-à-clef* readings in which I am engaged. Mito says that he would like the book to end there: "My story ends here, In this solitude. No one can continue it ... But solitude tells me that I'm not alone. That there's something else. I deny it. I am the narrator ..." (122; 156). He nevertheless continues, and in the next-to-last short section we are shown the orgy and the apotheosis filmed in his friend Giancarlo's castle; we discover that Giancarlo is Claudia's lover; Mito tells us that he has been in a sanatorium; Giancarlo escorts him to Paris to catch a plane back to Mexico, trying to convince Mito that it is all for the best, in the end roughing him up on the tracks of the Paris Métro. I reconstruct this sequence for you, but the chapter, entitled "Card Tricks," is not in chronological order; Fuentes has rearranged it so that the confrontation on the train tracks frames most of the chapter, just as the out-of-sequence conversation with Giancarlo on an Italian beach began the novel.

Two chapters in the center of the book set up the friendship more fully, first of a high school friendship coded through books like Gide's *Les Caves du Vatican* to insinuate homoeroticism, and then of a suggestive Christmas vacation spent in Giancarlo's family castle together, often naked, amidst ruined statue gardens, Baroque frescoes, and Giancarlo's collages of Italian silent film divas. There Giancarlo first seduces Mito, at first unsuccessfully, but when Mito is finally ready to respond Giancarlo suddenly rejects him, imposing a prohibition: "Don't touch anything, Guglielmo. [...] Desire, plead, kiss, but don't consume ... Only that is touching. Consuming" (82; 103).[13] Giancarlo then tries to explain his rejection away in mythological terms, of variations on the themes of Ulysses and the sirens, Circe, Penelope, Telemachus, and the divine half-brothers Apollo and Dionysos: the implausibility of the Giancarlo character, as he has been described up to this point, invoking an obscure variation of the Ulysses myth to tease and then disappoint his effeminate houseguest is for me the strongest indication that Fuentes has so much invested in the Giancarlo figure that it is buckling the novel's structure. Although Fuentes is willing to write the first-person novella from the emasculated persona of María Félix's son (or of Pepe Donoso), he must frame this novel as Mito's confessions to a virile interlocutor who effortlessly gains access to the phallic woman who has repeatedly denied Mito access to herself. While this interlocutor romances Claudia, he betrays all Mito's secrets to her and to the film director; the result is that Fuentes's three obsessions of European mythology, cinematic magic, and autochthonous *mexicanidad* can combine in "Gian/Carlos's" deification and possession of a Mexican Circe.

Sadly, obscure mythology is not the only terrain Gian/Carlos argues on when he explains his conduct to Guillermito at the Parisian train station. Mito has poked holes in the analogies Giancarlo has offered;[14] without defending himself as mythographer, Giancarlo shifts his ground from the mythical back to the psychosexual in a rather uglier tone:

> *Cretino*, and if I succeed in humiliating her?, and if I act in your name?, and if I break her and transform her and offer you her in all her weakness, behind her aggressive words and false strength?, [...] if I surrender your real mother to you, naked, maskless, insulted, finally revealed by an imagined man who offers her the last surprise: the surprise that, despite all appearances, I don't reflect her?, [...] do you want to see her like that, do you want me to give her back like that? (139; 183)

This is the last in a long series of images in the novel in which, in a direct reversal of Lacanian mirror-stage theory, Claudia expects the men in her life to reflect her, although she is supposedly also still hoping to find the man who can restore her femininity to her and tame the tigress. For Gian/Carlos, to re-feminize is to humiliate. Such sentiments toward the phallic woman may not be different in kind from the frequent ambivalence Mito has expressed, but due to Mito's narcissism every criticism of Claudia that he makes involves wounding himself, too. The transvestism scene is shot through with witch-hunt imagery, for instance, but Mito eventually concludes that Claudia would seduce the judges—might Gian/Carlos be one of them?—leaving him what he sees in the mirror: "this prince of mockery, [...] this puppet smeared with cosmetics, [...] this ravenous dog who can no longer hold himself up on these high, gigantic heels, stilts, and falls scratching the glass" (141; 186–7). Fuentes, safe in his position as Giancarlo from participating in the abjection of this transvestite image, goes on to strip Mito of even the voluptuous ambivalence of narcissistic transvestism in the novel's final scene, asserting the right of the mythmaker over the psychological realist by transforming Mito into a dog. Fuentes may claim the dog to be part of the myth of Circe, but now you may see Fuentes backhandedly acknowledging that the friend he is punishing often used dogs as punishments in his own fiction.

Sarduy knew there was something suspicious about a novel that isn't sure whether its *zona sagrada* is around the phallic mother or around the emasculated son. By omitting the frame of the relationship between Mito and Giancarlo Sarduy misses the energy invested in neither of those spaces, but rather in the Italian castle where effeminate men are teasingly flirted with and heterosexual orgies are performed and filmed, where Mexican film stars can claim to be the legitimate inheritors of Italian silent divas. Accounts of Fuentes and Donoso in the summer of 1965 help us see that in this novel the untouchable seducer double-crosses weaker storytelling performers and builds a holy place around a fantastic, Europeanized version of himself.

Conclusion I: The Place without (Literary) Autonomy

José Donoso may have been a closeted homosexual[15], or he may, in a deadpan way, have merely enjoyed playing with the emasculated position, as he did in *The Charleston and Other Stories, The Garden Next Door,* and most complexly in *The Obscene Bird of Night.* In either case, the Queer Sixties enabled Donoso to produce this fiction in which an emasculated man is triple-crossed by a powerful man he loves and envies, and then Donoso punishes the Donoso character for being taken advantage of; and in a package deal Carlos Fuentes writes a response to that text almost before Donoso has published it, in which an emasculated man fails to double cross his mother, and then Fuentes punishes the Donoso character for trying to do so. Whether a drag queen torn apart by dogs in a ditch or a whimpering dog watching his maid and her lover wreck his fin-de-siècle interior, Donoso comes out the loser. Perhaps this should not be a surprise: in a triple cross, the patriarchal position recoups what it seemed to have lost in its bet with any kind of phallic woman.

I have risked some wild simplifications in the defense of all these complex transvestite figures and in the defense of these complex literary fictions. The sexism of the Queer Sixties contributed to the complexities of these works. In order to interpret them I had to reject the Sarduyan idea that literary language is the place without limits, and I returned Fuentes and Donoso to the rather gossipy milieu in which they lived and wrote. It may be a mark of my own queerness that I savor the complexities I find there, *because*—not in spite of the fact that—these fictions never achieve a "literary autonomy" from the gaudy, anxious, gender-bending era that fuels them.

SEVERO SARDUY'S FLAMING CREATURES

Divinity School

> COBRA: *"My God"—on the record player Sonny Rollins, of course* [como es natural]—*why did you bring me into this world if it wasn't to be absolutely Divine?"*
>
> (*Cobra* 3; 8)

To approach the fictions of Sarduy's Queer Sixties from the matrix we have established in our readings of Fuentes and Donoso poses some exciting problems, exactly around the issue of "literary autonomy." Donoso's text, with its recognizable characters in a specific sociological milieu, foregrounds a character who would like to free himself from his biological gender but is brought back brutally to the place without limits. Fuentes's text actually frees itself from conventional verisimilitude in its last chapter, but the best explanation for this move resides in the characters portrayed, and quite probably also in Fuentes's reactions to the characters of the people in his house while he was percolating the novel. Neither is really best interpreted in terms of an achieved literary autonomy: character keeps getting in the way, as do the desires and anxieties which are catalyzed in the presence of the marginal male subjectivity of the drag queen and the transgressive image of the phallic woman, La Manuela and La Japonesa, Mito and Claudia, the paper doll and the spider woman. It would seem to be a strange methodological mistake to try to extend this mode of analysis to the fictions of Sarduy, where language cites without referring, where the conventional notion of character is eliminated in a play of masks and discourses. But if the presence of desires and anxieties in a text can signal a lack of some kind of autonomy, then the fiction of Sarduy may not be as serene as it appears on first reading. The first words of Cobra, on the first page of *Cobra*, suggest such a demand for literary autonomy. Or if you prefer, for Cobra (for *Cobra*) autonomy is not enough: she/it must have Divinity. Sarduy's novel is a sort of divinity school, in which the character has an earnest lesson to learn, and the novelist shows off the lessons *he* has learned.

In this novel, to achieve divinity is the equivalent of achieving the perfect performance of Woman. What is "natural" is merely what best expresses a feeling and a moment: "*como es natural, Sonny Rollins.*" Because Sarduy wrote the novel during that Golden Age of Literary Theory, the Sixties of Barthes, Lacan, and Derrida, achieving Divinity also means achieving a literary language that transcends the quotidian plane of reference.

A risky word, "transcends," insofar as there is a long history of using religious language to "transcend" the body and "transcend" the material. The tension between the materialist and antimaterialist readings of the desire for literary autonomy informs the search for literary autonomy from Kant through the fin-de-siècle to the present day. I examine this drive toward literary autonomy as a narrative drive, as a desire within the text to achieve, or to show that the text has already achieved, an independence from constraints. This sets the text up in potential conflict with the novel's protagonist, who does not yet feel perfectly free on the first page of the book. Sarduy's novel sincerely parodies the usual *Bildungsroman* in which a protagonist embarks upon a quest to embody those values most prized by his culture—in this case, the subculture of men who worship the image of woman.

The first half of *Cobra* focuses the desires and anxieties present in any linguistic artifact onto the very question of literary autonomy. It allegorizes the desire to achieve a particularly "divine" notion of literary autonomy: how wonderful it would be if words did not have to refer to things, signifiers were not ineluctably linked to signifieds, if a polyvalent sign could move its reader absolutely anywhere! Such a desire is a limit case: words without referents are a glossolalia; he who speaks in tongues may as well be silent. To take wing and fly away from this sublunar world of relatively limited signs is not the desire of the cobra but the desire of the bird, indeed as we shall see a very specific sort of *pájaro*; and in the case of Sarduy's novel *Cobra* this desire to achieve literary autonomy from the field of signification is in contradiction with the biggest binary opposition of them all, between male and female: sometimes to become a sign without referent is the equivalent of getting beyond male and female altogether—indeed, beyond the human—for our literary heroine; however, in other moments this desire to become a sign without referent is the equivalent of a male's desire to become a female.

Whenever this tension is operating in the text, a novel that his critic and friend Roland Barthes had described as "a paradisiac text" in which "a kind of Franciscanism invites all words to perch, to flock, to fly off again" (8), in which everything is permitted, becomes instead a much more conflictive space, not the playground of a Kristevan semiotic but instead a subtle battleground in which something—the best way to transcend the limits of masculinity, of the conventions of deciphering a sign—is at stake. If even this text, if even Sarduy in the heart of Tel Quel, cannot narrate the success of a striving to achieve literary autonomy; if character and referent always lie in wait to tax and eventually bankrupt "the millionaire of language," what hope does the Word have of freeing itself from the Body and from History in the texts of others?[16] I propose to perform a conflictive reading of the first half of the novel *Cobra* in terms of the differing claims of the book's (1) aesthetic ideology (*Cobra*), (2) its characters (especially Cobra), and (3) its referentiality (especially "Cobra").

Let me back up, and try not to repeat myself, so to speak. Once upon a time we readers opened a book called *Cobra*. As with any novel, we begin with the possibility that its view on the world, and on writing or art, may be sufficiently unified and prominent that we can feel that we are asked to agree with it. So Sarduy's task is to propose that we agree with *Cobra*, the novel, and it is traditional in literary criticism to give this level the highest priority. On the first page Sarduy presents us with a character, Cobra, although over the course of the novel it becomes clear that the conventions of characterization are being rewritten before our very eyes. Nevertheless, there is a certain amount of unity of characterization in the first half of the novel. Cobra is the star performer in a drag theater, the Teatro Lírico de Muñecas: Cobra performs Woman, and she makes money for herself and for the Teatro's madam, La Señora, by inciting the desires of the audience. Cobra herself, in the first half of this novel, is also defined by her desire: she wants to perfect her performance of Woman, which will make her absolutely Divine; she is convinced that her performance is being spoiled by her protruding ... feet. As the various treatments she undergoes to reduce her ... feet become more absurd, including an episode in which she somehow produces a dwarf double of herself who becomes named Pup, Cobra becomes more and more desperate. Finally, and against the advice of La Señora, she goes to Morocco for a sex-change operation which will in the process kill Pup. The operation seems to succeed; it seems not to succeed; the ending of the first half of the novel is most ambiguous. So we can express the second level thus: Do we agree with Cobra the character? Is the Divinity of Woman real and desirable for a biological male? And can it be achieved and guaranteed by correcting one's anatomy?

Posing and answering these two questions is more than enough to provide aesthetic pleasure from this most complex, most superficial artifact that is Sarduy's *Cobra*. Although to answer these questions in the end requires us to return to the text of the novel itself, they also tempt us to consult Sarduy's other texts, on writing and on transvestism and on desire: naturally, the most tempting of all is the 1969 essay "Writing/Transvestism," which claims that transvestism, properly understood, is the best metaphor for writing, properly understood. And yet, an enthusiast of the novel *Cobra* will eventually come upon a third Cobra of interest. I don't refer to the cobra in Octavio Paz's poem "La boca habla," quoted in the novel, nor the CoBrA group of painters, although Sarduy lists them in the novel (and some of the scenes in the second half of the novel take place in Amsterdam, if not in COpenhagen or BRussels). Either of them would send us in the direction of artistic codes, not in the direction of the body.[17] No, the third Cobra to whom I refer, neither a poem nor an artistic school, is the subject of the anecdote that, Sarduy frequently informed us, was the source of the novel's trajectory. In most interviews, he kept the anecdote short: he overheard someone say, "Cobra died in a jet plane over Mt. Fujiyama," and he knew that "Cobra" was a well-known Parisian transvestite; and the image of a drag queen dying in a mountain plane crash in the Far East evolved into a novel in which the first section tells of Cobra's attempt to transform into a woman, the next section tells of a gay leatherman named Cobra who is mummified by four totemic figures, gang members or perhaps Tibetan monks, and in the last section Cobra is carried up an Indian or Nepalese mountain to some kind of apotheosis. Told in this way, the original anecdote determined very little of the incidents of the novel. Eventually, however, not Sarduy himself but his lover François Wahl told a longer, and I think more interesting version of the anecdote, in the essay included in Sarduy's posthumously collected *Obra completa*:

> Severo told several times how the novel was born. He found himself in the summer of 1967 on one of the beaches of Cannes—"L'Ondine," in his personal language "Ondina Beach," to which he returned whenever he could, even if only in passing, an instant, each year—when an old drag queen set out to recite his memories in the middle of a circle of young men aspiring to enter the career. At a turning point of the tale, the narrator pronounced, "Cobra died in a jet plane over Mt. Fujiyama." Severo knew instantly that he had his book. (Cobra was in fact the pseudonym of a celebrated, and ravishing, transvestite, who died in an airplane accident on the way back from a contest in Japan.) ("Severo de la rue Jacob," *OC* 1484; my translation)

This is not the only piece of information Wahl offers us about what Sarduy does and doesn't know about the world of the real-life Cobra:

> On the other hand, one would be mistaken to think that the author was an habitué of drag performances. In Paris he probably saw no more than three, seduced above all by the one in a club that no longer exists, "The Carouzel"—that misspelling (a single s instead of two) drove him half mad—on Rue Vavin. Rather, it was by borrowing from the schemes of drag queens seized upon here or there, notably in [Sarduy's regular café the Café] Flore, that he, fantasizing freely, constructed the Lyrical Theater of dolls. Not without slipping in that taste for the backstage which followed him since [his first novel] *Gestos*, and not without projecting, for its topography, a much less imaginary knowledge of saunas. (*OC* 1484; my translation)

This, then, is the third question: after reading the novel, might we agree with "Cobra," that is to say, with the world and world view of the real person Cobra? Fantasizing freely over not just a single sentence overheard vaguely somewhere, but over the experiences of a broad range of his acquaintances and friends who belonged to a loosely connected yet international theatrical community, Sarduy wrote a novel named after a member of that community. Does *Cobra* agree with "Cobra"?

Of course this question is a risky one for a literary critic: to ask it might give the impression that one is more interested in attending the divinity school of an old drag queen's admirers than in interpreting the words and ideas of Sarduy himself (or the ideas of those other deities of the Café Flore, his teacher Jacques Lacan and his friend and teacher Roland Barthes). I deny that charge, although I am tempted to plead guilty to a lack of interest in the second half of the novel, the mummification of Cobra. Critics have remarked of the second half of the novel that it is more experimental in its rejection of narrative: there is nothing in the text to show that any of its major sequences happen before or after the other ones.[18] In its hewing to the rituals of the Tibetan Book of the Dead, the second half is also the space of desirelessness. I will suggest in the end that what the transvestite as figure brings to Sarduy's fiction is the narrative of desire, and the desire for narrative.

The second reason why asking oneself about the transvestite demimonde which Sarduy eavesdropped upon is risky is because it can lead all too easily into a naïve questioning of real transvestites, as if we could somehow receive these truths about The Life in an unmediated way, as if "Cobra" as we reconstructed her would unproblematically have priority over Sarduy's character, or as if Sarduy were the only artist here. Yet of course the theatricality of transvestites is what most interested Sarduy; and just as the Neo-Baroque artist takes previous artifices as the ground of his further artificing, so too we will examine this moment of the cultural milieu of the Queer Sixties not through transvestites who dressed up to pass for women, or just to incite desires in men, but through a drag performer.[19] This performer was a performer in every sense of the word, with an aesthetic interestingly comparable to Sarduy's own: a New York underground filmmaker and performance artist whom he may never have known personally, but who lived a life in parallel to Sarduy's own: Jack Smith (1932–89), director of the 1963 international underground film scandal *Flaming Creatures.*

Limp Penises and Other Paradoxes of Desire

Jack Smith on María Montez: "Cobra Woman is the best and worst Hollywood movie ever made."

(Tavel 99)

An ambitious boy from the country's central provinces comes to the big city to get involved with art history, but really to pursue art on his own. Fascinated with the performance of Woman, whether by men or by women, he works this into many aspects of his art. His imagination never seems to stray very far from a costume-jewelry view of the Orient, and in technique his art oscillates wildly between frenzy and stillness, abjection and apotheosis. Well-regarded by his avant-garde peers yet in his later years often feeling slighted or neglected, he dies of AIDS twenty years after his greatest successes.

Of course, the differences between Severo Sarduy and Jack Smith are more visible than the similarities. Camagüey is not Ohio. Certainly, Hollywood cannot be the same for non-Americans than for Americans, although the sort of "playing Scheherezade" which the drag performers in *Flaming Creatures* and *Cobra* indulge in undoubtedly has its roots not in Hollywood but in the last flourishing of fin-de-siècle ballet under Diaghilev and Nijinsky.[20] Neo-Baroque fiction, essays, and poetry are not experimental cinema, photo-collage, and performance art. Smith, who bullied his friends and declared most of them at some time his enemies while raging against his landlords, is temperamentally the opposite of Sarduy's persona as professional and *boulevardier* (not that Sarduy always favors characters who share these traits, and, I repeat, we might prefer to give priority to some of Sarduy's characters over his public authorial persona). Most relevantly, there is an interest in conscious intellectual pursuit in Sarduy which was totally absent in the projects of Jack Smith. Susan Sontag calls attention to this difference between the American avant-garde and its European versions in the 1964 essay which, when collected in 1968 in *Against Interpretation*, no doubt refocused Sarduy's interest in Smith as one of the many figures who think through the possibilities of transvestites as the stuff of art in the Queer Sixties. Sontag was a lifelong friend of Roland Barthes and Philippe Sollers, and I presume she knew Sarduy too, and when she praises the film *Flaming Creatures*, she does so in language that may recall to the reader the praise that Barthes would later bestow on Sarduy's *Cobra*.

Possibly Sarduy never saw the movie itself, since the only European performance, in Belgium in 1963, was in Jonas Mekas's hotel room after the film had been banned from an experimental film festival there (but Godard, Polanski, and Varda were in the audience). The forty-two minute black-and-white film begins with harem music and many false starts as characters cross in front of the credits, displaying "puckered mouths, wagging tongues, and—without any warning—a fondled penis" (Leffingwell et al. 155). Two female characters, only one biological, are introduced to the strains of a 1930s rumba, "Amapola." Another drag queen joins them, and much time is spent applying lipstick; what seems like a radio announcement for lipstick is interrupted by an obscene question. The first drag queen and the woman get into a comic fight; the woman is thrown to the ground and her breast is exposed. A general orgy ensues, which seems to trigger an earthquake, a glass-paneled lantern swinging wildly. Dust and debris rain down like snow; everyone screams and shrieks; someone tries to lick someone else's toe. The main character gets up and swoons in the arms of another woman, a rose in her teeth; now petals rain down and the music is classical. After an interval in which we watch a veil and a fly on the wall, a transvestite vampire comes out of a coffin and throws herself on the first transvestite. After this strange undead rebirth, and perhaps due to the Cuban 1930s bolero "Siboney" being played, the space once again becomes carnivalesque, as everyone foxtrots, including a sailor apparently picked up that day from the streets, and we follow a star turn by another drag performer, Mario Montez; the scene is crosscut with that of a haughty, silent courtesan, surrounded by equally fake Arabs, one pointing to her breast. Curtain.

We can take our cue from Susan Sontag in how we are to judge the film: "*Flaming Creatures* ... is crowded with visual material. There are no symbols, no commentary on or critique of anything in *Flaming Creatures*" (65). That is to say, it follows Sontag's own ambivalently pursued search for objects that are against interpretation, this search creating a space in which the highest late modernism overlaps with what we call post-modernism.[21] Yet it is hardly like a novel by Blanchot or an absurdist play like Ionesco. Instead, it shows a way out of the pessimism that such high modernist masters tended to produce, much the same way that Barthes praised Sarduy's carnival of signification as a literary *jouissance*: "*Flaming Creatures* is that rare modern work of art: it is about joy and innocence. To be sure, this joyousness, this innocence, is composed of themes which are—by ordinary standards—perverse, decadent, at the least highly theatrical and artificial. But this, I think, is precisely how the film comes by its beauty and modernity" (66). The young American facing the older Europeans, Sontag is of course ambivalently proud of Smith's innocence, like his anti-intellectualism;[22] Sarduy, who cites Baroque painting and the essays of Lacan instead of Marlene Dietrich and Maria Montez vehicles, could never be praised, or accused, of innocence in *Cobra*. Yet of course there are moments when Cobra *the character* is innocent, childish, petulant, her bulb as dim as any American's in Paris, and it could be said that *Cobra* the novel achieves its sophistication in contrast with Cobra the character's naïveté. When we judge which of the Cobras in our reading experience has priority, we must consider the level of calculated innocence with which Sarduy endows his heroine, the better to surround her with doctors and artists, and world-weary octogenarian madams.

One might use *Flaming Creatures* to highlight other aspects of Sarduy's novel. With its loose non-plot and its several orgy scenes, the film feels more democratic or anarchic than does the novel's social hierarchy. In this novel, there is a diva, a Queen; her nominal boss La Señora is as much her servant as her employer; her costumer/body-painter/lover is also defined in relationship to Cobra, as of course is her dwarf-double Pup, as is her rival the scheming Cadillac and the Tangiers doctor Ktazob.

Instead of a plot sequence in Smith's movie we get a sequence of scenes that has the character of a ritual: preparation, celebration, death, rebirth, more celebration. The entire novel *Cobra* has also been compared to a cyclic sequence of transformations: Cobra's treatments for reducing her feet have many ritual elements; halfway through the novel Cobra is castrated and Pup is killed; yet, in the second half of the novel, Cobra is still a man, indeed, is now the macho travesty of a gay leatherman, who is then mummified in another ritual by the gang of Tibetan lamas. That these rituals are presided over by a head lama who is first seen giving a blow job in an Amsterdam bathroom is somewhat on a par with Smith's own approach to his flaming creatures: the divine is juxtaposed not so much with the secular but with the abject. Both novel and film are full of junk, full of debris, full of spatters and shards.

There are few sex scenes in *Cobra*: as René Prieto is the most recent to have pointed out, sexual desire is transferred onto various scenarios of violence, of shredding of the body.[23] (And yet there are no rape scenes in *Cobra* as there is, though a deliberately unconvincing and unconsummated one, in *Flaming Creatures*.) When Cobra engages in a love affair with the Indian body painter, she goes "offstage" to do so, and we follow the antics of Pup and La Señora instead. Also instead, we are given scenes in which Cobra *incites* desire in her audience (and thereby incites envy in her fellow artistes). As Stefan Brecht has pointed out in *Queer Theater*, part of the scandal of *Flaming Creatures* is that, when the penises of the drag queens protrude past their skirts and flop on the shoulders of other characters, they are limp, and remain so. Giving no proof of being aroused, of having visible desires of their own,[24] these flaming creatures do not promise the pleasure of a conventional pornographic film, nor the pleasure of feeling superior to creatures trapped in yearnings and desires which we do not share. Just as María Montez in *Cobra Woman* is proven to be a star because the movie is otherwise so terrible, Sarduy hopes to create a literary artifact in which the divine and the abject coexist, in which Cobra becomes more divine the more abject her surroundings and behavior become, from the sheltered if tawdry stage and backstage of the Teatro Lírico to the poverty of Franco's/seventeenth-century Spain (although there is a shelter there, too, an oasis of Caribbean flora and fauna) to the grimy dangerous streets of Tangiers.

Most obviously, this copresence of the divine and the abject is the splitting of Cobra into Cobra and Pup. Pup is Cobra's limp penis, ugly and small but very visible whereas for a conventional biologically male protagonist the

penis is rampant and enormous but always concealed. One way to perfect
your femininity, Cobra thinks, is to kill off your Pup. Not perhaps as limp
as the penises of Smith's movie, Pup is noisy, rude, a spitfire, yet childlike.
Fully using the language of abjection, Doctor Ktazob in Tangiers performs
a surgery in which all of Cobra's pain is transferred to the poor innocent
albino dwarf:

> With all your strength now, direct your pain toward the dwarf: she is dia-
> bolic, needy and ugly [...] She is nothing but your waste, your gross residue,
> what comes off you formless, your look or your voice. Your excrement, your
> falsies, how disgusting! body fallen from you that is no longer you. [...] you
> who will be perfect. lean, like an icon?
>   Pup's *chest began heaving. The whole of her tongue protruded from her
> mouth; her eyes grew paler* [...] She was now lifeless, the poor innocent, on
> the amianthus sheet. (65–6; 115–17; Sarduy's italics)

In the final paradox of desire, when Cobra has killed her Pup and achieved
her desire (a desire that confused the Performing of Woman with the Being
of Woman, transvestism with transsexuality), she becomes an asocial creature,
her head the head of a bird, not a woman, no longer human (hence fully
divine) but also without Madam, without Theater, without admirers, without emulators (hence fully abject): "*Her make-up is violent, her mouth painted
with branches [...] Up to her neck she is a woman; above, her body becomes a
kind of heraldic animal with a baroque snout*" (70; 126; Sarduy's italics). Here
the intertext is no longer the real drag queen Cobra or some general drag-
culture performer but Marmori's *La storia de Vous*: Sarduy uses the same paragraph which he quoted in his 1968 essay "From Yin to Yang" (*Written on a
Body* 5/ *OC II* 1130). Divinity, Cobra thinks, is achieved by lifting up away
from the abject intertext of the Teatro Lírico/Carrousel and into the loftier
literary intertext. No wonder there is a serious doubt that it succeeds.

I asked whether we agreed with Cobra the character in her pursuit of the
perfect performance of Woman as a proof of Divinity, and I now suggest
that shifting her strategy from the field of the Image to the field of the Real,
from transvestism to transsexuality, must be counted her mistake. Insofar
as we disagree with Cobra, we do so from the perspective of the aged theater owner La Señora.[25] Even though in the end she helps Dr. Ktazob carry
out the operation, La Señora is the last person to try to talk her out of her
resolve to kill her Pup

> My dear, [...] You think that in the evening, after the benign extraction,
> without further torment than a slight indisposition, a Biscayan nurse will
> bring you [...] a hand mirror where, rather than yor own image, you will

contemplate on a background of twilight [...] Greta Garbo in close-up....
Get off of that cloud: [...] Rather than into your delirium, look at yourself
in the mirror of others: they flee crestfallen, as if they had just lost a ruby on
the sidewalk, so that, like Veronica Lake, or like lepers, their hair conceals
their faces. [...] They talk to themselves. They set the table for a dead friend.
With their clothes on they shoot up in the subway's urinals. The Indonesian
maid finds them [...] "Air in the needle, as usual"—and she just continues
sweeping. (57; 103–4)

This is not the language of misogyny; rather, it is the language of abjection
and social alienation. In that sense, all the disasters visited on Cobra in this
portrait (which all come true, ten pages later) really come from leaving the
Teatro Lírico, not from her sex-change operation per se: allegorically from
leaving the realm of the Image in favor of the realm of the Real. If we agree
with La Señora that the transvestite is a better performer of Woman than a
real woman would be, we must accept as inevitable that La Señora returns in
the last paragraph to interpellate Cobra as neither woman nor transvestite:
"Her bony forefinger very close to my lips, she shouted: 'It's him' " (72; 130),
thus reminding the reader that, if we are to speak of Reality, Sarduy the
author (and Cobra the real drag queen, dead in a jet plane on Mt. Fujiyama)
never abandoned his male privilege, reserving the right to keep his bony
index (finger), the right to point and name which is so characteristic of
Lacan's symbolic field. Sarduy will have to try another tactic in the second
half of the novel: Cobra will now be a male protagonist, but one without first-
person speech (until the last section, The Indian Diary, and even there spar-
ingly), without interiority, and, through mummification, without choice or
will or (apparently) pleasure in the process. A different sort of deity, one without personality or desires: more absolute, yet less lovable.

Let us retreat from that failure, and return to Jack Smith's divinity school
for another lesson. Perhaps surprisingly, it will be a lesson in failure.

Retouching Oneself in Public

*Smith was, of course, a performer in many underground films, with a persona quite
indescribable, based on the human potential within us for allowing human effort,
will, and purpose to be deflected and brought to a kind of transcendent, oscillating
standstill by the minutiae of every moment lived in the course of "trying to perform."*

(Foreman, in Leffingwell et al. 26)

So far I have spoken about a way to rethink Sarduy's artistic milieu in terms
of the image-repertoire which is made possible by a long history of gay

orientalism. Knowing nothing of the real transvestite Cobra, I turned to Severo and Cobra's New York contemporary Jack Smith to see an example of orientalized transvestism as provocation and scandal, not just a proliferation of signs detached from their kitsch contexts (although Smith's movie is that, too). Yet Sontag and Barthes would be correct to see the orchestrated sloppiness of *Flaming Creatures* as inimical in style to Sarduy's version of transvestite semiotic collage. Surprisingly, we can turn to Smith once again to help relate Sarduy's characteristic writing style in *Cobra* to his display of the hieratic, imperiled drag queen.

Smith abandoned film in the late 1960s, possibly due to its expense, possibly due to the scandal around *Flaming Creatures*, and turned to other art media, including performance art.[26] His shows would start impossibly late, the stage no more than a seemingly random pile of rubbish. Sometimes they were slide shows; sometimes they involved a deliberately inept one-man performance of Ibsen, say, or Shakespeare. Often they involved Smith, in full Cleopatra or Blonde Cobra drag (and trademark goatee—he *embodied* María Montez, he did not *impersonate* her), reclining upon a chaise longue. What his audience and colleagues most remember about these evenings was the incredibly slow pace of the performances, in which up to five minutes would pass between lines: in these pauses Smith would constantly fiddle with his costume, how it would drape along his leg, or rearrange the detritus on the stage set.[27] Filmmaker Jonas Mekas called the Jack Smith of these performance pieces "the keeper of the graveyard at the end of civilization" (50), in part because of Smith's love for these lost pieces of trash culture, but also because in some of these pieces Smith kept up a constant self-critical murmur about how badly things were going: the experimental playwright Richard Foreman called such strategies "confounding devices" and felt that "in Smith's case the great slowness [was] informed by a feeling that 'everything was going wrong'" (26). The difference between the ordinary viewer's experience and that of the cognoscenti was that the cognoscenti accepted the substitution of display with commentary upon the display, the substitution of narrative with the pauses between narrative, the substitution of the direction of the gaze with the (constantly unsatisfactory) tableau which the gaze would be forced to take in without direction. Above all, the cognoscenti appreciated the fragmentation of the conventionally significant gesture and pose into a series of constant retouchings and corrections.

If Sarduy as a prose stylist is very far from the everything-goes ecstasy of *Flaming Creatures*, he is temperamentally very close to the constant retouching of the later Smith. In its larger units, the novel's narrative starts up, stops, backs up, starts all over again: the first paragraph is repeated, word for word, eighteen pages later; in a marvelous tour de force, a series of four sections each beginning "La escritura es el arte de" give alternate biographies for the Indian body painter; the tale of the two white dwarves, Pup and the Square Root of the Señora, is itself a sort of false start that needs to be corrected. Cobra's stay in Tangiers involves many false starts and dead ends. But then, narrative delays are typical of quest literature; what makes Smith and Sarduy equally unwatchable to the general reader, equally fascinating to the cognoscenti, is that this also all takes place on the level of the pose and gesture, or on the level of the sentence. In order to write smoothly, Sarduy must engage in pastiche or in parody. In *Cobra*, the long sentences either are imitations of Lezama's ponderous similes (labeled as such immediately afterward) or they are entire passages imitating the prose of the seventeenth century while Cobra, la Señora, and Pup make their way through Franco's Spain.

While Sarduy's start-again, stop-again style is indeed appropriate to his own theoretical pronouncements, it is also consonant with Smith's other contribution to the transvestite art, thematizing the constant retouching which invokes narcissistic perfectionism and an aura of failure. Sarduy seems suspicious of the "return to narrative" which he associates with books that are easy to read, like those of the Boom, and prefers to remain in the realm of the avant-garde on that front. As Gustavo Guerrero has noticed in his stylistic analysis of Sarduy, the ratio of description to action in his texts is very high: a suspicion of action reigns throughout his literary universe. Indeed, there is a suspicion of the function of a paragraph's topic sentence: one-sentence paragraphs abound. (Indeed, there is a suspicion of clearly framing a passage at its beginning: most notoriously, *From Cuba With a Song* connects up the four sections of the novel only at the book's very end, and apparently Sarduy was reluctant to do even that.) (Indeed, there is a suspicion of description as a framing for action: some descriptions merely cite famous paintings, and do not set up actions, and one or two apparent scene-setting descriptions turn out to be descriptions of calendar art or cigar box illustrations.) Indeed, there is a suspicion of any predicate: paragraphs are full of sentence fragments; the subject and its verb are frequently separated by appositions and prepositional phrases, adjectives separated from their nouns, making them difficult to connect; all major forms of interruptive punctuation—parentheses, double dashes, colons and semicolons—are routinely used to break up the sentence into its constitutive words. No amount of parallel syntax or repetition of scenes with variations or meta-narrative commentary can prevent an air of stagnation from hovering over Sarduy's paragraph (as over the one you have just read).

For Barthes and other avant-garde cognoscenti, this procedure freed each word into a joy of bliss, much as Benjamin once said that collecting a book freed it from the drudgery of being useful. One of Sarduy's eleven footnotes (also an interruptive strategy) refers to the thesaurus, one way to organize words so that they might be of use to others, but they do not tell a story and Sarduy gives us a list of six synonymous phrases that slows the reading further. The thesaurus is an artificial way to increase one's own language, frozen by exile. Having found a phrase one had forgotten, then displaying it to the reader, is like waving a mechanical toy or batting a big false eyelash at the audience. Words become fetishes, in every sense: the religious sense (microcosmal presence of the Divine text); the Marxist sense (commodities wrenched out of their original contexts which thus conceal the labor of their original production, although we may admire the packaging as much as the word itself);[28] the post-Freudian (*not* Freudian, since these words do not defensively conceal a castration; rather, they are celebrations of the powerful yet still vulnerable phallic Woman, the power of the mother tongue, Spider Woman as Cobra Woman).

Smith prevented his performances from falling completely into narcissism through theatricalizing his own dissatisfaction with his self-display. Sarduy keeps narcissism at bay, again just barely, through the technique of splitting: he is both Cobra and La Señora (and La Señora's relationship to Cobra careens from owner to servant to whistleblower). He is more than that, invested in almost any of the characters who speak, Pup, Dr. Ktazob, the envious rival Cadillac; perhaps only the Indian body painter and the adoring desirous crowds are described regularly as outside this constantly splitting author-function. As we have said, proliferating narcissism is a structuralist's, not a narratological, perversion; how appropriate for such antinarrative texts like *Cobra* and Jack Smith's performance pieces. A successful castration which somehow simultaneously perfected both Cobra's biological status as woman and her performance of Woman would bring the Real and the Imaginary perfectly into line for Cobra: it would be literary autonomy, but it would also be psychosis. Better to thematize the sabotage of this operation/narration instead.

Not a desire emanating *from* one's gender (either heterosexuality or homosexuality, where one knows one's preexisting gender, and desires a specific gender in the other) but a desire *for* a gender for oneself, transvestism and transsexualism are always about the retouching and redressing of Self before any movement out to the Other. Certain kinds of transvestite labors foreground the failure of the self to coincide with its ideal image. Placing Sarduy next to Jack Smith in a literary and cultural history of the Queer Sixties partly involves the tragicomic persistence of the body, and of the body's bony finger (the act of symbolizing), within a milieu (and a general desire) for transcendence, for abstraction and for the absolute. As such, it is also a lesson for literary history.

Conclusion II: Baroque Recreations and the Neo-Baroque International

Flaming Creatures is, like Antoine Watteau's early eighteenth century painting A Pilgrimage to Cythera—a fête galante, baroque recreation in art of a theatrical entertainment—ambiguous about everything except the celebration it depicts, poignant because the celebration must end. For Smith, that was life.

(Leffingwell 73)

Literary history can learn some interesting lessons from thinking about the transvestites of Jack Smith in tandem with those of Sarduy's *Cobra*. In the early 1980s art history finally acknowledged that abstract expressionism was not the only art game in town; that Surrealism had laid the groundwork for subterranean movements which cut up preexisting bits of culture to mount their dream theaters and in which the human body is seemingly disfigured by desire. Not all of these experiments are as chilly as Andy Warhol, nor as historically flat, although many must route their history through the costume-jewelry and exoticist versions of history that we see in Joseph Cornell, Alfred Chester, Edmund White, Jack Smith—and Severo Sarduy. The word "baroque" comes to mind much more easily to a Latin American literary historian than to a European or North American literary historian to describe an object such as *Flaming Creatures*; and since the concept of "neo-Baroque" was used by some Latin American writers in the Queer Sixties to fend off the heroic Socialist Realism of Mexican muralists and Cuban Afro-Antillanists and revolutionaries, there is no reason not to use the same term in world art history to fend off the demand for macho heroics in 1960s French *auteur* cinema or existentialist theater or action painting. Such posturing, also to be found in some of the Latin American Boom novelists (and, less often, in their novels), is challenged by the anti-macho posing and retouching of Smith and Sarduy's flaming creatures, although (due to the logic of perversion and perversity) they can never really threaten the centrality of the normal macho as they oscillate between the abject and the divine, and although (due to the logic of decadence) their poses simultaneously incite desire and disgust, bring desire onto the surface and deflect it from that dwarf double, the limp penis.

For Latin American literary historians facing the *oeuvre* of Severo Sarduy, one lesson to learn is that deciding between treating Sarduy as a Cuban writer or as a French writer is a false dichotomy. The Neo-Baroque, it turns out, is neither narrowly Caribbean nor less narrowly Latin American but part of a range of strategies used by many mid-century writers and other artists whose unorthodox desires, and not just their opinions about the relationship between sign and referent, put them at odds both with bourgeois realism and *machista* late-modernist attempts to combat that realism. In his critical writings Sarduy usually plays down his unorthodox desires, preferring to make theoretical pronouncements about the autonomy of language. To favor Sarduy's theoretical pronouncements over his theatrical practices is to choose to ignore the Cobras of his day, the other artists in the Queer Sixties who wanted to provoke the right kind of titillation from their audience. The character Cobra's negotiation with the mirror, and the mirror stage, is thematized by Jack Smith, and by Sarduy, and their texts' constant retouching shows a willingness to accept the failure of desire, which also corresponds to Sarduy's failure in his desire for fame: like Smith's unwatchable performances, Sarduy's unreadable novel places him as a treat for the cognoscenti, but also for the emulators, the pupils of the Divinity School, those who surrounded that old drag queen in Cannes to hear stories of the master as they prepare to enter the career themselves. When *they* read this book, they feel the tension more than do the lockstep Barthesians between the quasi-Divine protagonist and the inhuman bird fetish that she became.

I'm not sure I can overidentify with pre-op transsexuals as I can with effeminate homosexuals, fetishists, masochists, and the more abject transvestites of Fuentes and Donoso. My promise to Molina in chapter one to identify "always with the heroine, dummy" is not really fulfilled, as I identify more with La Señora and her sage advice, with angry Pup, as much a victim of the plot as Foción is of the plot of *Paradiso*, and above all with the entourage at L'Ondina Beach hanging on a drag queen's anecdotes. But otherwise I have now brought the story of the perverse back to where I started, to the 1970s of Manuel Puig; and meanwhile I have strayed quite far from the continents of Latin America. Where should a "perverse literary history of Latin American literature" go from here?

Conclusion/Epilogue: Perverse Narratives on the Border ∽

PERVERSE NARRATIVES ON THE BORDER

When California graphic novelist Gilbert Hernandez began to publish *Love and Rockets* with his brothers Jaime and Mario in 1981, it is not at all clear that he knew where he intended to take his imagination. In the first year his contributions to this extraordinary black-and-white quarterly large-format comic book were predominantly parodies of science-fiction scenarios (his brother Jaime also began with what would be his favorite heroine, bisexual punk Chicana Margarita Chascarrillo, as a "prosolar rocket mechanic," although his story lines too have become rigorously realistic over the years). Beginning in 1982, however, he chose to take one of the minor figures from that era named Luba, and develop her in a realistic—although, at times, magical-realistic—milieu, the little pueblo of Palomar, somewhat south of the border and away from everywhere, Hernandez's Macondo or Yoknapatawpha County. As sarcastic little Carmen says about Palomar to the audience, here "men are men and women need a sense of humor." But these are certainly strong women. The mayor is a woman named Chelo (many years later, Luba too will become mayor), and Carmen's best friend Pipo will become rich in America running a big sportswear company. (The first of the Palomar women to make her way north will be Luba's eldest daughter Maricela, since she knows that Luba would not tolerate her lesbianism.) When Luba arrives in Palomar and sets up shop as a *bañadora* or bath-house operator and to run the town's movie projector, she is a woman of few words, very big-breasted but not otherwise especially attractive (although the town's adolescent boys think otherwise), already a single mother assisted by her older cousin Ofelia. As the years went on and we learned more about Palomar, we also learned more about Luba, and in 1988, Hernandez decided to spend much of the next six years writing a sort of prequel, an extended flashback that gives all of Luba's history up until the moment she arrived in Palomar, a story which was published separately in 1994 as *Poison River*.

Poison River is full of plot, and plotting. However sophisticated, its medium is the comic book (and comics gained another round of sophistication at exactly this moment in American history[1]), but it also freely draws on soap opera and melodrama. Perhaps because it is a comic book, there is an air about this prequel which brings to mind the "secret origin" stories of the superheroes, like the murder of Bruce Wayne's parents or Jor-El sending Kal-El away from the exploding planet Krypton, and so over the course of *Poison River* we discover not just Luba's parentage (her mother, a bored, amoral society woman named María, got pregnant from dallying with one of her dark-skinned groundskeepers; the groundskeeper takes María and Luba away to the city to look for work, but María abandons them and Luba's father dies of a stroke); but also the first time Luba worked as a *bañadora*, the first time she defended herself with a hammer or wore clogs, the first time she went to the movies, and other idiosyncrasies of her character which fascinated the adolescent boys of Palomar in 1982. This, too, is the period in *Love and Rockets* when Hernandez regularizes the chronology of his story, and the prequel includes episodes from cousin Ofelia's leftist youth in Cardenista and post-Cardenista Mexico. Ofelia's present-day back pains turn out to be from an attempted assassination: paramilitary groups were hired to wipe out leftist protests in the 1950s of the labor strikes. Still, much of Luba's story has an almost deliberate vagueness about time and space (Luba prefers anachronistic clothes and movies from the 1950s; early on Hernandez committed himself to a Palomarian geography which must be near the Pacific coast, but how close it is to the California border is never made clear); the narration, while drawn in a bold, somewhat Expressionist style, retains some of the story told about the old country by one's immigrant aunt or grandmother.

Young Luba was rescued from life as a poor relation by a much older man, Peter Río, a conga drummer and manager of a small traveling orchestra. Peter at first sight is authoritative in macho ways: he clearly likes it when Luba calls him "Daddy" when they are married; he makes all the decisions for the couple; Luba never asks him about his work when he changes jobs and moves them up north. Yet their married life is not perfect, in part because Peter has a fetish: he gets so aroused by Luba's navel that he seldom has normal sex with her, and for a long time she does not get pregnant.

Prequels within prequels: we learn that Peter is the son of a hired strangler Fermín Río, who beat Peter's mother until she committed suicide; Fermín is connected to a gangster Salas, who runs both a clandestine

adoption clinic and a series of strip clubs, at least one of which specializes in she-male (pre-op transsexual) dancers; Peter already has a "wife," Isobel, one of the she-males, who is rearing a child they got from the clinic; now in order to afford his second family, Peter has had to return to Salas's gang far enough to take a job managing one of the strip clubs. (Peter's homosexual bandmate Blas joins him, and helps rescue Peter and Luba from the novel's violent dénouement.) Further prequels: three of the seventeen chapters of narration take place while Peter seems to be asleep (we discover that he is having a stroke). Here we discover that the meeting of Peter and Luba was no accident: his father Fermín had had an affair with one of the molls of rabidly anti-communist gangster Garza: this woman, it turns out, was Luba's mother María. Peter has slept with his father's girlfriends before, but none of them had ever performed in the 1948 Miss Ionosfera Beauty Pageant talent contest by cracking walnuts with her navel … Peter promised María that he would scour Mexico looking for her daughter Luba, even after mob politics takes María herself out of his grasp.

The graphic novel also contains a sort of absolute prequel. Look at the page in which Peter, after a stressful encounter with his first "wife," goes to a belly-dancing establishment to worship navels. Hernandez shows that the power of the sexual experience for Peter is in part a (subjective) memory of the day when Peter first ejaculated. The panels can and should be read in normal comic-book fashion, and so the time frame moves back and forth from the adult Peter, brought to the belly-dancer by characters Peter already knows to be gunmen involved with the clandestine adoption clinic, to the

child Peter, lugging his father's suitcase and traveling with Fermín's ruthless yet fiercely loyal bodyguard Gorgo to be brought face to "face" with the belly dancer's navel itself. Seeing the navel in the present turns out to be a repetition of the sight of the navel in the past. When Peter comes in the bottom left panel, it is as if the ejaculation happens for both child and adult Peter at the same time. However, the page also suggests a centripetal rather than a linear sequence, experience spiraling into the desirable cavity. Note that the childhood scenes are drawn in such a way that it is as if it is the story that Peter tells himself, not in the "objective" style of all of the many other flashbacks in the book; also note in the bottom left panel that other detached body parts are implicated as well. The navel is in some sense an absolute beginning: the story never shows Peter's mother, although he clearly loved her and hated his father's abuse of her; conversely, neither Peter nor any of the more florid speakers at the belly-dancing establishment allude to cosmic myths about the Omphalos: while not totally unjustified, to see this navel as a stand-in for Peter's mother or for the Great Mother is not really supported by the text. But it is clear that Luba's navel *is* a stand-in for María's navel *is* a stand-in for that earlier navel—if only we could be sure that it really existed, and is not a fantasy reconstruction of Peter's.

In another sense, however, all these navels are by no means absolute and cannot transcend the contexts in which Peter finds them, much as Molina in *Kiss of the Spider Woman* is aware that the prison romance he is enjoying with Valentín is not the pure innocence that Valentín at some point claims that it is. Fermín and Gorgo bring little Peter to that first navel; Fermín and the gangster Garza have prior claim on María's navel; Isobel's navel was on

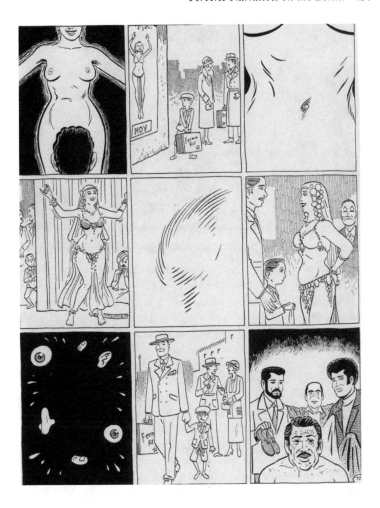

display at a belly-dancing establishment (and when she is taken out of circulation between men, Peter loses interest in it); Luba and her navel were
found by Gorgo and his decrepit father, who has a miraculous power to
trace women; and the navel in the center of this page is only rented from
these younger gangsters, who hover over the scene almost as if Peter preferred to have them there. For the goodness of the Phallic Woman to have
its greatest power over him, Peter seems to need to feel that he has stolen
her or rescued her—or just borrowed her—from the evil inherent in
machista masculinity. These evil father figures are, often enough, literally
his father: the novel maintains a tension in its political scenes between the

faceless capitalism of their baby-selling and drug operations and the more melodramatic mafia logic by which all politics and economics are merely quarrels within and between families. In the 1960s all the gangsters are rabid anti-communists who hate hippies, so they are often in deals with the police; Luba, now addicted to speed, is blackmailed into regular sex with Capitán Ortiz. Ortiz's relationship to Luba's hair is no less fetishistic than Peter's to her navel, except that he dumps her when it suits him, cutting off some of her hair for a souvenir.

This section of the novel ends in a gangland bloodbath, with Luba spirited off by the aged but loyal Gorgo; but Peter (who was thought to be fully paralyzed by his stroke) has already killed his father Fermín as he was taunting his incapacitated son by bragging about killing Peter's mother as well as his she-male first wife Isobel. Constantly aware of the presence of the violence which frames the scene of Peter's sexual arousal, Hernandez would be as diffident as Molina is in *Kiss of the Spider Woman* to agree with Valentín that sex is the space of innocence itself.

I choose to end my book on narratives of the perverse with *Poison River* for several reasons. A novel written in the 1980s and 1990s, full of homosexuals, fetishists, sadists, masochists, pre-op and post-op transsexuals "playing Scheherezade," with a narrative organized around defiant and resourceful, often powerful women: are we beyond Oedipus at last? It would have been a fantasy for Hernandez to say absolutely yes. The range of male subjectivities in the novel is still organized around the totems of machismo. As Paz argued in 1950 and (or so Hernandez thinks, to judge by other Palomar stories) as is still true today, machismo will even permit the homosexual in the active role to maintain his male privileges. But

Gilbert Hernandez and his Peter Río are much more resistant to this phallic posturing. He certainly would not be fooled into equating violence against women with a politically liberatory act of sadism, as Cortázar did.[2] Nor does Hernandez employ the masochistic suspense games of the Gothic or a Cortazarian neo-Gothic. Peter's erotics brush close to, but do not actually obey, Deleuze's reading of the masochistic scenario when he is in bed with María, the coldest of his women, but he is reluctant to fully have her beat the Old Man out of himself in order to usher in the New Man. His quest to find María's daughter suggests instead the chivalrous behavior of the courtly lover; when he finally does murder his own father, however, we realize that (unlike the Oedipal prediction) he did not grow up to become just like him, even though he actually did sleep with the women that his father had first enjoyed. Hernandez implies, in the end, that certain kinds of non-machista male subjectivities are no longer condemned to remain marginal to the most egregious versions of male domination.

These various marginal male subjectivities have all had their particular inflections. Unsurprisingly, Peter is most like a Felisbertian character, since he is after all a fetishist. His adoration of the big woman's navel renders him an adolescent, even a child. Looking can replace touching, and it is always related to the perversion of voyeurism. Peter abstracts an aspect of Woman which deprives the real women around him of agency, but then hands over to that abstraction a power over him. (Here we see the return of male dominance, at another level: the abstraction is not necessarily handed over to the woman who wields the navel, but to the men who run the strip clubs.) Insofar as it is an abstraction, the fetish can be detached from any individual woman—in Peter's case, it need not be on a biological woman at all—; and, like Felisberto, it generates backward-looking narratives that tempt us into a language of the absolute to explain the power of the fetish. Insofar as it is a fixation, it will always have a centripetal logic to it.

Does this novel, like Felisberto's *Las Hortensias*, also have a centrifugal or aberrant logic that counterbalances or complements the centripetal logic of the fetish? None of the centrifugal energies of the novel come from Peter's desire per se. As in *Las Hortensias*, the women of *Poison River* keep the men in motion: María sends the plot forward as well as the narration backward; Luba's reluctance to be merely a navel for her husband brings further plot complications. On a different level, the shift in genre from 1981 to 1982 to 1988 in Hernandez's use of Luba suggests the mobility of a fixated object of desire which, as I have argued, is characteristic of a fetish in a general way. Luba was introduced in a science-fiction parody; she is made realistic to ground realistic adolescent fantasies; her past is then narrated as the centerpiece of political melodrama. Felisberto's Horacio shifted in his fetishistic attraction from one aspect of an object to another, and eventually from one object to another; Hernandez lets the object, Luba, grow and show its different facets over the course of time. Likewise, the multiple mini-narratives and flashbacks that make *Poison River* so complex are generally (though not strictly) equivalent to the Felisbertian simile.

Instead of a drift in fetishistic desire, however, we have a different aspect of fetishistic logic altogether, neither the simile nor the metonym. Neither Luba's navel nor her hair is the most outsize aspect of her body, to put it mildly, and in the present of her Palomar years the adolescent boys and some of her boyfriends make it clear that Luba's breasts are absolute and incomparable. If there is evidence of fetishistic behavior in the writing and drawing of *Poison River*, then, we should treat all this talk of navels as displacing talk about a different body part, neither the navel that the pre-op transsexuals do not need to modify, nor the penis that they refuse to modify, but the breasts that they do indeed modify.[3] For the length of this particular novel, Luba's breasts are her open secret, on display even when covered, even when her men show no interest in them, and the air of knowingness and superiority we felt while reading Lezama's almost eroticized ambivalence towards his father partly obtains when we look at Gilbert's Luba: Gilbert thinks we believe that he is talking about navels; he may himself believe he is talking about navels, but "we know better." (If Cobra only could admit to herself that her worshiping audience knows all about her ... feet, even when most concealed! Vestiges of the logic of the open secret operate around her, too.)

A novella like Felisberto Hernandez's *Las Hortensias* certainly gives us a variety of positions in which we can place ourselves as we read an author who isn't in control any more. Are we the innocent collateral victim, like his wife? Are we like the sarcastic twin maids, gossipy and independent-minded but somehow implicated, calling the doll Hortensia "the spy" while themselves spying on their employer's privacy? Are we merely intellectual "enablers," like the embarrassed *muchachos* at Horacio's birthday party, listening to a confession we never elicited? Surely we are not Facundo, the department store dollmaker, the mass marketer of what was at first an individual's fantasy; yet there is always the fear that we are the crowds at the department store window. ... Yet Gilbert Hernandez is not a narrator out of control, as Felisberto was. He writes in a medium and genre that permits if not indeed requires improvisation—a quarterly installment on a growing cast of characters over twenty years!—but by 1988 it is the controlled improvisation of a writer who already knows his business. Moving the content of a character's fetish sideways from his own, Gilbert Hernandez masters some of the embarrassment that must accompany almost any sort of confessional speech about the overvalued objects of desire—I say "almost" because we have taken Felisberto's stories as a model of shameless speech. This embarrassment also almost always inheres around desires one traces back into childhood. Indeed, embarrassment and shame may inhere around literary genres, such as comic books, which form part of one's childhood. We see Luba learning to read from comic books: Ofelia is disgusted that she has picked the stories of "Pedro Pacotilla," a stereotype of a prank-filled lazy cowardly dark-skinned Mexican boy (Peter tells Luba that he uses the English form of his given name because he associates "Pedro" with Pedro Pacotilla). Luba defends the comics, and in general is open to a range of contemporary culture that Ofelia and Peter cannot accept.

There is no doubt that Gilbert Hernandez still worries that consuming or producing comic books is an embarrassment, despite a great amount of support from distinguished writers like Angela Carter (who reviewed his work enthusiastically in the mid-1980s) or U.S. Latino writers and spokespersons like Dominican-American Junot Díaz (whose story in the summer 2001 fiction issue of *The New Yorker* was illustrated by Gilbert; the story's narrator praises the Hernandezes by name), or tastemakers like autobiographer and editor Dave Eggers. Even after you get past your own embarrassment and shame, you encounter it all over again when your champions hope to take your work out of the small circle of like-minded individuals who already understand your genre, your medium, your subculture, your desires.

LITERARY HISTORY IN THE AGE OF CULTURAL STUDIES: TOO MANY ALTERNATIVES, AND NO ALTERNATIVE

To end a book that promises "perverse Latin American histories" with *Poison River* is also a challenge to the definitions that structure the field of Latin American literature.[4] I wonder if you saw it coming, even as we scolded Carlos Fuentes for superimposing Italy upon Mexico and classical mythology upon cinema. Puig wrote his novel in New York. Lezama's fanciful genealogies include Diaghilev, his character's bisexual episode occurs in New York, and his literary disciples scattered into exile despite his own insularism. In his own small way, Felisberto's *Las Hortensias* was written during a Paris trip, and his posthumous reputation depended on Spain (Peri Rossi in exile), France (Cortázar), and Italy (Calvino). Cortázar returns Pizarnik to a fin-de-siècle French boudoir as they rewrite Transylvanian countesses or Sade and Lautréamont. Most flamboyantly, Sarduy borrows from the nonliterary, only semi-narrative cultural forms of his day. We have quoted that great canonizer Harold Bloom: dare we open the Pandora's box of nonliterary narrative material, written by Latinos north of the border, in order to tell the next event in the literary history of the Latin American perverse?

Literary critics have shifted from relating novels to other novels, and placing them within historical, sociological, and political contexts, to relating novels to aspects of popular culture, and situating the novel as a discourse among other discourses. This would be perfectly fine if the novel as a discourse, defined as a mode of speech with a specifiable social context and variable social effects, still had the prestige that Modernism and late Modernism had won for it, if the novel could still change the way we see the world. But now we don't think that it can; some of us no longer think that the non-fiction narratives of the *testimonio* can, either.[5] The most overt defender of the shift to an examination of popular culture (despite his own position on the faculty of Amherst College) is Ilan Stavans, who has also positioned himself as a spokesperson for U.S. Latinos and especially Chicanos. Within the academy, it is easier to critique the systemic aspects of the popular; but the growth of cultural studies within the academy shows that professors qua professors are also less sure that we should be studying novels and other complex narratives in isolation from other cultural objects. An extraordinary collection of essays such as José Quiroga's *Tropics of Desire* devotes its first chapters to the interstices of canonical and semi-canonical writers such as Lezama, Rodríguez Feo, Elizabeth Bishop, Villaurrutia, Cabrera, and Piñera, and then moves foursquare to popular culture: the feints with official culture in *Fresa y chocolate*, the *bolero*, Ricky Martin and the gay tchothcke Carlos doll, all under the larger mantle of "sex tourism" as a model for the dangers of appropriating the Latin/o Other. (An interesting exception, to which we'll return: the art-house cinema of Frances Negrón-Montañer's *Brincando el charco*; but even that is described only in passing.) With its last chapter critiquing the relationship between queer Latino leadership and many of the grass-roots constituents' lack of interest in the only sorts of power that these leaders can broker, Quiroga has left the field of the literary altogether. Preserving a certain kind of Latin American focus, and certainly preserving a kind of historical methodology in the center of his political deconstructions, Quiroga abandons the literary. Likewise, Gareth Williams's searching and empathetic 2002 book *The Other Side of the Popular* grants Piglia's 1992 novel *The Absent City* an almost fetishized status, the only novel studied before chapters on history and theory and chapters on nonliterary cultural phenomena, like an El Salvadoran refugee who explains why she joined a Los Angeles gang.

Idelber Avelar, in an equally extraordinary book *The Untimely Present*, also performs a close political reading of *The Absent City* amidst readings of recent novels from the Southern Cone in a book that is weakened only somewhat by a pre-queer-theoretical Freudian reading of melancholy and the Oedipal in literary history. Yet Avelar abandons the field of Latin American literary history from a different direction: he argues that one of the effects of the dictatorship years and of neo-liberal Latin American economic policies is that local intellectuals are now forced to define their projects in national terms, not the continental terms of the Boom Era. There is still literary history, but in all honesty it can no longer be considered Latin American but "merely" Chilean, Argentinean, Nicaraguan, etc. Avelar's justification for examining the novel in its isolation from other genres of a culture is, we might say, funerary: the novels of the present post-dictatorship world rewrite the novels of the past because those earlier novels had had the ebullient arrogance to speak for Latin America, and the sepulchral fictions of a Piglia, Eltit, or Santiago are a grieving for the lost potential of the medium as well as a grieving for Latinamericanism. I find this melancholy position extremely attractive even if, as I hope to have shown, the solidity of the Boom's sexual politics turns out to be something of a mirage on closer inspection, and thus, much care must be exercised to argue that, as a moment in Latin American history, they pursued an Oedipalizing project.

With his Jamesonian affiliations and his foregrounding of mourning and melancholy, Avelar is the closest of those I have discussed to Alberto Moreiras, author of two powerful recent books which should bear on the relationship between Latin American literary history and cultural studies, *Tercer espacio* and *The Exhaustion of Difference*; yet it is not clear that they do, in part because of Moreiras's rigorous suspicion, almost phobia, of carrying meaning through narrative. Moreiras brings to bear the *dernier cri* of the French avant-garde (Blanchot, Tel Quel, and Derrida) and writes in a tone of voice reminiscent of Adorno at his most rebarbative, to critique facile narratives, especially the narratives of what Carlos Alonso called modernity and autochthony, the narratives which derive political and moral virtue from imitating the West (modernity) and the ones which derive political and moral virtue from refusing to imitate the West (autochthony).[6] His willingness to inhabit, austerely, the space of negativity means that, for him, Latin American literary history is only useful as a weapon to upset the smooth categories of world literary histories: it would be unwise to create a positive Latin American literary history, however perverse. In his refusal to connect books to other books in a significant narrative, he is insistent that if there is a subject of literary history, it is a Lacanian subject, or perhaps even a Deleuzian one; literary history does no more than invent narrative secondary revisions to create imaginary continuities whereas each original novel is a trauma, or a Barthesian *punctum* that wounds the surface of the comfortable literary history in which the book is supposed to serve. His best readings are allegorical—Borges's "Tlön, Uqbar" sparks a meditation on the relationship between history and literature's "ur-objects"—or overtly philosophical—Lezama's theories of cultural transmission in *Las eras imaginarias* can be aligned with, even correct, Heideggerian and Adornian theories in which the artist carries over the unthought potentials in language and culture even when the artwork itself does not think out that potential.[7]

To prefer allegorical and philosophical readings of narratives suggests some distaste for actual narratives, and Moreiras follows a long tradition of the avant-garde, mostly French but recognizable in authors positioned as far apart as Paul de Man and Diamela Eltit, which uses "poetic" and "anti-narrative" as honorifics. In both his books Moreiras expresses at crucial moments a fear of or distaste not just for Lyotardian master narratives, but narrative *tout court*.[8] The ideal of critical thinking for Moreiras is the opposite of telling stories about books, and we would be wrong to see his books, in chapters in roughly chronological sequence, as exercises in "literary history." (In any case, his powerful reading of the novel-essay-suicide note by Arguedas, *El zorro de arriba y el zorro de abajo* (The Fox From Above and the Fox From Below), in an essay that marks both the critique and the death of the Boom project, implies that there is no fiction to be read after the end of the utopian projects of the 1960s—his brief reading of Eltit is of her 1994 proses on photographs of the insane—). It would be equally wrong to argue that the chapter on Galician writer Xosé Luis Méndez Ferrín is Moreiras's attempt to write himself and his own peripheral-Peninsular roots into *Tercer espacio*; but if anyone were to insinuate that this were actually the case, that same someone should no doubt heap contumely on this epilogue of mine, which directs the history of Latin American narrative (and I have repeated that I *do* believe in literary history) through *Poison River* by Gilbert Hernández, a U.S. North American, queer in the broader sense of the word, who speaks English as his first language, who is about my age, and who tells stories in a medium that is as pre-critically mine as the *bolero*is for José Quiroga or his childhood photograph is for Moreiras: how embarrassing.[9]

So I am constructing my perverse Latin American literary histories in the teeth of excellent advice not to do so, more than a little dismayed by the company I am asking you to keep (Freud? Sacher-Masoch? Harold Bloom?), and excruciatingly aware that I have begun in my last chapter and here in the epilogue to drift. From the strictly literary I have chosen to drift in the direction of narrative artifacts which mix words with pictures, in less prestigious genres (underground movies that cite B-movies, comic books) which are often only the domain of cultural studies. I do not think that I am doing cultural studies. For one thing, I have not invoked one of the necessary phantoms of a sociological or cultural studies reading, an audience or readership other than myself, as the audience who is interpellated by that novel and its discourses. What sort of cultural studies interprets a culture of one? And yet I do not speak an idiolect, either; neither do any of the writers I have very hastily summarized here. If you and I understand each other, but know that we are not the general readers sought after by, say, Stavans's autobiographical memoirs, we must take into account the status of this segmented readership in the post-Boom, post-modernist moment in Latin American studies. I do so with a concept that may be almost as embarrassing, almost as tacky, as the open secret of Luba's breasts which I have had to present on the page to you while supposedly talking about the reconstruction of absent origins: the concept of "alternative culture."

The word is as much a product of the 1980s as the alternative comic book store, which stands as an instance of it. Alternative culture is opposed to 1960s counterculture, which had utopian and separatist aspirations; alternative culture has always understood that the naïveté of these aspirations was too easily exploited.[10] In contrast, alternative culture knew from the beginning that it was a product of the city and of the very same capitalist circuits that it distrusted. (It is tempting to correlate this focus with the urban focus of the novelists I have treated, and the way that the marginalities that queer theory studies most thoroughly are also urban marginals: the drag prostitutes of "Mema's House" in Mexico City or the streets of Nestor Perlongher's Sao Paulo. La Manuela's brothel may be in rural Chile, but I have focused on the libidinal urban chaos of Fuentes's Coyoacán house in which Donoso wrote the novella.) Alternative culture may never have been as atopian as Moreiras's demand for a "dirty atopianism" would like,[11] but it was certainly dirty; and it certainly could be argued that Michael Taussig's "savage hybridity" (quoted approvingly by Moreiras) or Greil Marcus's praise of Adornian negativity *Lipstick Traces* were the theories while modern primitivism and punk music were the practice, just as in the 1980s and early 1990s Sedgwick, Butler, and Crimp supplied the queer theory for which gender-bending rock stars, black and Latino voguing houses, and ACTUP supplied the practice. (And in each of these hasty examples, the relationship between the theory and the practice is probably articulated differently, not to mention the piles of awful theory or appalling practices sitting next to the good stuff on the book shelf or the bar stool: in alternative culture, as in any culture, you can choose your friends, but you can't choose your acquaintances.) Indeed, insofar as I distrust Moreiras's "atopianism," I do so because I distrust the equation of thought with culture. It may be the case that thought, and novels such as our narratives of the perverse, exceed the location in which they are thought, written and read, but the persistence of some spaces is absolutely necessary for collective decision-making, and sex of all kinds, and political action. By this I neither mean the Lacandón forest of the Zapatistas, nor the abstract and gray space of Postmodernity, but rather the institutions where books are actually written, read, and talked about, and alternative sexualities are actually engaged in: not The University but the college town, not The Library but independent bookstores; independent record labels; art-house cinema; gay and gay-friendly bars, the ghetto, the nude beach, the bath house.

Alternative culture was chronicled and at times theorized *avant la lettre* by writers such as Carlos Monsiváis and Edgardo Rodríguez Juliá in the shadow of the failures of the monolithic state and of a monolithic leftist opposition to that state; still, the concept will inevitably sound more American to your ears than "subaltern"; but most of the examples dear to subaltern studies could be fruitfully thought of as alternative cultural phenomena. The term would then show, to give an example out of García Canclini, that the new producers of rural handicrafts have something in common with the threadbare U.S. magazines in which the handicrafts are advertised, and often also with the people who purchase them. To survive at all is the goal of many of the alternative cultural spaces of the Third World, and to deploy some version of Benjamin's aura strategically, to let some narrative of authenticity cling to the objects they make and circulate into the First World, can be something of a theoretical embarrassment, but may not in the end be objectionable. After all, those who live in the alternative culture spaces of the First World are in need of authenticity. They propose to survive in a capitalist milieu without valuing it: if the alternative cultural spaces in the First World think, indeed often brood, in terms of what might seem to be an outmoded concern with authenticity, integrity, and not selling out, it must be acknowledged that we put the post-separatist, post-counterculturalists in an extraordinarily difficult position. The self-policing strategies of these alternative cultural figures are remarkably similar whether in the First or the Third World: shaming. By choosing an embarrassing example for my epilogue, I hope to suggest that academia, too, in many of its manifestations, is an alternative cultural space, especially for those of us on the fringes of respectability and institution-building.

First World alternative culture does differ from Third World alternative culture, of course. First World culture coexists with or even thrives on the avant-garde demand for constant novelty and constant motion. Whereas hybridity theories have (slowly) given permission to indigenists to evolve their inherited forms, and theories of praxis (occasionally) permit leftists to change, nevertheless, either can also remain faithful to lifelong practices without embarrassment and shame. However, a novelist who does not renew the form of the novel with each work is held to have stagnated. Queer theories have also defined themselves against lesbian and gay identity politics by privileging sexualities in flux: activists repeatedly tell the theorists that it is easier to organize a movement if you convince your constituency that we were born that way and that the deprogrammers can't change us, but we continue to question the coming-out narrative as the privileged narrative form in gay literature in our search for the Fociós and Fronesises whose senses of self just don't fit that paradigm. But the avant-garde demand for novelty is not only in collusion with the capitalist marketplace—a point numbingly clear to the queer movement as it watched glossy magazines co-opt and destroy its politics of style. Since so much of alternative culture revolves for better or worse around matters of style, not just lifestyles but specific institutions can look absurd within ten or five years' time. The alt.culture entrepreneur has the thankless task of creating an alternative cultural public space for people, one that must be publicized (since the space or practice did not exist before he or she created it) through alt.culture media that themselves constantly mutate, and then in the best of cases he or she must know when to walk away from the lucrative yet "inauthentic" mainstream circus it will have become. The gesture of walking away from a space that has been co-opted makes for a dangerous analogy with the field of cultural studies, since there the object of study often cannot fold its tents and move on like Lollapalooza once it has been co-opted by capital, or the habitués of a special area of the bushes in a city park once it has been made an example of by the police. And even in the realm of the "purely" literary, some novelists resent being told that it is time to move on to something else.

So I am well aware that I import many problems into the debate around cultural studies by preferring the term "alternative culture" to "subaltern culture." I am not temperamentally afraid of inhabiting the embarrassed position, the pervert's position. Naturally, I have chosen this term in part because so much of this book has been about alternative sexualities. Conversely, it could be tenably argued that I have been speaking all along about "subaltern sexualities," making a strict analogy between hegemonic First World economic and political systems and hegemonic Oedipal heterosexuality. But my reluctance to claim myself as a subaltern, and the space of literary history published by an academic press as a subaltern space, will I hope be appreciated by the reader.

For make no mistake: I am arguing that to read novels by Puig, Lezama, Hernández, Cortázar, Donoso, Fuentes, and Sarduy *is* to take part in an alternative culture. I have hoped not just to read representations of alternative sexualities but also to bring alternative erotics of reading to the fore in my analyses of texts, to perform reading like a homosexual, like a voyeur, like a masochist, above all to read like a fetishist, since the fetishist's "over-valuation" of the object he worships (a woman's navel, say, or the exiguous oeuvre of a failed Uruguayan concert pianist) bears the most similarities to our present conjuncture, both as readers and as students of culture. Our training as close readers is not easily distinguished from the situation of Peter Río in the belly-dancing brothel, surrounded by more or less sinister enablers, reenacting, with a difference, a close attention to something exciting and shameful. The reader, like the fetishist, crouches in the brothel of class (and structurally male) privilege. The alternative to this sort of fetishism is to take the role of *Poison River*'s policeman, indulging sadistically in the same pleasure as Peter but refusing to let that pleasure change the structures of power by which he acquires the long dark-haired women that *he* abuses. Peter's chivalry, his willingness to let the women he worships mark and change his life, is much more like the claims that we academics make about how literature has changed and shaped our lives, how we were seduced from a pre-med or pre-law track in college, dazzled by the fireworks of the Boom novel and lured away from our native American fiction, mobile in our way as we move from novel to novel (from navel to navel) and willing to experiment with other genres/genders provided that they, too, elaborate upon some narrative that both transfixes us and sets us into motion. We know that from the position of the real men's world of guns and drugs and stranglers we will seem disappointingly fixated, mere paper dolls chasing our spider women of fictional narratives which, we happily acknowledge, do not have the archetypal status that a Jungian awards them nor (more interestingly) the corroborative status of case histories that exemplify Freudian fictions. We can use our fictions to challenge the Freudian fictions, and have done so, while perhaps in the process giving those Freudian fictions in our critiques more credit than they get in the real men's world of guns and drugs and stranglers. Our alternative culture values desires that are more varied and complex than can be found in that world.

In our constantly shifting compromises with the no-alternative of global capitalism, we are, at times, faced with too many alternatives as to where to take the story next. José Quiroga's Carlos dolls, Gareth Williams's gang-member sound bites, and Alberto Moreiras's non-narrative dirty atopianism all abandon the story of Latin American narrative fiction. If the story of Latin American narrative fiction continues despite them, it may take on more and more features of alternative elite culture, like opera and poetry, a writing dedicated to Barthes's mandarinate, "the Society of the Friends of the Text," and indeed the writing of Barthes's friend Sarduy prefigures this option. But we might also on pragmatic grounds declare that Latin American literature expands to U.S. Latino literature, as Carlos Alonso has done in various presentations to the MLA, and in doing so we open up our alternative elite culture to the growing numbers of U.S. Latinos (whether bilingual or not) who make it to United States institutions of higher education. Although she misses Palomar, in the present time of my writing [December 2003] Gilbert Hernandez has actually sent Luba to the United States, staying with her half-sisters and with the three of her daughters who have moved here permanently, although she refuses to learn English. Whether the direction that Alonso advocates radically changes which texts we read in our Latin American syllabi and how we read them, or is merely a liberal gesture of inclusion and an institutional power play between U.S. Spanish departments and English or American Studies departments, depends partly, I argue, on whether or not we unleash different desires in ourselves and in our students as readers.

To publicize to others our desires is a risk; it is not at all surprising that we would prefer to limit that risk by participating in alternative public spaces, spaces convoked for the satisfaction of desires, preferably spaces hostile to large-scale capitalist mechanisms for satisfying desire like the mainstream market, and hostile to infinitely replicable small-scale mechanisms like the nuclear family. I further expose myself to risk (I hope you do too) by sidestepping certain avant-garde tastes and demanding narrative, heroines to identify with, omniscient narrators to disagree with, authors' biographies to compare their fictions with, popular stories to read perversely against the grain. Insofar as the greatest fear of avant-garde queer theorists and narrative deconstructionists is the elimination of possibilities that takes place with a premature closure (and the hidden coerciveness of the concept of maturity hidden in the word "premature"), I am pleased that a focus on the erotics of reading in the history of Latin American literature does not bring the story to a natural or violent end, as Avelar's and Moreiras's grimmer tales of the destruction of the Boom era's faith in a unified Latin American emancipatory narrative does indeed do. Like a twenty-years-and-running graphic novel in quarterly installments, the history of Latin American narrative fiction, perversely read, may no longer be unified or emancipatory but neither does it have any reason ever to end, as long as the alternative cultural spaces north and south of the border continue to negotiate the troubled relationships between norm and aberration, fixation and mobility, and no alternatives and too many alternatives.

Notes

PREFACE AND ACKNOWLEDGMENTS

1. Except when the original is required for the argument, all quotations will be in English translation throughout the text, with English source first, then the Spanish.
2. I can't resist quoting Ellis Hanson's good-natured dismissal of Kaja Silverman's book, insofar as it comes across as "defending perversions": "Silverman comes to the defense of those many, seemingly inevitable pleasures, reassuring us that masochism is okay if it is male, fetishism is okay if it is female, idealization is okay if it glorifies the downtrodden, and identification is okay if it is with someone we are not supposed to be" (*Out Takes* 13). Hanson thinks that it would be better to write essays without the moralizing of any ethical criticism, even feminist-psychoanalytic moralizing. But I hope you'll be keeping a scorecard for my perversions anyway.

CHAPTER 1: ENTER THE SPIDER WOMAN

1. In the novel's many avatars in play and film, Puig kept Molina's age to be the same as his own, while Valentín remained twenty-six years old. I thank Benigno Sifuentes for this insight. Levine's biography of Puig certainly emphasizes the chatty, gossipy, storytelling side of him, in part because of her extensive use of the letters he wrote home to his mother, another point of identification between Puig and Molina, whereas Valentín's family has nothing in common with his author's.
2. One of the first critics to relate Foucault to Molina's discourse of clichés is Alicia Borinsky in her *Ver/Ser visto*. Carlos Alonso's *The Burden of Modernity* underlines Vargas Llosa's insistent attempt to define the post-Boom moment as one of essentially light and trivial literature, "like Puig's," a misreading that shows his distance from Puig even as it enables him to write *Tía Julia y el escribidor*. For a more comparatist perspective on the new respect for cliché in the writings of the '80s, ushered in by Puig and by Angela Carter, see Michael Wood's *Children of Silence*, essays honed from his articles in *The New York Review of Books*.

3. The most recent works which I have found useful for charting a path relating narrativity to desire in a European, mostly nineteenth-century context, would be Barthes's *S/Z*, Peter Brooks's *Reading for the Plot*, and Ross Chambers's two books, *Story and Situation* and especially *Room to Maneuver*, which ends with a reading of Puig and with a reading of a novel about Ovid, David Malouf's *An Imaginary Life*.

4. Similar criticisms have been labeled against the canons studied in Anglo-American and French literature: Sedgwick, Moon, D.A. Miller, Lucey, have all found more energy studying the male canon than the female. Fortunately, both Judith Roof's *Come As You Are: Sexuality and Narrative* and Terry Castle's *The Apparitional Lesbian* insist on a specificity of women's experience in their examples.

   For my own project I am saddest about excluding the short stories and novels of Silvina Ocampo, surely the Latin American woman writer who has the most right to be considered a narrator of the perverse. Ocampo engaged in a relationship with lesbian poet and essayist Alejandra Pizarnik, whose relationship to Sadeian discourse and to Cortázar forms part of my chapter 4. A more detailed view of the "Rioplatense feminine perverse" would include Borinsky's *minas crueles*, Molloy's nouveau-roman lesbians and gay men, and Peri Rossi's faux-male *solitarios de amor*, whom I hope to study in a future project.

5. In this essay he refrains from explicating his theory of sublimation, one aspect of which argues that love is to sex as the upper parts of the body are to the lower parts, but it is a distinction that Molina and Valentín in their prison understand implicitly: Molina asks Valentín for a kiss only after they have been having sex regularly, a proof to him that the relationship is not simply physical but also romantic:

   [Molina]:—Well, but as a farewell, I do want to ask you for something ... [Valentín]:—What?—Something you never did, even though we did a lot worse things.[...] A kiss. [...] I'm curious ... would you feel much revulsion about giving me a kiss?—Mmm. It must be a fear that you'll turn into a panther, like with the first movie you told me.[...]—It's very sad being a panther woman; no one can kiss you. Or anything.—You, you're the spider woman, that traps men in her web.—How lovely! Oh, I like that (260–1/264–5).

6. For an analysis of the complicity between Ellis and one of his sources the Symbolist author John Addington Symonds, see Koestenbaum's brilliant essay, "Crouching Among Sailors" in his *Double Talk*.

7. Laplanche and Pontalis base the reading of the primal scene on a lovely narrative of the perverse, the Wolf Man case history. Besides their *Vocabulary of Psycho-Analysis* on the primal scene, see also their contribution to Burgin et al., eds., 1989.

8. Zizek's use of fantasy as fiction is far more subtle than this, except whenever he wants to make a political point: see *The Plague of Fantasies*, which is also marred by a sort of vanguardist suspicion of narrativity. A closer example of circular reasoning would be Marjorie Garber's use of the maverick psychoanalyst Robert J. Stoller's formulation about fetishism, "a fetish is a story in the form of an object"; see my discussion in chapter 4.

9. One danger which may not be obvious to many academic critics is how easily identifying with characters permits a slide from a generally Freudian analysis to a generally Jungian one. Many of the Latin American authors in this study, particularly Borges, Cortázar, and (as we shall soon see) Paz, were quite sympathetic to Jung. All the more reason to prefer a reading of The Spider Woman as a position which Valentín invents and into which Molina insinuates himself, not some preexisting Dark Goddess with its pre-existing symbolic content.

10. Elizabeth Abel's *Virginia Woolf and the Fictions of Psychoanalysis* demonstrates persuasively that Freud singled out a patriarchal trend in European anthropology at a moment in which a matriarchal vision of prehistoric societies was equally available to him. The central text for a critique of the collusion between psychoanalysis and structuralist anthropology is, of course, Deleuze and Guattari's *Anti-Oedipus: Capitalism and Schizophrenia*, and I follow some of its insights in my main text.

11. See his *Myth and Archive: A theory of Latin American narrative*, especially chapters one and four.

12. Ilan Stavans's brilliant if uneven *The Riddle of Cantinflas: Essays in Hispanic Popular Culture* (1998) alludes to the trajectory I stretch out here (48), noting that the Paz-Ramos line of national character essays is extended by Roger Bartra's 1987 *The Cage of Melancholy*, which is likewise haunted by a sense that the lower-class vulgarity of certain Mexican males is the key to understanding all Mexican men; Stavans tends to agree, but celebrates what Ramos and Paz deplore.

13. Of interest structurally: Paz seems astonished that the pachuco, although between two traditions, participating in neither, is nevertheless not paralyzed but in some anarchic ways hyperactive and excessively visible (just as queer culture claims to reject both straight culture and gay culture). Of interest prophylactically: although mixing certain signs of masculinity and femininity by 1940s standards, the pachuco dandy does not deviate from the level of misogyny of the cultures he stands between (just as we cannot presume that queer theory and culture shake off inherited male privileges). Paz also makes his appearance in lesbian and gay studies, the tamer precursor to queer theory, insofar as Almaguer and Lancaster cite some remarks from *The Labyrinth of Solitude* to bolster their claim that the active role in gay sex is not, or not very, stigmatized among Mexican (and other Latin or Latino) men, only the passive role. And Valentín, albeit in a prison cell, does not feel his masculinity threatened by penetrating Molina.

14. Rosario Castellanos, Mexico's premier first-wave feminist writer, skewers the traditionalist reading of Eve and Malinche both, not to mention a good half-dozen other stereotypes of Mexican women, in her posthumously published satirical play *El eterno femenino* (1975).

15. For queer readings of Moctezuma, see José Piedra, "Colonial Sissies"; for the larger context of marginalizing masculinity in the colonial enterprise, see Margarita Zamora, "Reading in the Margins of Columbus."

16. There are no real criticisms of Paz in the North American academy, except of the historicizing kind: Jason Wilson suggests that Paz's position is of a piece

with Surrealist doctrines of love on the one hand and discourses emphasizing the alienation of modernity on the other, implying that these are the truth about love and the truth about modernity. Straddling the North American and Mexican academies is Claudio Lomnitz's critique of centralist thinking in his *Exits from the Labyrinth*. In Mexico, criticisms of Paz blur into criticisms of his role for twenty years as the gatekeeper to official literary culture (even when literary culture was at odds with political culture). Probably the best independent critique of Paz from within Mexico, though not without flashes of bitterness, is Jorge Aguilar Mora's *La divina pareja*, which, instead of opposing the European intellectual tradition which Paz employs from some "autochthonous" or empiricist position, founds his critique in the dissonant voices of the European tradition—Nietzsche, Deleuze—which Breton and Sartre could never fully silence, much the way that, say, Greil Marcus in his book on punk music's roots in a "secret history of the twentieth century" critiqued Surrealism and existentialism for undervaluing the negative moment of Dadaism and other movements with which they were in competition.

17. While casting about at the beginning of the chapter for the Mexican sense of self as an archetype, he discards the possibility that the working-class man could possibly be the subject of Mexican history, blending Marx, Lukács, and D.H. Lawrence into a straw man that he can comfortably reject (his real opponent, Diego Rivera, is of course never mentioned by name). He almost goes so far as to say that the working-class man will never become the subject of modern history, then retreats to the position that if this should ever become the principal criterion of modernity then Mexicans will never accede to it. In this way he rehearses the moves that, as we shall see, blur the difference between a uniquely Mexican national character and a more generalized characterization of all modern man.

18. Similar criticism can be leveled at Paz's *Postscript to the Labyrinth of Solitude* (1970), which combined a denunciation of the government's massacre of student protesters in 1968 with a historical comparison of traditions of centralization and sacrifice to Aztec practices. Side by side with an Enlightenment hope that knowing one's history can help one refrain from repeating it is the modernist poet-anthropologist's (NOT the pre-Columbian's) insistence upon seeing events in the present as the fulfillment of mythical cycles: the latter insistence cannot help but annul the former hope.

19. See Stacie Widdifield's shrewd analysis of this painting in *The Embodiment of the National in Late Nineteenth-Century Mexican Painting*.

20. See Sandra Messinger Cypess's chapter on Ireneo Paz (68–97) in *La Malinche in Mexican Literature*.

21. Jean Franco has already submitted this novel to an analysis partly in terms of its relation to the Malinche figure in her book *Plotting Women*; but also see Amy Kaminsky's different approach to the novel's unreliable narrator and the inevitably gendered misreadings he produces.

22. Laurita does not quite have the sad double consciousness of Mia Farrow's character in *The Purple Rose of Cairo*: "I just met the most wonderful man the other day. He's fictional, but I guess you can't have everything."

23. It is somewhat puzzling that Paz could not or would not find such examples in the popular or political culture of his day in 1950: Anne Rubinstein in *Bad Language, Naked Ladies, and Other Threats to the Nation* runs off in a footnote (168, n. 10) a quick list of a variety of powerful women shadowing the dichotomy of the *mujer moderna* versus the *mujer tradicional*; and I examine Fuentes's use of the Golden Age film actress María Félix in chapter 5.

24. This is probably as good a place as anywhere to warn ourselves of the danger of equating all women with mothers when dealing with Freud. Upon close examination, any hope that his theorizing about the Oedipus complex could remain persuasive is limited to the Oedipal complex of male children; but to presume that all the women in a male infant's development have the same function and valence as the mother limits the range of positions much too much. The preservation of the triangle at the expense of weighing the uniqueness of governesses, uncles, family friends, and older siblings is the sort of Freudian and Lacanian thinking castigated by Eve Sedgwick in "Tales of the Avunculate" in her *Tendencies*, as we see in chapter 2. The most novelistic of the case histories, *Dora*, is an excellent place to examine the importance of adults who are neither the father nor the mother in a patient's neuroses, and Kahane and Bernheimer's collection *In Dora's Case* remains exemplary.

25. All of the footnotes have secondary or local purposes. A section on anal eroticism as a possible characteristic of homosexuality follows beneath the scene in which Valentín, whose food has been poisoned by the Warden, loses control of his bowel movements and Molina helps clean up his diarrhea. The long press release on the Nazi film supplements Molina's retelling starting from the moment when he, too, has knowingly eaten poisoned food so as not to break his cover; that is, from the moment when Molina gets sick from bad material which he knowingly (but under compulsion) consumed.

26. The events of the novel are supposed to be taking place in 1975 and the novel was pubished in 1976: in that sense, the footnotes' pro-Marcusian sexual politics can serve as an interesting counterpoint to Foucault's attack on Marcusian liberation theory in his introduction to *The History of Sexuality*, published in 1975 but which Puig gives no indication of having read, nor of Foucault's most relevant Rive Gauche precursor Guy Hocquenghem. In "Progresos de la doctora Anneli Taube," Daniel Balderston argues that Puig carved the complete narrative in the footnotes from only two of his sources, D.J. West and Dennis Altman.

27. The most subtle reader of García Márquez's willingness to use and then transgress such aspects of anthropological and literary structuralism is Josefina Ludmer (Ludmer 1972).

28. Not surprisingly, *novelists* who include scenes of primitivist transmission emphasize orality (or telepathy!)—that is, a transmission outside written history—and gender it male if they are male (Carpentier, Vargas Llosa) and female if they are female (Allende, Esquivel).

29. Other textual sites to examine García Márquez's response to the threat of decadence in the fin de siècle would be his comments on fellow Colombian José

Asunción Silva for the centenary edition of Silva's prose (García Márquez, 1996), and the portrayals of Rubén Darío and the sadistic Saenz de la Barra in *Autumn of the Patriarch*. In order to praise *modernismo* in these moments, García Márquez defuses their subversive sexuality; even to critique *modernismo*, the sadist's sexual drive must be ruthlessly sublimated.

30. Pedro Lemebel's *Tengo miedo torero* (2001) is the most loyal revisionist narrative; less complete hommages to Puig can be seen in novels by Santos-Febre and Bayly, although in both cases the realist novelist's desire to describe a milieu is a higher priority than the formal experimentation of Puig's recreation of a world of refunctioned clichés through voice and storytelling alone.

CHAPTER 2: ELLIPSING LEZAMA LIMA

1. As is well known, Lezama published the early chapters of *Paradiso* in the influential Cuban magazine *Orígenes* in the early 1950s; these autobiographical chapters, although they include homosexual minor characters, never achieve the level of scandalousness the novel attains beginning with chapter VIII; Lezama's mother dies in 1964 and the novel is published in 1966. Any reading of Lezama's prose is an imperfect translation, and I have kept my second-guessing of Gregory Rabassa's heroic 1988 English translation to a minimum, marked in square brackets in the citations.

2. Vargas Llosa wrote an encomium of the book in the Lima magazine *Amaru*, a review that was criticized in the Paris-based *Mundo Nuevo* for leaving out the theme of homosexuality altogether; when Vargas Llosa wrote in to defend his review, claiming that rumors about *Paradiso* had led people to believe it was nothing but pornography when really its homosexual thematics were quite limited, Monegal clarified his position that Lezama's eroticism seems to blur the difference between genital and nongenital eroticism, as well as between heterosexual and homosexual attraction, but then Monegal provided a long checklist of virtually every scene in the novel with homosexual content anyway. I thank Ben Sifuentes for helping me with these polemics.

3. I suspect that the irritation some gay and queer writers expressed toward *Fresa y chocolate* came not just from the film's more conciliatory approach to heterosexual anxiety than in Paz's original story (see Smith, 1995), but also from the reduction of the difficulty of Lezama and his initiatory rhetoric in the democratic medium of film; Lezama becomes little more than a photo on the wall, *Paradiso* little more than a cookbook.

4. Gustavo Pellón 1989 is the main disputant, with Lihn as a precursor, although Gustavo Pérez Firmat also takes the topic as far as a conventional methodology can get one. In 1992 Foster praised it on p.1 of his book and then ignored it throughout. By 2001, however, Emilio Bejel can squeeze Lezama's entire oeuvre into a brief chapter, insofar as he is interested primarily in the relationship

between homosexuality and Cuban nationalism, and insofar as Arnaldo Cruz-Malavé's fine 1994 book presents a sharp reading of Lezama's gay love triangle chapters in the context of his larger philosophical project. In his work Cruz-Malavé pays more attention than I do to the moves within the three friends' debate and less attention to the novel's melodramatic plot manipulations.

5. The Castro regime's turnaround on gay issues is remarkable, some (like Smith) would say cynical. Besides Smith's 1995 book, one can examine two 1997 documentaries, DeVries's *Gay Cuba* and Gilpin's *Mariposas en el andamio*. This story is covered by Emilio Bejel. Apologists for the Castro regime defended Revolutionary homophobia by claiming that the radicals saw homosexuality as part of the island's Tropicana culture of pre-1959 casinos and tourists; if so, the regime hasn't learned anything, since it is still associating gays with tourists and a culture of prostitution, which it now encourages for economic reasons. For the best recent reading of queer desire in an international context, see José Quiroga's *Tropic of Desire*.

6. Up to here I follow closely Enrico Mario Santí's brilliant essay "Parridiso," which sets up a similar tension between the narrator/author's praise of the Colonel and the flaws that the reader can see within that portrait. Santí's project is more purely deconstructive: it wishes to show that the son is a flawed copy of the father, but also that the father is a flawed copy of himself.

7. Reinaldo Arenas's autobiography, not entirely to be trusted, speaks of nights spent with Lezama in the Havana bathhouses of the 1960s: "Virgilio [Piñera] liked tough men, blacks, and truck drivers, while Lezama's preferences were Hellenic: the extremes of Greek beauty and, of course, adolescents" (84).

8. By using parts of their methodology for a gay male book I suppose I am implicitly disagreeing with any claims to a lesbian specificity that their theories make. But insofar as both Castle and Roof work variations on the trope of "lesbian invisibility," and insofar as the phalloi of *Paradiso* are aggressively visible even as the book propounds a defense of sex in the closet, it could be argued that their theories and this novel reinforce a basic difference in gay as opposed to lesbian representations in writing under compulsory heterosexuality.

9. For an essay taking this as a point of departure, see Dianna Niebylski's excellent "Transgression in the Comic Mode: Angeles Mastretta and Her Cast of Liberated Aunts."

10. Rabassa has eliminated a short passage here in which Cemí recalls having heard that Alberto once successfully teased an aristocratic friend's father (by means of a pun that Rabassa presumably found untranslatable) for his pretensions to fine china and fine bloodlines. Like Foción, Alberto attacks his friends' fathers for them. Mocking the aristocracy from within is also characteristic of the avunculate.

11. In the Vitier edition, one of the "notas finales" (483) details another discrepancy between the novel and real life: "«La muerte del tío Alberto es una verdadera creación: José Lezama Lima le dio la muerte que le correspondía: en la realidad Alberto queda esa noche preso y en la mañana siguiente amanece ahorcado.» (*C.* 341)." Vitier approves of Lezama's poetic justice.

12. I leave for another occasion how an "avuncular literary history" would analyze Lezama's readings of the military patriarch José Martí and the bachelor uncle Julián del Casal, a project also inspired by Cruz-Malavé's 1994 book.

CHAPTER 3: FELISBERTO'S PAPER DOLLS

1. Interestingly, Julio Cortázar begins his introduction to the 1975 anthology of Felisberto's stories, *La casa inundada y otros cuentos*, by making comparisons between Felisberto and Lezama, too, and he too is amused by the juxtaposition of a titan and a *tímido*: "A riesgo de provocar la sonrisa de no pocos críticos literarios," he begins; and he proceeds to argue that "Como el poeta y narrador cubano, Felisberto pertenece a esa estirpe espiritual que alguna vez califiqué de presocrática" (Rela 27). The argument follows a common practice of Cortázar's, to praise an Other for never achieving, or never aspiring to achieve, the fall into discursive thought that living as an intellectual in Europe entailed for Cortázar himself (but not for the "insular" Lezama or the poverty-stricken Felisberto). Insofar as both Felisberto and Lezama have intellectual pretensions, Cortázar goes on to say, they think through objects or the poetic image; and Felisberto in particular is praised for describing his esoteric desires for objects without intellectualizing his desires or apologizing for them.
2. I like everything about Harss's 1993 translation except his anglicizing of the characters' names and will refer to "Hortensia," "Horacio," "María," and "Facundo" throughout in my only departure from his English text. Citations from the Siglo XXI complete edition follow each quotation.
3. As far as I can tell, the first critic to demonstrate Felisberto's familiarity with Freud's writing is the novelist-critic Juan José Saer in his contribution to the 1973–74 seminar compiled in *Felisberto Hernández ante la crítica actual*. Insofar as Felisberto's understanding of Freud was almost certainly second-hand, it is worth reminding ourselves that Breton and other mediators of Freud's ideas into the postwar France that Felisberto visited were not particularly accurate or thorough, and Felisberto's reading habits were themselves somewhat scattershot.

    From my own "actualidad" I find it surprising how resistant the 1973–74 essays and discussions, often excellent, are to any analysis of Felisberto's eroticism. (Almost all the discussion of psychoanalysis in the seminar sets out to revise previous readings of Felisberto as an autodidact philosopher of consciousness.) While there is a spirited discussion on the value of sociological criticism (in which Felisberto appears, we might say, as an autodidact philosopher of alienation), spurred on by a strong essay by Jaime Concha and a reactionary response by Saul Yurkievich (63–102), nevertheless something like a conspiracy of silence occurs on the topic of the erotics of the Felisbertian *oeuvre*.
4. Any essay on the relationship between psychoanalysis and Felisberto's oeuvre should take into account Frank Graziano's exhaustive 1994 *The Lust of Seeing*. Its flaws are also its virtues. It eclectically combines a range of Freud and

Freudian theory from Jung to Lacan without critical distinction; it juxtaposes quotations from Felisberto's texts with statements from real-life narcissists, voyeurs, and fetishists, without critical mediation; its own neutral narrative voice comfortably embodies the masculinity which it excoriates Felisberto the man and the narrator for abandoning, without critical reflection. (Graziano's dedication of the book to his daughter, "who may not read it until she is eighteen" (5), particularly grates on me.) I rather fear I re-enact the pervert's parasitic obeisance to normality when I stubbornly refuse to imitate Graziano's anti-theoretical eclecticism, encyclopedic psychobiographizing, and mature self-confidence. Graziano's most comfortable theoretical sources are Khan's *Alienation in Perversion* and the above-mentioned Stoller book, which form a continuum of thought committed to psychoanalysis as morality in a clinical context (although each author has his moral idiosyncrasies). See Sedgwick, *Tendencies*, for one of the limits to Stoller's sexual liberalism.

5. I find this to be the only limitation to Enrique Pezzoni's and Roberto Echavarren's excellent Lacanian readings of Felisberto. Perhaps it is not surprising that most of these paternal castrating figures occur in the most realistic of the autobiographical pieces, such as the dentist/scoutmaster in "Tierras de la memoria." Yet it would be more exciting as a theoretical project to acknowledge how *seldom* Felisberto's stories provide all three points to the Oedipal triangle.

6. The best reconstruction of this scenario in Felisberto's biography is Graziano's (133–65, especially 147–51). Note that, following a very standard Freudian interpretive protocol, even though none of the women Graziano finds is actually Felisberto's mother they nevertheless are all "the mother imago" (151); such thinking remains within the Oedipal triangle as critiqued in my previous chapter.

7. Most of what follows derives from Apter and Pietz (1993), although McClintock (1995) and Foster (1995) were also helpful to me.

8. Besides Taussig's excellent contribution to the Apter and Pietz collection and his 1982 work on Colombia and Bolivia, see also his *Mimesis and Alterity*.

9. But then, I once sublet an apartment from a prostitute, a San Francisco Lesbian Avenger who was the daughter of a Cornell professor, and perhaps my dearest friend for years in Brooklyn had had to spend three years on the street as a hustler after his parents threw him out of their house for being gay; so my ambivalence on the issue of commodity fetishism and prostitution is ambivalent in many directions at once. I return to the question of alternative cultures, the narratives of the perverse, and the triumphalist narrative of global capitalism, in my epilogue.

10. The most polemic voice in the debate is Donald Morton's; for convenience's sake we might take Andrew Ross (1988; not cited in Morton) as the advocate for a rethinking (which claims to remain on the left) of the mid-century intellectual's moralizing anti-capitalism.

11. Mulvey's much-anthologized 1975 essay on the male gaze in narrative cinema is certainly appropriate for Felisberto's fictions. For her attempt to preserve an Enlightenment space for desire while not abandoning her

Enlightenment-feminist disapproval of fetishism, see her 1996 collection *Fetishism and Curiosity*.

12. Valerie Steele's *Fetish: Fashion, Sex, and Power*, a somewhat breezy and picture-filled but basically serious essay by a fashion historian, brings out a series of possible sources for such investigations in her section "Neosexualities and Normopaths" (26–31), while commonsensically noting, "This type of 'field-work' is crucially important, yet informants do not always tell the whole truth because as insiders their perspective is inevitably one-sided and may entail a degree of denial" (28).

13. Naomi Schor's brief but persuasive essay in Apter and Pietz 1993 elaborates on this relationship.

14. The essay "The Uncanny" has a solid history in recent literary theory: see Cixous and Hertz for close readings of the text; Jackson and Todorov for a debate over its usefulness in defining the genre of the fantastic. I think that Freud's essay is especially apropos for Cortázar's neo-fantastic.

15. Everything Ian dislikes about these aspects of literary modernism is uncritically put on display in Lucien Mercier's comparison of Felisberto with Marcel Duchamp's *The Bride Stripped Bare By Her Bachelors, Even*; Ian's treatment of male ambivalence suggests that both the phallic mother and "máquina célibe" are strategies for avoiding the real conflicts between men and women. Although I disagree with some of Ian's critical premises and the early moves in her argument, I enthusiastically praise the way she discovers a hidden theological—and not-so-hidden patriarchalist—move in the writings of Julia Kristeva, starting in the mid-1970s; Ian takes advantage of this devolution in Kristeva's writings to attack Tel Quel and post-structuralism's never-fully disavowed belief in the autonomy of literary language.

16. Permit an exasperated homosexual to remark that it seems very strange that Freud should invariably think that the male child is incapable of finding a mother's genitalia desirable either despite, or even because of, the absence of a penis.

17. From a biographical perspective, it certainly seems as though the women in the Hernández household were strong, conflicted, at times arbitrary, and often in conflict with each other: if your mother is shown not to wield the phallus because she is humiliated by your grandmother, who is also threatening you, might this create a fantasy life that is neither fully Oedipal nor fully fetishistic?

18. I leave for another occasion the examination of the "Felisbertian" aspects of Cristina Peri Rossi, Rosario Ferré, Alicia Borinsky, and Sylvia Molloy.

19. As I write this chapter I have been noting an absurd parallelism between my hesitation as to whether to refer to the Hortensia doll as "it" or "she," and the obligatory hand-wringing footnote in essays about transvestites in the real world or in fiction in which the author carefully sets out why and when the pronouns "he" and "she" were employed.

20. A tradition from Barrenechea through Rama, Ludmer, and Panesi highlights defamiliarization as a central aspect of Felisberto's *ars poetica*, summarized in her typically telegraphic style by Josefina Ludmer as follows: "El chico aparece como

doble del artista en dos sentidos: porque el mito filosófico y estético que funda los cuentos es siempre el de la 'mirada nueva' (asombro filosófico, *ostraninie* literaria), y porque debe aparecer siempre como 'travieso' (inocente-perverso)" (112).

21. See the essays by Concha and Fell in Sicard, ed., including the seminar discussions after their papers (61–126). Although he does not distinguish metaphor from simile, Sicard's comment on intentionality is worth quoting at length: "En Felisberto [...] hay siempre una intención en el nivel de estas maquinerías [...] que él fabrica *intencionalmente* para liberar un proceso metafórico cuyo carácter no siempre es intencional. Estas maquinerías, estos artífices (la casa inundada, el túnel de 'Menos Julia', las muñecas de 'Las Hortensias') son metáforas destinadas a producir metáforas o a crear las condiciones de la experimentación metafórica. Cada cuento de Felisberto funciona como una máquina. Existiría por supuesto un tercer nivel: no intencional, inconsciente (el nivel en que 'te intencionan', como dice Felisberto [in the short story 'El taxi')], donde podría intervenir el análisis psicoanalítico" (123–4).

22. The truly bizarre discovery in 1995 (Díaz 126–9) that Felisberto's third wife, the Spanish refugee dress-designer to whom he dedicated *Las Hortensias*, was in fact a KGB spy who had materially abetted in the assassination of Trotsky ten years before she met Felisberto, and who married Felisberto in all probability in order to get Uruguayan citizenship, takes this aspect of the story to another level, especially since Felisberto's right-wing opinions make it inconceivable that De Las Heras ever confessed her past seriously; I'm guessing that she "invented" a similar story and they used it in sex games that he then borrowed for this novella.

23. A child is also the messenger of the atrocities of public space, this time Nature, when Horacio takes el Tímido's Hortensia out for an adulterous afternoon: "vio, en un bote, un muchachón de cabeza grande haciendo muecas horribles; ... sólo movía la boca, horrorosa como un pedazo suelto de intestino" (223) and making a disturbing rumbling sound. The boy, a reminder of the materiality of the adulterous occasion, should be compared not just with the more phallic mass-public boy of the trip to the department store, but also with the simile of the noise of a shipwrecked steamship, mentioned below.

24. See Fombona (2001) for a witty and creative use of post-structuralist ethics in the Lacoue-Labarthe/Agamben mode to describe the obsessive euphemizing that *el pudor* imposes on the *pudenda* in the novella.

25. For a brilliant juggling of Lacanian theories of desire and Frankfurt School theories of commodity fetishism in the context of the American Gilded Age consumer culture (and the Golden Age of the MGM musical), see Stuart Culver's 1986 reading of L. Frank Baum's *The Wonderful Wizard of Oz*, "What Mannikins Want." His analysis turns on a passage in the novel, omitted in the film, in which live porcelain figures warn Dorothy that if she takes them back to Kansas they will stiffen and harden. Culver argues that the proper goal of a theory of desire within consumer capitalism would be to free desire from ownership, to let it play on the world without having to buy anything to (think that you will) satisfy it.

26. A powerful and elegant recent demonstration of this position is Reinaldo Laddaga's chapter on Felisberto, which nevertheless passes over—indeed, must pass over—the "fetishistic fictions" I have treated here, since here the author and the characters take pleasure not just in the formless "desconocido sin vida" found in the objects but also in the odd theatrical/narrative machinery through which these objects are displayed.

27. In some of the secondary sources I hear a biographical correlation: *Las Hortensias* was written during his stay in postwar France, which at first stoked his vanity but eventually disillusioned him, and where he eventually withdrew from social circles.

CHAPTER 4: CORTÁZAR AND PIZARNIK READ "THE BLOODY COUNTESS"

1. Cortázar's *Libro de Manuel* contains a long and serious defense of masturbation by one of its more eccentric characters, Lonstein. Meanwhile, at other points of the novel characters mention in passing the tactics their parents, both in France and in Buenos Aires, used to stop them from masturbating. For a brief version of the "normalization" of masturbation and its implications for sexology and literary theory, see Eve Sedgwick's "Jane Austen and the Muse of Masturbation," in *Tendencies*. For an excellent historical overview of the rise and fall of onanism as a practice to be invigilated in France, see Vernon Rosario.

2. I say this despite Steven Boldy's intelligent use of Derrida to read the poetics of displacement and deferral at work in *62* in his *The novels of Julio Cortázar*, by far the most thorough and helpful reading of this book in English. Boldy does not claim that Cortázar was reading Derrida, only that Derridean theories help explain strategies in the book.

3. The *tártaros* do not function merely as a group that protects against individual loneliness or merely as comic relief, or merely as a band of anarchists to *épater les bourgeois*: in a novel with a deliberately skewed time scheme in which the main characters at times wander in an ambiguous metaphoric landscape which transcends time and space, the *tártaros* are the inhabitants of an intermediary zone that permits zany behavior but remains within conventional space-time parameters. Yet even these characters are not traditional literary characters per se: one is a shadowy half-character named "mi paredro," who begins as a linguistic device and only solidifies into a character halfway through the novel, and another is the enigmatic/moronic Feuille Morte, who only says "Bis bis" and seems unable to take care of herself. Within Cortázar's own oeuvre, as is well known and as he makes explicit in the novel's title and prologue, this experimental disregard for traditional characterization, and for sexual and literary maturity, is defended by the novelist-philosopher Morelli in Chapter sixty-two and other "dispensable chapters" in Cortázar's Boom best-seller *Rayuela* (1963).

4. The poem and the two essays were compiled in 1993 and translated and compiled together in Paz (1998).

5. Here, I think, is the basic way in which this chapter differs from that of Feal's "Queer Cortázar," not just in her decision to limit herself to reading the short fiction: Feal accepts the legitimacy of Freud's coining of the term sado-masochism, and then crisply uses it to show the ways that the reader of Cortázar's stories moves back and forth between the dominant and dominated position. Feal accepts the pleasure of being a "lector hembra" only after trying out Debra Castillo's "lectora hembra" (a position which values traditional stereo-types of femininity, but in a contestatory mode, à la Rosario Castellanos) and then trying out her own "lectora macho" (a feminist "lector cómplice" who is savvy enough to wrest Cortázar's authorial stance away from him). The advantage of treating sadism and masochism as different and competing discourses, instead of a reversible continuum, is partly that in this way I explain just how the resistance to their being a single impulse led to overcompensations by writers such as Cortázar.

   Somewhat to my own surprise, neither Feal's nor my essay make anything of the rumors laid down in 1994 by Ilan Stavans that Cortázar experimented with bisexuality and that (now confirmed by Cristina Peri Rossi in 2001, although she claims the cause was tainted French blood transfusions) he died of AIDS, possibly infecting his wife Carol Dunlop first. The men in the novel I am prin-cipally treating, *62: modelo para armar*, are rigorously and unproblematically heterosexual: straight men have always been given permission by both conven-tional and avant-garde society to be aroused by lesbians. Peri Rossi declares thst Cortázar had a constant fascination with lesbians in his Paris years.

6. Such Frankfurt School mixtures of history with philosophy and ethics were com-mon throughout the 1960s, and indeed Adorno's name was so well known at the time that, as he recounts in *La vuelta al día en ochenta mundos*, Cortázar decided to name a stray cat whom he adopted "Teodoro W. Adorno."

7. An excellent summary of this aspect of Surrealist infighting is Stoekl's collection and translation *Visions of Excess*.

8. The 1998 memoir by Juan Jacobo Bajarlí *Alejandra Pizarnik: anatomía de un recuerdo* portrays a Pizarnik infuriated by her mother's restrictions (the memoir covers only two years, when Alejandra was eighteen to twenty); Piña has a more complex reading of Pizarnik's relationship to her father, whom she loved and who supported her vocation, in a distant and not really comprehending way, but who supposedly became identified with Death itself after his own death in 1966.

9. Piña's biography of Pizarnik, chatty and repetitive and irritatingly proud of its discretion over Pizarnik's sex partners (see Chavez-Silverman's thoughts on this subject), mentions a half-dozen times the small obsession Pizarnik had over Bataille in her Paris stay of 1960–64: Piña claims that Bataille's blue eyes link him to Pizarnik's father's blue eyes, and a figure in Pizarnik's later poems, "the man in the blue mask," representing death. See Melanie Nicholson's smart, concise 2000 essay.

10. There are suggestions that Penrose does offer a psychological reading of the Countess's sadism, amid all the astrology and heredity, and that Pizarnik is choosing to ignore it: in a nice piece of ventriloquism, after the Countess has been immured, Penrose has her staring into the mirror and thinking, "So who was this personage possessing the rights of Erzsébet, the last of the Báthorys, and whom I have never been? Why am I here, so harshly accused, to expiate what my desires did, but which I, myself, never felt I had done? My desires satisfied themselves outside of me, without me; my desires have missed their goal" (178). Pizarnik in effect edits out such passages as these from Penrose's book.

11. Molloy, Nicholson, and Scarafía and Molina are all drawn to the change of tone that takes place in the chapter "El espejo de la melancolía": after so many brief chapters in which Pizarnik plays the mute mirror, copying without comment the horrible acts of the Countess, she speaks of the Countess's custom-made mirror and moves into a first-person essayistic tone about melancholy which intensifies the position of everyone involved: Pizarnik *is* the Countess's mirror, and can speak as herself only when the Countess looks into it.

12. The phrase is Hal Foster's, and is used to invoke the Freudian dynamics of repetition compulsion and obsessive behavior in the theories of the Surrealist painters and poets.

13. This story was also commented on by Emir Rodríguez Monegal, the Uruguayan critic who founded in Paris the Boom-novelist-friendly magazine *Mundo Nuevo*; in his essay "Le fantôme de Lautréamont" he footnotes Pizarnik's essay. Clearly a fashionable interest in Paris and perversion had some institutional support in the Latin American Rive Gauche of the 1960s.

14. Sarduy's essay is also footnoted by Emir Rodríguez Monegal.

15. The capital letters here are my own to tantalize myself and the reader into wondering if there could be a connection between this odd masochistic scenario and the political debates over "El Hombre Nuevo" in Cuban society, debates which Cortázar incorporates fully into his 1973 novel *Libro de Manuel*. Cortázar's hero-worship of Che Guevara works itself into much of his writing of the 1960s and 1970s.

16. Countess Bathory had two residences, one in Vienna and one in Transylvania; girls were tortured in both palaces, but the more outrageous evils took place in the castle. Pizarnik omits all mention of the Viennese residence.

17. *Dracula* is, notoriously, the first of the great vampire tales to heterosexualize the lesbian vampire scenario elaborated by Coleridge, Nerval, and (most relevantly for *62*, according to Boldy) Sheridan LeFanu.

18. In the critical tradition, the only writer to note a discrepancy between Erszebeth Bathory and Frau Marta is Ana María Hernández. Hernández's Jungian methodology keeps her from making any use of this distinction: by the end of her essay she is praising Austin and Celia for killing the bad pervert who does not know how to love, and remarks with satisfaction of Juan that "He is a victim of his own monster" (114).

19. Freud, who considered courtly love and other structurally unrequited love to be a form of sublimation, found himself also developing these ideas further in a lesbian context; see his "A Case of Homosexuality in a Woman" and the ripostes by Findlay and Merck for queer theory perspectives; see also Gossy on Peri Rossi's *Solitario de amor* for a creative use of this dynamic.

20. For an acceptably orthodox version of this theory, see Laplanche and Pontalis; also relevant would be the essays in Victor Burgin ed., *Formations of Fantasy*. I don't wish to suggest, by repeating the Freudian term primal, that this scene is necessarily closer to Cortázar's textual erotics than the cold mother—sick son motif. Following what will be said later about the mechanics of disavowal, it is worth noting that in this novel both fantasies about Juan are attributed to Hélène, not to Juan himself.

21. The most obsessive and ambivalent of the Surrealist dollmakers was Hans Bellmer. Hal Foster's book demonstrates how these dolls can still trouble a critical discourse despite its being sensitive to gender, psychoanalytic theory, and the ugly history of calling some artwork "degenerate."

22. Paley-Francescato was the first to upbraid Cortázar for the novel's conservative sexual politics.

23. Illegibility is, of course, relative. Writing in a series which expects to be some readers' first encounter with literary criticism, Peter Standish rushes past the entire novel in a handful of pages, stressing the book's difficulty. Conversely, Lucille Kerr's sharp 1998 essay footnotes profusely, to show that not only have academic readers found *62* to be readable, but that they all find the novel to say roughly the same thing, in part because all of them repeat the hermeneutic strategies proffered extensively, in Cortázar's many paratexts ("Una muñeca rota," "Cristal con una rosa adentro," and the many interviews), as well as within the text itself (the *coágulo en fuga*, the advice in the preface, etc.): "To read like Juan is, in a sense, to read like Cortázar, and that is the only reading, the 'master' episode suggests, which can get one through this text" (102–3). Although agnostic on the sort of psychoanalytic reader-relations theory I use in this book, Kerr certainly leads us to ask, Are we professional readers of *62* accepting the authority of the figure of the author in the same way that the masochist accepts the authority of the Deleuzian dominatrix, especially in the way we demand, and are hypnotized by, a ritual of re-reading and repetition, and in the promise of a "pessimistic" text that will cause us (exquisite) pain?

24. Uncannily, Pizarnik anticipates this strategy of posthumy too, more confrontationally than Cortázar himself. In a 1983 letter to Ana María Barrenechea (*Cartas* 1765–6) Cortázar dispels the rumor that *Rayuela*'s La Maga was based on Alejandra—the book was finished before he met her—but adds that, two months after her suicide, he somehow received a brief letter in the mail from her with a photo of her sunbathing naked on a beach. Naturally, Cortázar tells Barrenechea not to divulge this information, so we can only read about it some twenty years later: conventional posthumy upon uncanny posthumy.

CHAPTER 5: FUENTES, DONOSO, SARDUY, AND
THE QUEER SIXTIES

1. The most obvious attempt to write Boom and post-Boom literary history this way is Lindstrom (1994), who bases her arguments on John Beverley's *Against Literature* and on Raymond L. Williams; Phillip Swanson (1990) makes very similar moves, citing Donald Shaw and David W. Foster. The most rigorous and long-running attack on the Boom's elitism comes from Jean Franco, in her 1999 collection *Critical Passions*. For an extraordinarily sophisticated use of Bloom's Oedipal language to describe Latin American literary history, which nevertheless defers the question of Foucault's critique of Oedipus, see Avelar (1999).

2. I have no room to discuss the cross-gender signs of Claudia Nervo, or of her spinster secretary Ruth. Fuentes is explicit that "Claudia Nervo" performed the role of Catalina de Erauso, the sixteenth-century lieutenant nun, in a movie: for María Félix's portrayal of the *monja alférez*, see Velasco (2000).

3. Yoking James and Joyce as "roughly realist" novelists is quite a shorthand statement. A good place to hear the tension between views of Joyce as realist and as anti-realist is the polemic intervention on the topic by Leo Bersani in "Against *Ulysses*," in *The Culture of Redemption* 155–78. It is also useful to consult Franco Moretti on Joyce in his invigorating book *Modern Epic*, since in that work Moretti is elaborating an argument about the role of magic realism in world literature. By calling Donoso's novel realist I realize that I disagree with Magnarelli's larger point in her excellent *Understanding José Donoso*; to my mind, the sort of Jamesian perspectivism in which we receive most of our facts only as filtered through various consciousnesses is still realism.

4. The word *mayate* is taken from Mexican Spanish, in recent anthropological studies by Joseph Carrier (*De Los Otros*, 1995) and Annick Prieur (*Mema's House*, 1998). Both authors emphasize the extreme difficulty they had in actually interviewing nominally straight men who take the active role with passive homosexuals or, for Prieur's study, transvestites.

5. In his recent excellent work on Lacan, psychoanalysis, and narcissism, Tim Dean attempts to yoke together the powerful narrative of Freud's 1910 essay on Leonardo and his 1914 essay on narcissism, in the end focusing on the differences between Freud's two attempts to grapple with the role of self-love in developmental psychology. In popular understandings of homosexuality, the 1910 narrative overrides the 1914 analytic treatment.

6. Such a formulation approaches those used by René Prieto in the chapter on Sarduy in his recent *Body of Writing* (2000). Indeed, his conclusion that his 1960s male authors all unleash upon women a "rage and idealization which seem to be men's revenge for having been evicted from their first home and then estranged from their first love (who, to compound matters, consented to the separation)" (247) is certainly more applicable to *Holy Place* than, in my opinion, to any of the Sarduy novels Prieto analyzes, certainly not to *Cobra*. By writing completely within the Freudian paradigm and paying no attention to queer

theory of any kind, Prieto also works within the framework of the incest/machismo boundaries I sketched in chapter 1; his final chapters on women authors allow him to condemn this paradigm in his male novelists, but not to reinterpret it.

7. When unreconstructed Lacanians invoke a discourse of the Real to found theories of sexual difference, I find them unconvincing in the extreme: Joan Copjec's "Sex and the Euthanasia of Reason," in her often brilliant *Read My Desire: Lacan Against the Historicists*, could nevertheless serve as an instance of a foundationalism that only preaches to the already Lacanian choir. Nevertheless, I accept as quite valid Lacan's reluctance to give any weight to what orthodox Freudians in 1949 were calling "the reality principle"—"a principle that is the expression of a scientific prejudice most hostile to the dialectic of knowledge" ("The Mirror Stage" 6). I would go further: the reality principle a transvestite like La Manuela takes leave of is not just a scientific prejudice, but a regime of normalization, whether in social life or on the level of realist representation.

8. What's not to love about Doctor Schreber? Schreber is not entirely forgotten by the French intellectual world during the Queer Sixties, but neither the old-guard of Sartre and Levi-Strauss (Fuentes and Donoso's France) nor the newer wave of Lacan-early Derrida-Tel Quel (Sarduy's milieu) made much out of him. (For the most complete placing of Sarduy in a social and intellectual milieu of French intellectuals, see François Wahl's long essay, "Severo dans le rue Jacob," in the *Obra completa*.) The French version of the anti-psychiatry movement, notably Foucault and most especially Deleuze and Guattari in their *Anti-Oedipus* (1970), are the first to take Schreber's attack on reality seriously, directed there perhaps by some early (1930s) texts on Schreber by Georges Bataille.

9. It is tempting to map the difference between La Manuela and Mito onto the exaggerated binary that the provocative but unscholarly J.Michael Bailey elaborates in his *The Man Who Would Be Queen* (2003); Manuela is the "real" homosexual while Mito is the "autogynephilic" man in love with the image in the mirror (in his case, an incestuous love, too). Bailey provides a checklist to tell the two types apart, and ruminates on the evolutionary-psychological paradox of non-procreative sex: isn't queer science reassuring?

10. By rewriting La Manuela as a being whose signs are all on the surface, rather than a literary character with an interiority that can be manipulated by other characters, Sarduy is hewing to what was understood in the 1960s as the difference between French and Anglo-American rhetorical criticism. (See Sarduy's frank admission that he knows little of the New Criticism in his interview with Emir Rodríguez Monegal in the *Obra completa* 1809–11.) When I focus on characters and their points of view, implicitly I invoke the Jamesian tradition set forth by Percy Lubbock and codified by Wayne Booth's *The Rhetoric of Fiction*; Donoso's enthusiasm for Henry James is well known. The French rhetorical tradition, by contrast, refuses to privilege voice, persona, or perspective, even in a text such as Donoso's where they figure prominently, making it

all the easier for Sarduy to conclude the first half of his essay with, "*El lugar sin límites* es ... el espacio del lenguaje" (1149). For a thorough attempt to use Genettian categories to examine Sarduy's own narratives while pursuing an argument about his relation to Baroque literature, see Guerrero (1987).

11. Here as elsewhere in this reading I am following Sifuentes Jáuregui (2002).

12. See de Guzmán (1972). Elena Poniatowska in her 1988 collection of interviews, *¡Ay vida, no me mereces!*, is diplomatic in her omission of any mention of the novel. More recent books, such as van Delden's *Mexico and Modernity*, no doubt omit considerations of *Zona sagrada* for more pragmatic reasons, as they groan under the weight of Fuentes's literary output.

13. Perhaps I am missing a cinematic intertext here. While bisexuality in Italy has a British prose pedigree that explains E.M. Forster and Patricia Highsmith novels which have become recent films (*Where Angels Fear to Tread*, *The Talented Mr. Ripley*), Gus van Sant's decision to send River Phoenix and Keanu Reeves to Italy in *My Own Private Idaho* has the feel of a purely cinematic allusion. These private scenes in the castle of course share aspects of a code of "decadence" that will be made manifest in the apotheosis-orgy filmed in the penultimate chapter.

14. This didn't stop Fuentes from citing all these same myths to Emir Rodríguez Monegal in a long interview in *Mundo Nuevo* as the book was being finished: in Apollodorus's version of the Odyssey tales, Circe had a son by Odysseus, Telegonus. Telegonus and Telemachus are half-brother doubles; Telemachus travels to Circe's island and sleeps with her, while Telegonus travels to Ithaca to kill Odysseus and sleep with Penelope (Giacoman 48–50). As Mito does in this scene, the critic Lanin Gyurko notes the discrepancies between Telemachus/Telegonus and Mito/Giancarlo (mostly, that Giancarlo has no mother to give to Mito in exchange for the mother Claudia whom he takes) and, giving Fuentes the benefit of the doubt differently than Sarduy does, concludes that Fuentes is mystifying himself with Apollodoran variations on Ulysses in order to conceal from himself the enduring power of the Oedipal myth in its Freudian form. Oedipal criticism colludes with mid-century Boom writers to bring Oedipus back into texts which proffer completely different mythical texts. Meanwhile, one can titillate oneself with the complexities of various *roman-à-clef* readings (Fuentes offering his wife and/or stepdaughter? Donoso offering *his* wife? Enrique Alvarez Félix offering his mother?), knowing that Fuentes will come out the winner, and his two emasculated "half-brothers" the losers.

15. Revelations of love letters to a younger man have surfaced in Donoso's papers, at Princeton and the University of Iowa, and were discussed in Chilean newspapers in the autumn of 2003. I thank the LASA-LGS list serve, especially Adán Griego, for keeping us informed.

16. The phrase "millonario del lenguaje," used with tender irony by his lover François Wahl in the essay "Severo dans le rue Jacob" in the *Obra completa*, is actually a quotation from one of *Cobra*'s footnotes, where Sarduy credits a Spanish thesaurus for his ability to generate a list of synonyms. Sarduy's

footnotes do not give us his "real" voice, by any means; they do, however, provide a break from the staccato rhythms characteristic of much of his descriptive prose, as I will describe below.

17. This is analogous to the self-imposed limitation of González Echevarría's reading of *Cobra*, which he summarizes as "The word that lies hidden under this elaborate series of mistakes is CUBA" (234). As in my own reading, he is fascinated by Sarduy's deliberate equivocations; rather than moving to find an interpretable bodily referent behind these feints, as I do, González Echevarría chooses to find an historical referent.

18. The methodology I am proposing for the first half of the novel could be applied to this part of the novel, too: besides the real subculture of 1960s leathermen, Sarduy is "fantasizing freely" through the mediation of gay personal ads, which he quotes in the English original, and through the cinematic intertext of Kenneth Anger's *Scorpio Rising*, also, as it turns out, a product of the New York underground cinema scene. James McCourt's introduction to the reedition of Jill Levine's translation, though more than scattershot in its erudition, is very helpful on Sarduy's intertexts.

19. A different way to take an analogous argument would be to compare Sarduy's aesthetic with that of his friend Copi (Raúl Damonte, 1939–87), the Argentine cartoonist, playwright, and drag performer. Copi also died of AIDS, and appears very briefly in Sarduy's (1986) *El Cristo de la rue Jacob*; his plays, written in French, permit an analogous expansion into this chapter's "international scene," as well as another way to suggest an internationalization and a queering of what is often too narrowly perceived as the Cuban/Caribbean/Latin American neobaroque.

20. Moon (1995) makes this argument most persuasively. While there has been a homosexualization of Europe's fantasies of North Africa over the last two centuries, focused on the Tangiers expatriate community (Gide, of course; but also recall that Cobra and the Señora actually meet William S. Burroughs in the novel when they make their way there for the sex-change operation), Moon argues that Diaghilev's choreographing of Nijinsky in *Scheherezade* in 1910 led to the queering of the libertine but hitherto heterosexual harem scenario. Recall that in Lezama's *Paradiso* Ricardo Fronesis's father as a youth rejected the advances of Diaghilev, which is given as an explanation for his homophobia towards his son's friendship with Eugenio Foción.

21. The best reading of the maneuverings made by the Pop intellectuals in general and Sontag's role among them in particular in U.S. intellectual life in the Queer Sixties is still Andrew Ross (1988).

22. Hoberman and other critics do what they can to emphasize how conscious and anti-spontaneist Smith's filming practices were, and we'll say more about that; but anti-intellectual he was.

23. Prieto (2000) makes clear his revision of his 1985 essay on Sarduy, emphasizing that now he reads the ambiguous ending of the first half of the novel as the *failure* of Cobra's attempts at castration. I must register here my dissatisfaction with Prieto's attempts to read Sarduy's "body of writing" through such an

orthodox Freudian methodology. It is unclear how he justifies putting such emphasis on a single, supposedly Oedipal, scene in *Maitreya* at the expense of the rest of the novel (and his insistence on identifying Sarduy only with the scene's dwarf, and not at the same time with La Tremenda); how he justifies reading this scene back into *Cobra* and forward into *Colibrí* (but not even further into *De donde son los cantantes* and *Pájaros en la playa*, or sideways into the essays of *La simulación* (where an extremely different Oedipal transvestite scene occurs)); finally, in a rather homophobic faux-Zizekism, how he justifies citing as the only transvestite for comparison Norman Bates in Hitchcock's *Psycho*. In short, through selective quotation and in his adherence to Freud and his most conservative interpreters (Bettelheim, Kristeva, Dinnerstein), Prieto privileges the Oedipal and therefore comes up with the conclusion that Sarduy's oeuvre both fantasizes about having sex with the mother *and* yearns vainly to separate from her. With no theoretical attempts to (in Garber's words) look *at* the transvestite instead of looking *through* her, Prieto is unable to think through the pleasures and dangers of wanting to Become Woman/Divine.

24. I emphasize "conventional" because in the film such great attention to lipstick and making up, while asking the voice-over narrator about lipstick and blow jobs, reminds the audience of other erogenous zones. In *Cobra*, I admit to wondering about the possible uses of Cobra's never described "juguetes mecánicos," one of which Pup is mistaken for when she is on the bed.

25. Their difference of opinion on this issue may remind you of the disagreement between the older and the younger drag queens in the documentary *Paris Is Burning*. Pepper LaBeija reminds her children that life on the streets as a black woman is not much better than life as a black drag queen. Or it may remind you of Garber's irritation at the gender-conformist narrative of Christine Jorgensen. While I respect the company of two such divas, I also respect the people who decide to undergo sex-change operations.

26. Since I am a fan of Cortázar's *Libro de Manuel*, whose turquoise penguin gives his all for the Joda, I cannot help but mention Smith's series of photo-narratives he composed while in Europe of himself and "Yolanda la Pinguina," a plush toy he had decked out in a '40s Hollywood showgirl turban, in the mid-70s. More relevantly for this argument, Smith also staged plays in decrepit theaters or in his own apartment, in which he would claim that the actors he hired had not shown up, and would replace them with his stuffed plush toys and members of the audience, who were handed scripts but placed on stage where the light was too dim for them to read them.

27. I never saw Smith perform; nor did I see the actor and performance artist Ron Vawter's paired one-man one-act plays, *Roy Cohn/Jack Smith*. But in late 1993—just as Sarduy was dying, coincidentally–the avant-garde documentarist Jill Godmilow filmed a performance of it. The second act recreates Smith's 1981 *What's Underground About Marshmallows* (Vawter 445). Vawter himself died of AIDS a few months after the performance was filmed. As recreated by Vawter, the piece begins with a speech in which Smith claims to live in a locked vault, from which he is allowed to escape whenever anyone needs to see a

specimen of one of the last non-commercial artists left in the world: this would seem related to the commemorative purpose of Vawter's (and Godmilow's, and my) taking Smith out of the vault to display him to an audience.

28. Is Cobra's desire to shrink her feet, sometimes referred to as "la base" (30, 32). an attempt to separate her base from her superstructure?

CONCLUSION: PERVERSE NARRATIVES ON THE BORDER

1. The roots of such experimental comic books lie in the underground comix of the 1960s. 1980 marks the transformation of the industry, in decline because of high paper costs (and possibly the effect of Vietnam/Watergate malaise on the concept of the superhero), when the first specialty shops opened which no longer needed to conform to censorship standards that presumed a pre-teen audience. Pulitzer Prize–winning *Maus* (1986, 1992) by Art Spiegelman, recasting an oral history of his father's experiences during the Holocaust as a macabre cat-and-mouse game between Nazis and Jews, marked the official acceptance of comics as an acceptable medium for serious narrative art. For the neophyte, the first best book to read about comics as "sequential art" is Scott McCloud's *Understanding Comics* (1992), an almost Aristotelian or Genettian formal treatise (narrated in pictures, of course) which covers Japanese *manga* as well as American superhero pulp as well as experimental writers like the Hernandezes.

2. I worry sometimes that he engages the reader in a sadistic relationship with respect to Palomar, which has been regularly visited with disasters: a plague from an old *llorona*; a serial killer among the crew of the local archaeologists; most recently an earthquake. These catastrophes structure large parts of *Love and Rockets* and seem to go beyond the usual requirements for comic-book plotting, especially since Gilbert is also extraordinarily skilled at real-life-scaled plots.

3. Simultaneously with this novel, Gilbert was producing *X*, which follows a huge cast of characters in Los Angeles in the present, including María's two daughters by a later husband: both share the family trait of huge breasts, and one of them, Petra, has surgery to get hers reduced.

4. I use the word "literary" not as an honorific per se but in the sense of a formally complex verbal artifact. There is of course nearly a half-century of criticisms of this definition. First, ideological critique has called into question whether the complexities that the critical tradition has historically valued are better than other sorts of complexities hitherto undervalued; second, since the linguistic turn it has been difficult to maintain that words have either a specific or hegemonic status in the construction of artifacts. Many of the authors I discuss glancingly below will have staked out a position that listens more sympathetically than I do either to ideological critique or poststructuralist linguistic critique, or both.

5. The most subtle recent approach to the *testimonio* as a textual genre which challenges our habits of appropriative reading is Doris Sommer, *Proceed With*

Caution, When engaged with minority writing in the Americas (Harvard UP, 1999). Sommer's book and mine are almost antinomian: she reads texts that short-circuit unethical desires for mastery of the minority other; my book has pursued desires for the unethical, a desire for something in the other that the other does not recognize in itself. Sommer emphasizes how often the minority other is wounded or endangered in these readings; I am drawn to those moments when it is the reader who is wounded or endangered.

6. Moreiras calls these two stances mimesis and identity. Given their similar commitment to deconstruction and their utterly different styles and points of reference (Moreiras to the post-colonial theorists around Spivak and the Subaltern Studies Group, Alonso around more traditional Hispanists), it would be interesting to stage a more thorough comparison between *The Exhaustion of Difference* and *The Burden of Modernity*. One might start with the different uses of suicide (Quiroga's, in Alonso; Arguedas's, in Moreiras), or the differing critiques of the Boom novelists, although each must pass very rapidly over the Boom years (Moreiras does read a 1976 Cortázar short story in *Tercer espacio*; Alonso attacks Vargas Llosa's 1976 understanding of postmodernism directly, but sympathetically reads Fuentes's *La campaña* (1990) and García Márquez's *El general en su laberinto* (1989): the Cortázar story is a political fiction about a beleaguered revolutionary government, while the Fuentes and García Márquez novels are melancholy reflections on the birth of the Latin American republics).

7. A more detailed and rigorous version of such an argument is available in Levinson (1997 and 2002); *The Ends of Literature*, too, is in dialogue with Beverley's *Against Literature*, and also treats Rigoberta Menchú as an endpoint of sorts.

8. In *Tercer espacio*'s exergue, a meditation on a photo of himself as a one-year-old: "el lugar intelectual es a medias lugar filosófico y lugar crítico-exegético, lugar político y lugar privado, lugar poético y lugar de odio a lo poético, aunque el verdadero odio está en la narrativa, porque la narrativa no es aquí más que pre-texto para buscar en ella los momentos constituyentes de desnarrativización, los momentos en los que la historia y las historias se hacen indistinguibles de su propio desastre: cuando la lengua común resulta ajena, oscuro goce, espacio críptico" (37). In *The Exhaustion of Difference*, the equivalent claim is in the penultimate paragraph of the book: Moreiras defends a subalternist position, provided that it does not give in to an easy hybridity narrative but rather shares in "a savage hybridity which is, in Spivak's words, 'the absolute limit of the place where history is narrativized into logic' ('Subaltern Studies' 16)—and therefore also an absolute refusal to narrativization itself. But from this refusal, from the nakedness that results, something like a force able to confront 'the central axis of conflict' begins to emerge. I think Latin American cultural studies is in at least as good a position as any other discursive field to open itself to it—provided that we do not tell ourselves stories" (299).

9. For those who think that secondary sources or theoretical reflection can assuage embarrassment, I recommend Eve Sedgwick's reflections on shame and

shaming in "Queer Performativity: Henry James's *The Art of the Novel*," and her work with Adam Frank reviewing *Shame and Her Sisters*, both in *Touching Feeling*. The source for many of these reflections is Erving Goffman's *Stigma: Notes on the Management of Spoiled Identity* (Englewood Cliffs, NJ: Prentice Hall, 1963).

10. Awkwardly spliced into the end of *Poison River*, after Luba has left Peter and reunited with her cousin Ofelia and aging aunt, the women travel in search of the aunt's home town and come upon what seems at first to be a beautiful hippie commune of love and peace and equality between men and women. The idyll, Gilbert's take on early 1970s countercultures, ends as Luba's sexual attractiveness threatens the other women of the commune, but also when Luba and Ofelia realize that the commune is a marijuana/cocaine operation that has cut deals with the police and drug dealers who killed Ofelia's leftist friends many years ago.

11. "An untranslative excess, then, must mark Latin Americanist reflection as its last and first condition of critical existence: as the possibility of its existence as a theoretical practice and a community of friends. For the same reason, locational thinking must give way to a sort of dirty atopianism, a supplement to location, without which location comes to the end of itself and becomes a ruin of thought. Dirty atopianism is here the name for a nonprogrammable program of thinking that refuses to find satisfaction in expropriation at the same time that it refuses to fall into appropriative drives. It is dirty because no thinking proceeds from disembodiment. And it is atopian because no thinking exhausts itself in its conditions of enunciation. This does not free us from criticism: rather, it makes critique possible" (23–4). I quote at such length to show that Moreiras, despite his rather forbidding prose style, believes in a community of friends, too.

Bibliography

Abel, Elizabeth. *Virginia Woolf and the Fictions of Psychoanalysis*. Chicago: University of Chicago Press, 1989.

Aguilar Mora, Jorge. *La divina pareja: historia y mito: valoración e interpretación de la obra ensayística de Octavio Paz*. México D.F.: Eds. Era, 1978.

Almaguer, Tomás. "Chicano Men: A Cartography of Homosexual Identity and Behavior," pp. 255–73 in *The Lesbian and Gay Studies Reader*, Henry Abelove, Michèle Aina Barale, and David M. Halperin, eds., New York: Routledge, 1993.

Alonso, Carlos J. *The Burden of Modernity: The Rhetoric of Cultural Discourse in Spanish America*. New York: Oxford University Press, 1998.

Amícola, José. *Manuel Puig y la tela que atrapa al lector*. Buenos Aires: Grupo Editorial Latinoamericano, 1992.

Apter, Emily and William Pietz, eds. *Fetishism as Cultural Discourse*. Ithaca: Cornell University Press, 1993.

Arenas, Reinaldo. *Before Night Falls*. Dolores M. Koch, tr. Harmondsworth: Penguin, 1993. [Sp., *Antes que anochezca*, 1992].

Avelar, Idelber. *The Untimely Present: Postdictatorial Latin American Fiction and the Task of Mourning*. Durham: Duke University Press, 1999.

Bailey, J. Michael. *The Man Who Would Be Queen: The Science of Gender-Bending and Transsexualism*. Washington, DC: Joseph Henry Press, 2003.

Bajarlía, Juan Jacobo. *Alejandra Pizarnik: anatomía de un recuerdo*. Buenos Aires: Ed. Almagesto, 1998.

Balderston, Daniel. "Progresos de la doctora Anneli Taube," pp. 271–80 in *Encuentro internacional Manuel Puig*, José Amícola and Graciela Speranza, eds. Rosario: Ed. Beatriz Viterbo, 1998.

Barrenechea, Ana María. "Ex-centricidades, di-vergencias, y con-vergencias en Felisberto Hernández," *MLN* 91 (1976), 311–36.

Barthes, Roland. *The Pleasure of the Text*. Richard Miller, tr. New York: Hill and Wang, 1975 [1973]

———. *S/Z*, Richard Howard, tr. New York: Hill and Wang, 1974 [1970].

Bartra, Roger. *La jaula de la melancolia*. México: Ed. Grijalbo, 1987.

Bataille, Georges. *Visions of Excess: Selected Writings, 1927–1939*. Allan Stoekl, ed. and intro.; Allan Stoekl, Carl Lovitt, and Donald M. Leslie, Jr., trs. Minneapolis: University of Minnesota Press, 1985.

Bejel, Emilio. *Gay Cuban Nation*. Chicago: University of Chicago Press, 2001.

Bersani, Leo. *The Culture of Redemption*. Cambridge: Harvard University Press, 1996.

Beverley, John. *Against Literature*. Minneapolis: University of Minnesota Press, 1996.

Blanco Arnejo, María D. *La novela lúdica experimental de Julio Cortázar*. Madrid: Ed. Pliegos, 1996.

Boldy, Steven. *The Novels of Julio Cortázar*. Cambridge: Cambridge University Press, 1980.

Brooks, Peter. *Reading for the Plot: Design and Intention in Narrative*. New York: A. A. Knopf, 1984.

Burgin, Victor, James Donald, and Cora Kaplan, eds. *Formations of Fantasy*. New York: Routledge, 1989.

Carrier, Joseph. *De Los Otros: Intimacy and Homosexuality Among Mexican Men*. Berkeley: University of California Press, 1995.

Carroll, Lewis. *Alice in Wonderland: A Norton Critical Edition*. Donald J. Gray, ed. Ithaca: Norton, 1971. [*Through the Looking-Glass*, 1871.]

Castellanos, Rosario. *El eterno femenino*. México: Fondo de Cultura Económica, 1975.

Castle, Terry. *The Apparitional Lesbian: Female Homosexuality and Modern Culture*. New York: Columbia University Press, 1993.

Chambers, Ross. *Story and Situation: Narrative Seduction and the Power of Fiction*. Wlad Godzich, foreword. Minneapolis: University of Minnesota Press, 1984.

———. *Room to Maneuver: Reading (the) Oppositional (in) Narrative*. Chicago: The University of Chicago Press, 1991.

Chávez-Silverman, Susana. "The Look That Kills: The 'Unacceptable Beauty' of Alejandra Pizarnik's *La condesa sangrienta*," pp. 281–306 in *¿Entiendes? Queer Readings, Hispanic Writings*, Emilie Bergmann and Paul Julian Smith, eds. Durham: Duke University Press, 1995.

Cixous, Hélène. "Introduction to Lewis Carroll's *Through the Looking Glass* and *The Hunting of the Snark*." Maclean, Marie, tr. *NLH* 13: 2 (Winter 1982 [1971]), 231–51.

———. "Fiction and Its Phantoms: A Reading of Freud's 'Das Unheimliche' (The 'Uncanny')," *NLH* 7 (1976), 525–48.

Copjec, Joan. *Read My Desire: Lacan Against the Historicists*. Cambridge, MA: MIT Press, 1994.

Cortázar, Julio. *Cuentos completos, t.1 (1954–66)*. Madrid: Alfaguara, 1996 ["El otro cielo," *Todos los fuegos el fuego*, 1966].

———. *Around the Day in Eighty Worlds*. Thomas Christensen, tr. San Francisco: North Point Press, 1986 [1967].

———. *62: modelo para armar*. Buenos Aires: Ed. Sudamericana, 1968.

———. *62: A Model Kit*. Gregory Rabassa, tr. New York: Avon, 1972.

———. *Libro de Manuel*. Buenos Aires: Ed. Sudamericana, 1973.

———. *A Manual for Manuel*. New York: Pantheon, 1978.

———. *Salvo el crepúsculo*. Madrid: Alfaguara, 1984.

———. *Cartas, 1937–1983*. Ed. Aurora Bernárdez, Madrid: Alfaguara, 2000.

————, and Evelyn Picón Garfield, *Cortázar por Cortázar*, Xalapa: Ed. Veracruzana, 1973.

Cruz-Malavé, Arnaldo. *El primitivo implorante: El «sistema poético del mundo» de José Lezama Lima*. Amsterdam and Atlanta: Rodopi, 1994.

Culler, Jonathan. *On Deconstruction: Theory and Criticism After Structuralism*. Ithaca: Cornell University Press, 1982.

Culver, Stuart. "What Mannikins Want: L. Frank Baum's *The Wonderful Wizard of Oz* and *The Art of Dressing Dry-Goods Windows*," *Representations* 21 (Winter 1988): 97–116.

Cypess, Sandra Messinger. *La Malinche in Mexican Literature*. Austin: University of Texas Press, 1991.

de Guzmán, Daniel. *Carlos Fuentes: A Critical View*. New York: Twayne's World Author Series, 1972.

Deleuze, Gilles. *Masochism: Coldness and Cruelty* (1967), and Leopold von Sacher-Masoch, *Venus in Furs*, Jean McNeil, tr. New York: Zone Books, 1989.

Deleuze, Gilles, and Felix Guattari. *Anti-Oedipus: Capitalism and Schizophrenia*. Robert Hurley, Mark Seem, and Helen Lane, trs. New York: Viking Press, 1977 [1972].

Díaz, José Pedro. *Felisberto Hernández: Su vida y su obra*. Montevideo: Ed. Planeta, 2000.

Donoso, José. *El lugar sin límites*. Barcelona: Seix Barral, 1991 [1966].

————. *Hell Has No Limits*. Suzanne Jill Levine, tr. New York: Sun Moon Press, 1995 [1st ed. in *Triple Cross*, New York: E. P. Dutton, 1972].

————. *Historia personal del «Boom»*. Santiago: Alfaguara, 1998 [1972, 1987].

————. *The Boom in Spanish American Literature: A Personal History*. Gregory Kolovakos, tr. New York: Center for Inter-American Relations, 1977.

Echevarren, Roberto. *El espacio de la verdad: Práctica del texto en Felisberto Hernández*. Buenos Aires: Ed. Sudamericana, 1981.

Faris, Wendy. *Carlos Fuentes*. New York: Frederick Ungar, 1983.

Feal, Rosemary Geisdorfer. "Queer Cortázar and the *Lectora Macho*," pp. 239–253 in *Reading and Writing the Ambiente*, Susana Chávez-Silverman and Librada Hernández, eds. Madison: University of Wisconsin Press, 2000.

Findlay, Heather. "Queer Dora: Hysteria, Sexual Politics, and Lacan's 'Intervention on Transference,'" *GLQ*, 1:3 (1994), 323–47.

Fombona, Jacinto. "Cuño, cuña, coño: Juegos de Felisberto Hernández," *Revista Iberoamericana* LXVI:190 (enero-marzo 2000), 25–36.

Foreman, Richard, "During the Second Half of the Sixties," pp. 25–27 in *Jack Smith, Flaming Creature: His Amazing Life and Times*, Leffingwell et al., eds. New York: The Institute for Contemporary Art, P.S. 1 Museum/Serpent's Tail, 1997.

Foster, David William. *Gay and Lesbian Themes in Latin American Writing*. Austin: University of Texas Press, 1991.

Foster, Hal. *Compulsive Beauty*. Cambridge: MIT Press, 1993.

Foucault, Michel. *The History of Sexuality, Volume 1: An Introduction*. Robert Hurley, tr. New York: Random House, 1978 [1976].

Francescato, Martha Paley, "The New Man (But Not the New Woman)," pp. 134–9 in *The Final Island: The Fiction of Julio Cortázar*, Jaime Alazraki and Ivar Ivask, eds. Norman: University of Oklahoma Press, 1978.

Franco, Jean. *Plotting Women: Gender and Representation in Mexico*. New York: Columbia University Press, 1989.

Freud, Sigmund. *Three Essays on the Theory of Sexuality*. Steven Marcus, Intro; James Strachey, tr. and rev. New York: Basic Books, 1975 [1905].

————. *Three Case Histories: The "Wolf Man," the "Rat Man," and the Psychotic Doctor Schreber*. James Strachey, tr.; Phillip Rieff, ed. and intro. New York: Collier Books, 1963 [1909].

————. "'A Child Is Being Beaten': A Contribution to the Origin of Sexual Perversions," pp. 107–132 in *Sexuality and the Psychology of Love*, Alix and James Strachey, trs.; Philip Reiff, ed. and intro. New York: Collier Books, 1963 [1919].

————. "The Economic Problem in Masochism," pp. 190–201 in *General Psychological Theory*, Joan Rivière, tr.; Philip Reiff, ed. and intro. New York: Collier Books, 1963 [1924].

————. "Fetishism," pp. 214–19 in *Sexuality and the Psychology of Love*, Phillip Rieff ed. and intro.; Joan Rivière, tr. New York: Collier Books, 1963 [1927].

Fuentes, Carlos. *The Death of Artemio Cruz*. Alfred Macadam, tr. New York: Farrar, Straus, Giroux, 1991 [1962].

————. *Zona sagrada*. Mexico, D.F.: Siglo XXI, 1992 [1967].

————. *Holy Place*. Suzanne Jill Levine, tr. New York: E.P. Dutton, 1978 [1972].

Garber, Marjorie. *Vested Interests: Cross-Dressing and Cultural Anxiety*. New York: Routledge, 1992.

García Márquez, Gabriel. *One Hundred Years of Solitude*. Gregory Rabassa, tr. New York: Harper and Row, 1970 (*Cien años de soledad*, 1967).

————. *Innocent Eréndira, and Other Stories*. Gregory Rabassa, tr. New York: Harper & Row, 1978 (*La increíble historia de la cándida Eréndira y su abuela desalmada*, 1972).

————. *The Autumn of the Patriarch*. Gregory Rabassa, tr. New York: Harper and Row, 1976. (*El otoño del patriarca*, 1975.)

————. "En busca del Silva perdido," pp. 9–29 in *Poesía completa; De sobremesa (Edición del centenario)*, José Asunción Silva, Bogotá: Ed. Norma, 1996.

García Pinto, Magdalena. *Historias íntimas: Conversaciones con diez escritoras latinoamericanas*. Hanover, NH: Ed. del Norte, 1988.

Generani, Gustavo. "*62/modelo para armar*: La tradición de la ruptura," pp. 129–38 in *Cortázar, 1994: Estudios críticos*. Buenos Aires: Ed. Academia del Sur, 1997.

Giraldi de Dei Cas, Norah. *Felisberto Hernández: del creador al hombre*. Montevideo: Ed. de la Banda Oriental, 1975.

González Echevarría, Roberto. *La ruta de Severo Sarduy*. Hanover, NH: Eds. del Norte, 1987.

————. *Myth and Archive: A theory of Latin American narrative*, Cambridge: Cambridge University Press, 1990.

———— "Plain Song: Sarduy's Cobra," pp. 212–37 in *Celestina's Brood: Continuities of the Baroque in Spanish and Latin American Literature.* Durham: Duke University Press, 1993.

Giacoman, Helmy F. *Homenaje a Carlos Fuentes.* Long Island City, NY: Las Americas Publishing, 1971.

Goffman, Erving. *Stigma: Notes on the Management of Spoiled Identity.* Englewood Cliffs, NJ: Prentice Hall, 1963.

Gossy, Mary. "Not So Lonely: A Butch-Femme Reading of Cristina Peri-Rossi's *Solitario de amor*," pp. 238–45 in David William Foster and Roberto Reis, eds, *Bodies and Biases: Sexualities in Hispanic Cultures and Literatures,* Roberto Reis and Dario Boim, Jr., intros.; Naomi Lindstrom, afterword. Minneapolis: University of Minnesota Press, 1996.

Graziano, Frank. *The Lust of Seeing: Themes of the Gaze and Sexual Rituals in the Fiction of Felisberto Hernández.* Lewisburg, PA: Bucknell University Press, 1997.

Guerrero, Gustavo. *La estrategia neobarroca en las novelas de Severo Sarduy.* Madrid: Taurus, 1987.

Guibert, Rita. *Seven Voices; Seven Latin American Writers Talk to Rita Guibert.* Frances Partridge, tr.; Emir Rodríguez Monegal, intro. New York: Knopf, 1973.

Hanson, Ellis, ed. *Out Takes: Essays on Queer Theory and Film.* Durham: Duke University Press, 1999.

Hernández, Ana María. "Vampires and Vampiresses: A Reading of *62*," pp. 109–14 in *The Final Island: The Fiction of Julio Cortázar,* Jaime Alazraki and Ivar Ivask, eds. Norman: University of Oklahoma Press, 1978.

Hernández, Felisberto. *Obras completas.* 3 vols. Maria Luisa Puga, ed. Mexico: Siglo XXI, 1983 [*Por los tiempos de Clemente Colling,* I:137–98; "Menos Julia," II: 92–110; "Explicación falsa de mis cuentos," II, 175–6; *Las Hortensias,* II: 176–233; "El cocodrilo," III: 75–90].

————. *Piano Stories.* Luis Harss, ed. and tr.; Italo Calvino, intro. New York: Marsilio Publishers, 1993.

————. *Lands of Memory.* Esther Allen, tr. New York: New Directions Press, 2002.

Hernandez, Gilbert. *Poison River.* Seattle, WA: Fantagraphic Books, 1994.

Hertz, Neil. *The End of the Line: Essays on Psychoanalysis and the Sublime.* New York: Columbia University Press, 1985.

Hocquenghem, Guy. *Homosexual Desire.* Daniella Dangoor, tr.; Jeffrey Weeks, 1978 preface; Michael Moon, intro. Durham: Duke University Press, 1993.

Ian, Marcia. *Remembering the Phallic Mother: Psychoanalysis, Modernism, and the Fetish.* Ithaca: Cornell University Press, 1993.

Jackson, Rosemary. *Fantasy: The Literature of Subversion.* London and New York: Methuen, 1981.

Kahane, Claire and Charles Bernheimer, eds. *In Dora's Case: Freud-Hysteria-Feminism.* New York: Columbia University Press, 1985.

Kaminsky, Amy. "Residual Authority and Gendered Resistance," pp. 103–25 in *Critical Theory, Cultural Politics, and Latin American Narrative,* Steven M. Bell, Albert H. Le May, and Leonard Orr, eds., Notre Dame: University of Notre Dame Press, 1993.

Kerr, Lucille. *Suspended Fictions*, Chicago and Urbana: University of Illinois Press, 1987.

———. "Betwixt Reading and Repetition (Apropos of Cortázar's *62: A Model Kit*)," pp. 91–109 in *Julio Cortázar: New Readings*, Carlos Alonso, ed. Cambridge: Cambridge University Press, 1998.

Khan, Masud R. *Alienation in Perversions*. New York: International Universities Press, 1979.

Koestenbaum, Wayne. "Crouching Among Sailors," in *Double Talk: The Erotics of Literary Collaboration*. New York: Routledge, 1993.

Lacan, Jacques. *Ecrits: A Selection*. Alan Sheridan, tr. New York: Norton, 1977.

———. "Kant with Sade." James B. Swenson, Jr., tr., *October* (1989) 51, 55–104.

Laddaga, Reinaldo. *Literaturas indigentes y placeres bajos: Felisberto Hernández, Virgilio Piñera, Rodolfo Wilcock*. Rosario: Beatriz Viterbo, 2000.

Lancaster, Roger. *Life Is Hard: Machismo, Danger, and the Intimacy of Power in Nicaragua*. Berkeley: University of California Press, 1992.

Laplanche, Jean and J.B. Pontalis. *The Language of Psycho-Analysis*. Donald Nicholson-Smith, tr.; Daniel Lagache, intro. New York: Norton, 1974 [1973].

Leffingwell, Edward. "Jack Smith, the Only Normal Man in Baghdad," pp. 68–87 in Leffingwell et al., eds.

Leffingwell, Edward, Carole Kismaric, and Marvin Heiferman, eds. *Jack Smith, Flaming Creature: His Amazing Life and Times*. New York: The Institute For Contemporary Art, P.S.1 Museum/Serpent's Tail, 1997.

Lemebel, Pedro. *Tengo miedo torero*. Santiago: Seix Barral, 2001.

Levine, Suzanne Jill. *The Subversive Scribe*. St. Paul: Graywolf Press, 1991.

Levinson, Brett. *Secondary Moderns: Mimesis, History, and Revolution in Lezama Lima's "American Expression."* Lewisburg, PA : Bucknell University Press, 1996.

———. *The Ends of Literature: The Latin American "Boom" and the Neoliberal Marketplace*. Stanford: Stanford University Press, 2001.

Lezama Lima, José. *Oppiano Licario*. Mexico: Biblioteca Era, 1977.

———. *Paradiso*. Cintio Vitier, ed. UNESCO: Colección Archivos, 1988 [1966].

———. *Paradiso*. Gregory Rabassa, tr. Austin: University of Texas Press, 1988.

Lihn, Enrique. "*Paradiso*, novela y homosexualidad." *Hispamérica* 8:22 (1979), 3–22.

Lomnitz, Claudio. *Exits From the Labyrinth: Culture and Ideology in the Mexican National Space*. Berkeley: University of California Press, 1992.

Ludmer, Josefina. «*Cien años de soledad*»: *una interpretación*. Buenos Aires: Ed. Tiempo Contemporáneo, 1972.

———. "La tragedia cómica." *Escritura* VII:13–14 (enero-diciembre 1982), 111–18.

Magnarelli, Sharon. *Understanding José Donoso*. Columbia: University of South Carolina Press, 1993.

Marcus, Greil. *Lipstick Traces: A Secret History of the Twentieth Century*. Cambridge, MA: Harvard University Press, 1989.

McClintock, Anne. *Imperial Leather: Race, Gender, and Sexuality in the Colonial Context*. New York and London: Routledge, 1995.

McCloud, Scott. *Understanding Comics: The Invisible Art.* New York: Harper Perennial, 1993.

Mekas, Jonas, "Jack Smith at the End of Civilization," pp. 48–50 in *Jack Smith, Flaming Creature: His Amazing Life and Times,* Leffingwell et al., eds. New York: The Institute For Contemporary Art, P.S. 1 Museum/Serpent's Tail, 1997.

Mercier, Lucien. "La cajita de música: Felisberto y las máquinas célibes." *Escritura,* VII:13–14 (enero-diciembre 1982), 229–41.

Merck, Mandy. *Perversions: Deviant readings.* London: Routledge, 1993.

Miller, D. A. *Bringing Out Roland Barthes.* Berkeley: University of California Press, 1992.

Molloy, Sylvia. "From Sappho to Bafo: Diverting the Sexual in Alejandra Pizarnik," in *Sex and Sexuality in Latin America,* Daniel Balderston and Donna J. Guy, eds. New York: NYU Press, 1997.

Moon, Michael. "Flaming Closets," pp. 282–306, in *Out in Culture: Gay, Lesbian, and Queer Essays on Popular Culture,* Corey K. Creekmur and Alexander Doty, eds. Durham: Duke University Press, 1995.

———. *A Small Boy and Others: Imitation and Initiation in American Culture from Henry James to Andy Warhol.* Durham: Duke University Press, 1998.

Moreiras, Alberto. *The Exhaustion of Difference: The Politics of Latin American Cultural Studies.* Durham: Duke University Press, 2001.

———. *Tercer espacio: Literatura y duelo en América Latina.* Santiago de Compostela: Universidad ARCIS/LOM Ediciones, 1999.

Moretti, Franco. *The Modern Epic: The World-System from Goethe to García Márquez.* Quintin Hoare, tr. London and New York: Verso, 1996.

Morton, Donald. "The Birth of the Cyberqueer." PMLA 110:3 (May 1995), 369–81.

Mulvey, Laura. *Fetishism and Curiosity.* Bloomington, IN: The British Film Institute and The University of Indiana Press, 1996.

Nicholson, Melanie. "Alejandra Pizarnik, Georges Bataille, and the Literature of Evil." *Latin American Literary Review* (Winter 2000), 11–23.

Niebylski, Dianna, "Transgression in the Comic Mode: Angeles Mastretta and Her Cast of Liberated Aunts," pp. 29–40 in *The Other Mirror: Women's Narrative in Mexico, 1980–1995,* Kristine Ibsen ed., Westport, CT: Greenwood, 1997.

Pallares, Ricardo, and Reina Reyes. *¿Otro Felisberto?* Montevideo: Ed. de la Banda Oriental, 1994 [2nd edition].

Panesi, Jorge. *Felisberto Hernández.* Rosario: Ed. Beatriz Viterbo, 1993.

Paz, Octavio. *The Labyrinth of Solitude/The Other Mexico/The Return to the Labyrinth of Solitude/Mexico and the United States/The Philanthropic Ogre.* Lysander Kemp, Yara Milos, and Rachel Phillips Belash, trs. New York: Grove Press, 1985 [*El laberinto de la soledad.* México: Fondo de Cultura Económica, 1950; *Posdata.* México: Siglo XXI, 1970].

Paz, Octavio, *An Erotic Beyond: Sade.* Eliot Weinberger, tr. New York: Harcourt Brace and Company, 1998 [1947, 1961, 1986].

Piedra, José. "Nationalizing Sissies," pp. 370–409 in *¿Entiendes? Queer Readings, Hispanic Writings*, Emilie Bergman and Paul Julian Smith, eds. Durham: Duke University Press, 1996.

Pellón, Gustavo. *José Lezama Lima's Joyful Vision: A Study of Paradiso and Other Prose Works*. Austin: University of Texas Press, 1989.

Penrose, Valentine. *The Bloody Countess: The Atrocities of Erzsébeth Báthory*. Alexander Trocchi, tr. London: Creation Books, 2000 [1970; French original, 1962].

Pérez Firmat, Gustavo. "Descent into *Paradiso*: A Study of Heaven and Homosexuality." *Hispania* 59:2 (1976), 247–57.

Peri Rossi, Cristina. *Julio Cortázar*. Barcelona: Ed. Omega, 2001.

Pierre, José, ed. *Investigating Sex: Surrealist Research, 1928–1932*. Malcolm Imrie, tr.; Dawn Adés, afterword. London: Verso, 1992.

Pizarnik, Alejandra. *Obras completas*. Cristina Piña, ed. Buenos Aires: Ed. Corregidor, 1999.

———. "The Bloody Countess," pp. 99–113. Alberto Manguel, tr. in *Pleasure in the Word: Erotic Writing by Latin American Women*, Margarite Fernández Olmos and Lizabeth Paravisini-Gebert, eds., Fredonia, NY: White Pine Press, 1993.

Poniatowska, Elena. *¡Ay vida, no me mereces! Carlos Fuentes, Rosario Castellanos, Juan Rulfo, la literatura de la onda*. Mexico DF: Joaquín Mortiz, 1985.

Prieto, René. *Bodies of Desire*. Durham: Duke University Press, 2001.

Prieur, Annick. *Mema's House, Mexico City: On Transvestites, Queens, and Machos*. Chicago: University of Chicago Press, 1998.

Puig, Manuel. *El beso de la mujer araña*. New York: Vintage Español, 1994 [1976].

———. *Kiss of the Spider Woman*. Thomas Colchie, tr. New York: Vintage International, 1978, 1979.

Quiroga, José. *Tropics of Desire: Interventions from Queer Latino America*. New York: NYU Press, 2000.

Rama, Angel. "Su manera original de enfrentar el mundo." *Escritura*, VII:13–14 (enero-diciembre 1982), 243–58.

Rela, Walter (intr., sel., and biblio). *Felisberto Hernández: Valoración crítica*. Montevideo: Ed. Ciencias, 1982.

Rodríguez Monegal, "Le fantôme de Lautréamont," pp. 167–78 in *Julio Cortázar*, Pedro Lastra, ed. Madrid: Ed. Taurus, 1981.

Roof, Judith. *Come As You Are: Sexuality and Narrative*. New York: Columbia University Press, 1996.

Rosario, Vernon A. *The Erotic Imagination: French Histories of Perversity*. Oxford: Oxford University Press, 1997.

Ross, Andrew. *No Respect: Intellectuals and Popular Culture*. New York: Routledge, 1988.

Rubinstein, Anne. *Bad Language, Naked Ladies, and Other Threats to the Nation*. Durham: Duke University Press, 1998.

Santí, Enrico Mario. "Parridiso," in *José Lezama Lima, textos críticos*, pp. 91–114, Justo C. Ulloa, ed. Miami, FL: Ed. Universal, 1979.

Sarduy, Severo. *Obra completa*, two volumes, Gustavo Guerrero and François Wahl, eds. Madrid: Colección Archivos, 1999.

———. *Written on a Body*. Carole Maier, tr. New York: Lumen Books, 1983.

———. *Cobra*. Barcelona: Edhasa, 1981 [1972].

———. *Cobra and Maitreya*. Suzanne Jill Levine, tr. and pref.; James McCourt, intro. Normal IL: Dalkey Archive Press, 1995 [1975].

Scarafía, Sylvia, and Elisa Molina. "Escritura y perversión en la *Condesa sangrienta de* Alejandra Pizarnik y *62/modelo para armar* de Julio Cortázar," pp. 89–114, in *Un tal Julio (Cortázar, otras lecturas)*, María Elena Legaz, coordinadora. Cordoba: Ed. Alción, 1998.

Schor, Naomi. "Fetishism and Its Ironies," in Apter and Pietz, pp. 92–100.

Sedgwick, Eve Kosofsky. *Epistemology of the Closet*. Chicago: University of Chicago Press, 1990.

———. "Tales of the Avunculate: Queer Tutelage in *The Importance of Being Earnest*," in *Tendencies*, pp. 52–72, Durham: Duke University Press, 1993.

———. "How to Bring Your Kids Up Gay: The War on Effeminate Boys," in *Tendencies*, pp. 154–62.

———. "Divinity: A Dossier, a Performance Piece, a Little-Understood Emotion (written with Michael Moon)," in *Tendencies*, pp. 215–51.

———. *Touching Feeling*. Durham: Duke University Press, 2003.

Sicard, Alain, ed. *Felisberto Hernández ante la crítica actual*. Caracas: Monte Ávila Eds., 1977.

Sifuentes Jáuregui, Ben. *Transvestism, Masculinity, and Latin American Literature: Genders Share Flesh*. New York: Palgrave Press, 2002.

Silverman, Kaja. *Male Subjectivity at the Margins*. New York: Routledge, 1992.

Smith, Patricia Juliana, ed. *The Queer Sixties*. New York: Routledge, 1999.

Smith, Paul Julian. *Vision Machines: Cinema, Literature, and Sexuality in Spain and Cuba, 1983–1993*. London: Verso Books, 1996.

Sommer, Doris. *Proceed With Caution, When engaged with minority writing in the Americas*. Cambridge, MA:Harvard University Press, 1999.

Spiegelman, Art. *Maus I and II: A Survivor's Tale*. New York: Pantheon Books, 1986, 1991.

Standish, Peter. *Understanding Julio Cortázar*. Columbia, SC: University of South Carolina Press, 2001.

Stavans, Ilan. *The Riddle of Cantinflas: Essays in Hispanic Popular Culture*. Albuquerque: University of New Mexico Press, 1998.

Steele, Valerie. *Fetish: Fashion, Sex, and Power*. New York and Oxford: Oxford University Press, 1996.

Stoller, Robert J. *Observing the Erotic Imagination*. New Haven: Yale University Press, 1985.

Taussig, Michael. *The Devil and Commodity Fetishism in South America*. Ann Arbor: University of Michigan Press, 1982.

———. *Shamanism, Colonialism, and the Wild Man: An Essay in Terror and Healing*. Chicago: The University of Chicago Press, 1987.

Taussig, Michael. "Maleficium: State Fetishism," pp. 217–247 in *Fetishism as Cultural Discourse*, Apter and Pietz, eds. Ithaca: Cornell University Press, 1993.

———. *Mimesis and Alterity*. New York: Routledge, 1993.

Tavel, Ronald. "María Montez: Anima of an Antediluvian World," pp. 88–104 in *Jack Smith, Flaming Creature: His Amazing Life and Times*, Leffingwell et al., eds. New York: The Institute for Contemporary Art, P.S. 1 Museum/Serpent's Tail, 1997.

Todorov, Tzvetan. *The Fantastic: A Structural Approach to a Literary Genre*. Richard Howard, tr.; Robert Scholes, foreword. Ithaca: Cornell University Press, 1973.

van Delden, Maarten. *Carlos Fuentes, Mexico and Modernity*. Nashville: Vanderbilt University Press, 1998.

Vargas Llosa, Mario. "*Paradiso* de José Lezama Lima." *Amaru* 1 (Lima: Universidad Nacional de Ingeniería, enero, 1967), 72–75.

Vargas Llosa, Mario, and Emir Rodríguez Monegal. "Sobre el 'Paradiso' de Lezama Lima." *Mundo Nuevo* 3 (1967), 89–95.

Vawter, Ron. *Roy Cohn/Jack Smith*, pp. 441–476 in *O Solo Homo: The New Queer Performance*, Holly Hughes and David Román, eds. New York: Grove Press, 1998.

Velasco, Sherry. *The Lieutenant Nun: Transgenderism, Lesbian Desire, and Catalina de Erauso*. Austin: University of Texas Press, 2000.

Widdifield, Stacie. *The Embodiment of the National in Late Nineteenth-Century Mexican Painting*. Tucson: Arizona University Press, 1996.

Williams, Gareth. *The Other Side of the Popular: Neoliberalism and Subalternity in Latin America*. Durham: Duke University Press, 2002.

Williams, Raymond. *Culture and Society: 1780–1950*. New York: Harper & Row, 1966 [1958].

Wilson, Jason. *Octavio Paz*. Boston: Twayne's World Authors Series, 1986.

Wood, Michael. *Children of Silence: On Contemporary Fiction*. New York: Columbia University Press, 1998.

Zamora, Lois Parkinson, and Wendy Faris, eds. *Magical Realism: Theory, History, and Community*. Durham: Duke University Press, 1995.

Zamora, Margarita. "Reading in the Margins of Columbus," in *Amerindian Images and the Legacy of Columbus*, René Jara and Nicholas Spadaccini, eds. Minneapolis: University of Minnesota Press, 1992.

Zizek, Slavoj. *The Plague of Fantasies*. London and New York: Verso, 1997.

Index 🙰